listen

Five Simple Tools to Meet Your
Everyday Parenting Challenges

More Praise for Listen

In this wonderful book, Patty Wipfler and Tosha Schore invite us to Listen in to our hearts to create a science-informed, practical strategy for parenting our children well. The Hand in Hand approach empowers us to become our best, finding support in others and exploring the important ways we can be secure attachment figures that nurture self-regulation, resilience, and compassion in our children. What a gift that will help our world be a better place for all of us to live!

— Daniel J. Siegel, M.D.
Author: *Mind: A Journey to the Heart of Being Human, Brainstorm,* and *The Developing Mind* and Co-Author, *Parenting from the Inside Out, The Whole-Brain Child,* and *No-Drama Discipline*

Patty Wipfler is quietly revolutionizing parenting by explaining emotions so that parents not only understand their child's behavior, but know exactly how to support their child to transform that behavior. You wouldn't think a parenting book would be a page-turner but this one is. Wipfler and her co-author Tosha Schore demonstrate the power of listening to children, with story after story of parents helping their child master the large and small traumas of everyday life. Every parent needs this book.

— Dr. Laura Markham
Author: *Peaceful Parent, Happy Kids: How to Stop Yelling* and *Start Connecting* and *Peaceful Parent,* and *Happy Siblings: How to Stop the Fighting and Raise Friends for Life*

The book is wonderful in every way—and that is very rare. I believe this book is going to be a blessing for everyone who picks it up, not only parents. Just this weekend I pointed a couple of dads toward Hand in Hand Parenting, as I have so many other parents. Thank heavens this book is finally going to be available!

— Bonnie Badenoch, PhD, LMFT
Co-founder, Center for Brain-Wise Living and Author: *Being a Brain Wise Therapist: A Practical Guide to Interpersonal Neurobiology*

Wow. This is the book I've been waiting for! *Listen* captures the heart and soul of Patty Wipfler's groundbreaking work with parents and families. This remarkable book describes the tools of Parenting by Connection with clarity, and then applies them with thoughtfulness and compassion to the real struggles of parents. I am thrilled about *Listen* for the thousands of people who—like me—have had a taste of these ideas already and have been itching for this book. I'm even more thrilled for those of you who are discovering these tools for the first time. You are in for an incredibly rewarding adventure.

— Dr. Lawrence Cohen
Author: *Playful Parenting, The Opposite of Worry: The Playful Parenting Approach to Childhood Anxieties and Fears*, and Co-author, *The Art of Roughhousing, Best Friends, Worst Enemies: Understanding the Social Lives of Children*, and *Mom, They're Teasing Me: Helping Your Child Solve Social Problems*

This book by two masters of the art of parenting is a helpful resource for parents of young children and expectant parents. The authors incorporate some simple principles drawn from the fields of neuroscience, psychotherapy, and attachment theory to give their advice a solid theoretical foundation. And don't be fooled by the subtitle: *Listen* contains a lot more than five tools; the entire book is chockfull of tools and strategies and techniques that parents will find useful.

— Stan Tatkin, Psy D, MFT
Stan Tatkin, Psy D, MFT is a clinician and teacher; he developed A Psychobiological Approach to Couple Therapy® (PACT), which integrates attachment theory, developmental neuroscience, and arousal regulation, and founded the PACT Institute.

Brimming with compassionate, insightful and practical advice, *Listen* provides parents and professionals with an essential guide to nurturing deep connections with children and lovingly navigating conflicts with them.

— Marguerite A. Wright, Ed. D.
Author: *I'm Chocolate, You're Vanilla: Raising Black and Biracial Children in a Race-Conscious World*

Listen: Five Simple Tools to Meet Your Everyday Parenting Challenges
by Patty Wipfler and Tosha Schore, M.A.

Books may be purchased by contacting the publisher and author at:
555 Waverley St., #25, Palo Alto, CA 94301

Tosha Schore, M.A. Photo Courtesy of *In Her Image Photography*

Library of Congress Control Number: 2016944390
ISBN: 978-0-9974593-0-2
1. Parenting 2. Self-help
First Edition (2016)
Second Edition (2017)
Printed in USA

Contents

Acknowledgments

It took a village to write this book!

Hand in Hand's Board of Directors has given both inspiration and exceptional support. Thank you to Jeff Crowe, our Board Chair, for twenty-seven years of believing in our work and leading us forward. And to Dr. Ellyn Bader, Craig Friedman, John Heltzel, Mary Lou Johnson, Ron Meiners, Kathy Neuman, Penny Righthand, Sushmita Vij, and Teresa Kelleher Zepeda. Your dedication has grown our work and strengthened it. We have benefited greatly from your generous outpouring of caring, time and expertise. Thanks also to Joe Hudson and the DBJ Foundation for the growth you've fostered, for expecting great things, and for spurring us on.

The Hand in Hand staff has contributed their enthusiastic and skilled support. Special thanks to Craig Appel, who ably managed the project; Julianne Idleman, whose campaign funded the book, and who dropped everything to help us stay on schedule; and Michelle Pate, whose leadership freed Patty to write. Elle Kwan, Elizabeth Elias, Molly Pearson, Paul Russell, and Martin Wilson have also worked hard, acquired new skills, and shared their considerable energy.

Marilyn Elias, our editor, worked swiftly and with great skill to separate the wheat from the chaff. Her encouragement and discerning eye were most helpful. Lawrence J. Cohen, Ph.D. shared valuable insights on our draft, and contributed to its clarity almost overnight. Matt Sanders at Trigger Design created a cover and design that communicates our message well, and Brian Aced's illustrations are treasures we are proud to share.

The Hand in Hand Instructors' work within their own families, and within their communities is reflected throughout this book. We feel privileged to be learning with them and from them as they face myriad parenting challenges and share their experience. Their generous outreach to parents all over the globe is the beating heart of Hand in Hand Parenting.

We are particularly grateful to Alaiya Aguilar, Lucy Allen, Lori Bakshi, Hannah Brobst, Georgie Bancroft, Merav Besser, Deborah Betz, Melinda Booth, Udaya Bryce, Michelle Carlson, Adriana Castillo, Emily Cernusak, Torri Chappell, Anna Cole, Maya Coleman, Paula De Francesca, Marilupe de la Calle, Zsuzsanna Egry, Christine Ashe Elizondo, Kristin Ellermann, Todd Erickson, Miranda Fairhall, Freddie Ferber, Sandra Flear, Allison Fluet, Tyralynn Frasier, Velma Gentzsch, Lana Harel, Zelon Harrison, Jamila Jackson, Melissa Jara, Kirsten Jensen, Julie Johnson, Esther Kamkar, Carol Kellendonk, Louise Omoto Kessel, Kristan Klingelhofer, Michelle Kokel, Jeni Leary, Lyra L'Estrange, Benn Lim, Rebecca Lippiatt, Otilia Mantilers, Tara McCay, Muftiah Martin, Heidrun Matties, Alma Mendoza, Shaheen Merali, Rita Mori, Skye Munro, Emily Murray, Roma Norriss, Joe Novotny, Liesl Orr, Stephanie Parker, Maddie Pemberton, Laura Podwoski, Zhen Rong, Jamie Russell, Sharon Ryder, Tara Rye, Jasmin Sanders, Usha Sangam, Keiko Sato-Perry, Sara Smith, Kim Sutton, Patricia Townsend, Annie Tyson, Sabina Veronelli, and Kristen Volk for their fine thinking and their willingness to share their personal stories in *Listen*.

Patty is grateful to the members of the very first parent group she worked with more than forty years ago. She is indebted to Lorraine Amerian, Andrea Borning, Margie Smart, Daphne Stewart, the late Diane Taylor, and many others for their adventurous spirit and their trust. Thanks to Sara Wood Smith for her friendship, leadership, and special genius. Thanks to Tim Jackins for believing we could figure things out, and keeping us on the path toward growth.

Additional and unstinting support from Ravid Aisenman Abramsohn, Jean Hamilton, Michelle Kokel, Martín Lamarque, Kirsten Nottleson, Scott Ross, Rachel Schofield, and Robin Setchko made writing possible for her.

Patty thanks Vahé Petrosian, Jacob Bricca, Lisa Molomot, David and Morgan Bricca, and Rory, Lucas, and Allison Bricca, for the cradle of love and support you've always been. And she is grateful to keep learning about love and family from the Bricca, Kamkar, Petrosian, Van Heusen, and Wipfler clans.

Tosha thanks her husband, David, and her sons Zakai, Adiel, and Paz for letting her disappear for hours—and sometimes days on end—to write. You are my deepest love and my inspiration for spreading these parenting insights. Did I tell you today that I love you? Thank you also to Ravid Aisenman Abramsohn for reminding me that I matter. Irit Ginsburg, thank you for that secret writing place, and for not telling a soul I was there! Tali Cohen Tzedek, thank you for your friendship, your encouragement, and for folding me into your desert writing retreats. And Café Yodfat, thanks for saving me "my table" and never making faces because I wasn't ordering more food.

And last but certainly not least, our gratitude goes out to the 746 supporters who generously funded the production of *Listen*. We are grateful to each and every one of you for supporting this project and cheering us on. Without your help, this book would not have come to be. To Blake Adams, Allison Carrillo, Jeff Crowe, Cecilia Hyoun, Jalayne Ladd, Robyn Moore, Sarah Neuse, Beth Ohanneson, Hao-li Ti Loh, and Teresa Kelleher Zepeda: we so appreciate the special measure of help you have given.

Patty Wipfler and Tosha Schore, M.A.

Patty's Preface

By the time I was thirteen, I knew kids inside and out. I was the oldest of six and already had years of experience taking care of younger siblings, cousins, and neighbors. At school, when rain kept kids inside for lunch, I was the one who the nuns sent to the rowdiest class. I knew how to keep the class—all fifty-two of them—from rocking off the rails.

I worked with children every summer during my teen years and through college, married at twenty-one, and, still gravitating toward children, became a teacher. So when I became pregnant with my first child, I knew I was going to be a good mom. I was an old hand. And I was eager.

Just after my second son was born, though, I ran into trouble. I got edgy. I started losing my temper. One day, when my two-year-old made a move to hurt the baby, I lunged at him. I checked myself just a split second before throwing him against the wall. I saw the fear in his eyes, and was shocked at what I had almost done.

One mother, two realities. I was a good mom—except when I wasn't. I was a natural, but sometimes out of control. I'd vowed at a young age that I would never, ever be harsh with a child. And until I had two children, I never was. What had happened to me? What could I do to help myself? My children? I told no one.

On a Saturday in 1973, I took a walk with an acquaintance, Jennie Cushnie, who asked me how it was to be a mother. Suddenly, I burst into tears and told her how frightened I was by what was happening to me. I told her my father had been harsh and explosive—he'd been under terrible stress throughout our childhoods—and now here I was, leaning in that direction! I sobbed uncontrollably with this virtual stranger. She just listened to me. She was kind. When I could collect myself, I apologized, but she was unfazed and reassured me that she was pleased to listen.

When I played with my children that afternoon, I felt patience and joy. My whole body felt lighter. The pleasure of parenting was back. I had no angry episodes for weeks afterwards. Whatever it was that she did, *that* was what I'd needed!

Jennie told me she'd taken classes in which people exchanged the favor of listening to one another's hopes and concerns. Slowly, as trust developed, they'd cry and laugh more often. This release of emotion was thought to be especially helpful. That explained why one fifteen-minute cry had helped me so much, and why I had cried with *her*. She knew how to listen, and somehow, I'd known. Listening had helped me regain my patience with my kids, and that's what I wanted, so I jumped in!

My first listening partner was an engineer, a somber guy my age whose wife had just walked out on him. She'd left him with a six-month-old daughter who had Down syndrome. He had no experience with infants, a demanding job, few friends, and no help. He and I exchanged listening time, an hour each way, every week for the next twelve years. On my end, family life warmed and lightened quickly. The benefits for my listening partner came more slowly but were just as concrete.

Then I had an experience that took my breath away. My two-year-old son Jacob came down with pinkeye. The doctor prescribed eye drops for several days. I knew he would be frightened by this. I envisioned having to pin his arms down with my knees and lean, dropper in hand, over his struggling body. If it went that way, his trust in me would be undermined three times a day for several days.

When the baby went down for his nap, I decided to try listening to Jacob's feelings about getting drops in his eyes. Perhaps that could help. Being listened to had certainly helped me. I had no idea how this would go, but what was there to lose?

So I showed him the bottle of drops and told him I needed to put some in each eye. He threw himself back on the bed and cried hard. I listened intently, right next to him. I told him the drops would help him get better. He kept crying. When he would slow down, I'd lift him gently to a sitting position, show him the bottle again, and say, "I need to put these in your eyes. It's going to help you." And every time, he cried hard.

After half an hour of this back-and-forth, I asked him if he wanted to see how the drops were squeezed out. He did. I filled the dropper, raised it, and squeezed drops back into the bottle. He watched, and then threw himself back on the bed for more crying. It went on like this: demonstration, crying; demonstration, crying.

Then Jacob asked whether he could try squeezing the dropper. After he'd tried it several times, I asked if he was ready for me to put the drops in his eyes. He wailed again, and I stayed close, keeping eye contact and murmuring that I was sorry it was so hard.

A few minutes later, his face cleared. He sat up and asked, "Can I put them in?" Let me tell you, in a hundred years I wouldn't have thought of a two-year-old giving himself eye drops! I said, "Sure, you can try. If you miss, I'll have to help, though." I asked him to lie down, and filled the dropper. I helped him position his hand over his eye. And I watched as he squeezed two drops into his open eye. He did the same for his other eye, then sat up, looked at me and grinned, and ran off to play.

I was astonished! In the following days, putting drops in his eyes was as ordinary as putting socks on his feet. His fear was gone.

Important ideas came together that day. I saw that much of the stress of parenting could be prevented. I'd grown up with good parents whose stress levels had skyrocketed. I had seen the world of hurt a good parent under stress could cause. Parents themselves needed an emotional outlet! And they didn't have to dominate their children. Children could go from balky to cooperative if a parent would listen. Families could be warmer and closer, as ours had become. Parents could trust their children, set necessary expectations, listen and connect, and their children would thrive.

I saw that listening was a way of giving love that was powerful and respectful. And in the end, it got things done. It felt great to parent this way—working *with* my child's feelings, rather than against them. I knew what I wanted to do with my life.

Since then, I've spent most of my waking hours raising our two boys and working to understand how parents can build the kind of support that makes parenting go better. I've had the privilege of working with thousands of parents and children over four decades, learning how parents can lift all kinds of difficulties out of their children's lives by connecting with them and listening to their feelings. The rewards can come quickly, as they did with my son that day, or the process can take some time. Either way, I am sure that we parents have the power to help our children surmount all kinds of hurdles. And by listening to one another, we too can grow.

After seeing again and again the great good that listening can do for parents and their children, I wanted to get the ideas out there where parents could reach them. So in 1989, with the help of friends and supporters, I founded what is now Hand in Hand Parenting—a nonprofit, parent-led organization. It grew slowly at first, while we rooted our work in our own solid experience. We are now helping parents in a big way.

Tosha Schore, M.A. came to one of my ongoing parent groups in 2005. She has used Hand in Hand Parenting brilliantly to bring her family through many challenges, including illness, trauma, and issues with school. Now the mother of three boys, she is a Trainer with Hand in Hand, and works internationally as a parent consultant, an advocate for boys, and a blogger. I love her embrace of the nitty-gritty, her fine mind, her courage, and her ability to keep good connections paramount in her parenting. I wanted Tosha's voice in this project.

Listen is grounded in all we've been privileged to learn. We're proud to bring you our experience, along with the stories of over seventy parents raising their children on five continents. *Listen* is a Hand in Hand-based team effort to bring you excellent tools for delivering your love to your children. I do hope it is helpful to you.

Patty Wipfler
Founder and Program Director, Hand in Hand Parenting

Tosha's Preface

I was born Heather Megan Schore—named after the beautiful purple ground cover that coated our neighborhood hills. My memories of my early years are sweet—full of rope swings, picking wild berries, sitting on the beanbag in front of the fire, and pouring salt on those pesky slugs, insistent on eating our beautiful garden vegetables.

When I was five, my parents divorced and the house I loved was sold. My dad moved out of state, and my mom and I moved far, far away from all of my friends. I became a very angry girl. I "hated" my dad, was furious at my mom, changed my name to Tosha, switched schools three times in kindergarten, and spent most of first grade in the principal's office.

Fortunately, I had a mom who never lost sight of my goodness. She remained my advocate, even when I kicked and screamed and got into trouble at school. She kept herself in good emotional shape so she could listen to me rage without taking it personally or losing her cool. Mom was my rock.

Now I'm the mom. I have a husband and three boys of my own, each with their own challenges. Becoming a parent is, hands down, the best decision I ever made. I love being a mom, but it hasn't always been easy.

By the time my second son was born, I started reacting to everyday challenges more harshly than I wanted to, which left me feeling badly. I knew I needed help. I wanted to know what I could do when my two-year-old went back to nursing every two hours at night while I had to get up for work in the morning. I wanted to know how I could say, "No" without yelling. I wanted to really, really enjoy my time with my kids because I knew that sooner than I would be ready, they would grow up.

My mom said, "Call Patty Wipfler. She's local, and she does amazing work with families." So I picked up the phone and called her.

A week later, I began attending Patty's two-hour parent support group and it turned out to be just what I needed. We were a small group who would sneak away from our busy lives as mothers, partners, and workers, and gift ourselves two hours of connection. In that room we were unconditionally loved and accepted. We were offered a safe space to cry and shake and rage about our children and the injustices we faced as parents. And we shared the joy of our successes with each other, knowing the whole room was rooting for us. We were never once judged.

Over a decade has passed since that first meeting. My kids are still very much works in progress. They are now nine, eleven, and thirteen years old. I'm still right here in the trenches, using the effective listening tools you'll learn about in this book day in and day out. When things get tough—and boy do they—even my teenager knows I'm here for him. And I've seen over and over again that when he needs me, he comes for help.

I shudder to think what shape my family would be in without my regular Listening Partnerships, which have given me the courage to listen to my boys' tears and tantrums, to connect with them deeply, to set limits firmly but lovingly, and to play wildly.

The Hand in Hand tools have been a road map for me, shaping my parenting into something I feel quite proud of. Am I perfect mom? Not even close! Are my kids straight-A students who wash the dishes without prompting and never talk back? No, they're not. But they work hard, and they know that I'm not going to let fear stop them from pursuing their dreams. They know how to wash dishes and do laundry. They know when they've done something out of line, and will apologize when they feel in their hearts that they're ready. But, most importantly, they know they're loved—no matter what. And when I kiss them goodnight at the end of the day, I know I've done my best and that they have as well.

I hope that this book helps you, too, feel your worth, increase your confidence, and create the change that you long for in your family.

Tosha Schore, M.A.
Certified Trainer at Hand in Hand Parenting
Founder, Your Partner In Parenting

Introduction

When love is flowing between us and our children, our lives burst with meaning. Our children thrive in our glow. We have the energy it takes to see that their lives go well. We sleep (well, sometimes we sleep) without worry.

But every well-loved child goes haywire at times, and some children seem to arrive unhappy right from the start. When the times don't roll easily, we consult fellow parents and we experiment with the parenting tools we've learned. But our children often outwit and outlast our strategies. They continue to drive us nuts.

To add to our difficulties, the parenting ideas we use must serve children of varying ages, and situations that go from infant panic when Mommy steps into the shower to a twelve-year-old's refusal to go to bed by ten. From sibling squabbles to homework woes; from fears in the night to a meltdown at dinner when peas on the plate touch the potatoes. That's a lot of behavioral territory to cover, through eighteen years of development!

When our children go off track, most of us use tools based on rewards and punishments. But when we threaten, give our child a Time Out, or offer a little prize for finishing a task on time, does lasting change come about? Our stress level rises, and most of us find that threats today turn into threats tomorrow; Time Out today begets Time Out tomorrow; and the ante goes up on rewards. A little prize this year turns into one with heavier sugar content or a bigger price tag by fifth grade. And none of these techniques will impress your child when he's fifteen.

When you use rewards and punishments, you focus on barter: your child learns to buy your love and other tangible prizes with his behavior. He also learns that your love is conditional; you will stop acting like you care when he acts out. Rather than developing better judgment over time, he has to focus on what you will charge for his misbehavior, and what he can earn by cooperating. This can take the warmth out of parenting and turn it in to a low-level power struggle with no end in sight. We can do better!

With Hand in Hand Parenting tools, you can turn your child's behavior around. You'll learn how to help your child recover his eager, cooperative, loving nature. The ideas work with children of all ages. You'll learn how to apply them as you read the stories of parents who live on five continents and come from many different cultures. You'll learn from parents of between one and eight children. They are single and partnered, fathers and mothers, gay and straight. We've included the experiences of African American, Latino, and Asian parents; adoptive parents; parents of children with special needs; immigrants; parents who were raised in stark poverty; parents breaking the cycle of abuse in their families; and more. Their insight, caring, and humor will inspire you.

The approach you'll find in these pages is based on four decades of working with children and families across the globe, and is validated by state-of-the-art research. Hand in Hand Parenting is founded on the core observation that parents and children are at their best when they feel close and connected. The troubles that exhaust you and complicate your child's life can be resolved by focusing on *connection*! And, because life has its unhappy moments, it's important to create emotional outlets for both you and your child. With a strong sense of connection between you, your child will thrive in good times and make gains even during difficult moments.

From this book you'll learn concrete, practical tools to lower your child's stress level, and your own. Parenting is hard work. You now hold in your hands a resource to help you with that work. At last.

HOW TO USE THIS BOOK

We wrote this book knowing that you probably don't have time to read it from start to finish. It's unlikely that you ever have several uninterrupted hours. If you can, by chance, read this book from cover to cover, you will close it with a solid understanding of the Hand in Hand Parenting approach, and the tools to build more fun and harmony into your family. But if you're juggling responsibilities all the time, you can come away with the same understanding and know-how by taking in the information ten minutes at a time.

Listen is divided into four sections:

I. A New Perspective on Parenting

II. Your Powerful Parenting Toolbox

III. Solutions to Everyday Parenting Challenges

IV. Our Future, Connected

We do recommend starting with Part I, *A New Perspective on Parenting*. This section presents an understanding of why we parents are so strapped for patience and energy. You'll find an introduction to our powerful new ideas about parenting, why they work, and a taste of the results you can expect to see.

Part II, *Your Powerful Parenting Toolbox*, is at the heart of the Hand in Hand approach. Using the five Listening Tools will change your life and your child's. These Listening Tools will help you work *with* your child's instinct to expel the tension that bothers him. And one of the tools is designed just for you. It will help you stave off worry, guilt, anger, and the exhaustion that comes with working so hard and caring so deeply. Using the Tools will help your whole family overcome struggles. So read all of Part II if you have time. Then, experiment! You can expect good things to happen.

However, if you feel you can't go one more night without sleep, or you simply cannot tolerate some nutty behavior your child has picked up, you can jump straight to Part III, *Solutions to Everyday Parenting Challenges*. There you will find information you can use right away, tucked under the topics of *Building Cooperation, Toward Sweeter Separations, Lifting Fear,* and *Moving Beyond Aggression*. We offer a unique perspective on meeting each of these challenges, and bring you parent stories that show how you can use Listening Tools to connect with your child and move things forward. Then, you can refer back to *Your Powerful Parenting Toolbox* to learn more about the ins and outs of using each tool.

One of the hallmarks of the Hand in Hand approach is that we consider your life and wellbeing to be at least as important as your child's. In Part IV, we offer fresh strategies for your worst parenting moments. We'll outline how you can build a support system for your important work as a parent. And we'll tell you a bit about how the young people who have grown up with Hand in Hand Parenting are doing. We will also sketch out the connected future we envision for hard-working parents. We hope these chapters will encourage you to reach out and build the support you deserve.

You've already got the right ingredients—love, caring, and dedication—for nurturing your child well. The Hand in Hand approach will show you new ways to use them. We want you to thrive as a mom, to love being a dad! We want your family life to be rich with joy and connection. And we believe we can help.

....

To make our book easier to read, we've written it as if we are one person. The personal stories we tell, of course, belong to just one of us, but each story exemplifies the approach we both know well. We're honored to have your precious time and attention; we hope that the ideas we bring will benefit you, and eventually, change the world of parenting.

PART I:

A NEW PERSPECTIVE ON PARENTING

1
Parenting Is Vital But Difficult Work

One of the best things about being a parent is the chance to love our children with all our hearts. Words fail to describe how deeply and completely we love our young ones. Every parent, of course, has moments when feelings about our children are less than lovely. We rebound, though—and love again.

Looking at your own family, you've probably noticed that each new generation tries to give their children a stronger, more loving foundation than they themselves received. Most parents, given halfway decent circumstances, succeed.

You are vital to the wellbeing of your children. They need your love, plenty of warm attention, and your confidence in their goodness. Every effort you make to understand and guide them is worthwhile. Your work as a mom or dad is done through small, commonplace interactions. You wipe a nose gently. You play catch outside till it's almost dark. You keep your thoughts to yourself as your child's slice of hot dog scoots, with a glob of ketchup, off his plate and onto the floor. At nine in the evening, you may feel as though you've gotten nothing done all day long. But if I'd been shadowing you, I could list a hundred quiet acts of caring that you are too tired to remember.

Unfortunately, your parenting work is almost invisible in the eyes of the world. No headlines appear when your child finally overcomes his terror of the dog in the downstairs apartment, or when you handle a fight between your children without blowing up. With zero fanfare and a million interactions, you build your children's character. Their sparkle, their curiosity, and their vigor would wither without the heart you put into your moments with them.

Through our years of experience listening, we have come to three basic understandings about parents.

- **We do our very best.** Dads will show up at the parent-teacher conference although they've worked twenty-four hours straight. When moms get the flu and spike fevers of 103°, they will continue to tend their little ones. Parents without insurance will sell everything they have in order to pay for medical treatment for their ailing child. Courage in parenting is not the exception. It is the rule.

- **We need good support.** To be at our best with our children, we need warm relationships with others, grounded in respect and appreciation. We need confirmation that our children are good at heart, and that they, too, are trying their hardest to do well. And we need a way to deal with the emotional stress that comes with parenting.

- **Parenting is a cradle of leadership.** When our children ask "Why?" again and again, we have the chance to think deeply about every issue important to the human race—fairness, compassion, integrity, civility, property rights, our relationships with other living creatures, peacemaking, reparations, how to foster the growth of character, and the meaning of life. To advocate for our children, we learn how to build good relationships with others and win their cooperation. To lead our families, we figure out how to guide and inspire right at the dinner table, or on the way to school in the morning. And when we can, we use our leadership skills to work for positive change in our communities.

Your importance as a parent is obvious—your children would face danger and heartbreak without you—but it's oh! so difficult to *remember* the importance of your work. If you're an at-home parent, you've felt your heart sink when you were casually asked what you "do," and found that your answer, "I'm a parent," ended the conversation. If you hold a paid job, it's hard not to feel like you're stuck on a treadmill, harried and unable to do it all. Whatever your situation, it's easy to lose sight of your importance, although you ensure your family's survival every day.

In the middle of gluing your child's glider wing back together, or cutting his orange slices just the way he wants them, you won't be aware that your nurturing will live on through many generations. However, your unsung kindnesses will ensure that your kids become even more attentive and wise with their own children someday.

Whether it is recognized or not, the parenting you do is vital work. You put the imprint of your love and judgment on your children countless times each day; they will keep it always. They will pass it on. It is work that lasts.

We're good people, we do important work, and our children are sweet and precious beings. So why is parenting so difficult? Why do we frequently trudge through our days and groan through dinner-and-bedtime routines?

We tend to blame ourselves for our lack of patience, or our children for their wildly maddening behavior. But the roadblocks that we parents run into are so universal that we suspect there must be some bigger dynamic at work. We had energy before we had children. Most of us had some patience then, too. And we felt that, even when we struggled, we could learn. We could grow. So what's going on?

WE FACE EXTERNAL FORCES THAT MAKE PARENTING DIFFICULT

In fact, there *are* bigger dynamics that make parenting hard—forces in our society that pull us away from the warm, nurturing times we need with our children and one another. In brief:

- It takes well over $200,000, together with incalculable warmth, generosity, and wisdom, to nurture a child for eighteen years. But there's no preparation, pay, or protection from overwhelming circumstances for parents. Parenting holds the economic status of a hobby.

- Parenting custom and employment law distance fathers from their children.

- Poverty, racism, sexism, and other kinds of discrimination intensify parents' struggles and stress, and hurt our children.

- Parents are open targets for criticism.

Let's look at each of these burdens more closely.

Parenting is utterly personal, night-and-day work that starts off with a bang—a three-year-long intensive care period. Beyond that stretches at least fifteen more years of dedication, guidance, research, advocacy, diplo-

macy, night work, mess patrol, grooming, tutoring, cooking, transporta-
tion, first aid, and more. Above all, you are called upon to model caring
and wisdom in small matters and large, day after day, at a moment's notice.

Moreover, for your child to thrive, he needs abundant attention. He
needs play—lots of play! And he needs you to be smitten with him. Love is
central to the job, and your life will be enriched by the love your child gives
in return. He'll also give you at least ten colds in his first two years, wake
you up often in the night, plunge you into spirals of worry, and to top it all
off, he's likely to look you in the eye and tell you you're stupid one day. Yet
your love will still be needed. Raising your child is no hobby!

Work pressure and the dated expectation that a mother's role is primary
can distance fathers from their kids and make nurturing harder for both
parents. When a father is present, but relegated to a secondary role in parenting, everyone loses. That said, when a father or a mother can't manage
to step into their parent role, the family isn't "broken." Resilience studies
validate what common sense tells us: it takes just one person, in love with
a child, to provide the positive regard that a child needs to get a good start
in life. But support for that one person is vital!

Many parents' energy is taxed by injustice. In the US, one in five of our
children are poor. Poverty goes hand in hand with unsafe neighborhoods,
hunger, poor health, and low-performing schools. Parents who face these
conditions lead stressful lives. Their children have fewer chances to play
freely and bask in the delight of the adults around them. And when a family is targeted by racism, homophobia, or any other kind of discrimination,
the potential of every member of that family is threatened.

Finally, you've probably found that your parenting is subject to criticism from those who know you, and even from random passersby. Adults
in the US are often impatient with young children. Many of us become
hard on our children in public as a defensive measure; we bluster at our
little ones out of fear that someone else will stride over and do it for us.

When children misbehave, people fault the parents. When children
struggle in school, people fault the parents. But every parent I've ever listened to has done their best to love their child. All parents face challenges
that they did not bring upon themselves.

WE FACE INTERNAL CHALLENGES, TOO

In addition to these societal hurdles, we face challenges that come from within. Some of our parenting comes from the best of what our parents gave us. Without knowing it, we might channel our father's sweetness at bedtime, or our mother's patience as our child learns to hammer a nail. But some of what we bring to parenting came to us when our parents felt embattled. So after a frustrating day, we might unleash stinging threats like the ones we heard from our father, or yank our child's arm like our mother did ours. And you have probably noticed that although you vow not to yell, spank, or throw flaming tantrums, raw emotion sometimes wins the day. We're good parents, but we can't help but carry some baggage.

PARENTING IS EMOTIONAL WORK

You can't predict ahead of time how you will feel once you become a parent. But you *will* have feelings. Big feelings! You'll be swept up by extraordinary hopes and gripping fears, waves of gratitude and bitter resentment, love and hate. There's worry; there's joy. One day, you'll feel proud and confident as you watch your child make a new friend at the park, just like that. But when he wails in pain from an earache at two in the morning, you'll feel pangs of helplessness. When a feeling comes along, it will come on strong.

Still, we can't match our children's emotional chops! Good children don't just cry: they are wracked with sobs. They don't register complaints, they have tantrums. Perfectly normal children scream and throw things. They run yelling through the house. They kick. They tremble with rage. Have a child, and you're living with an emotional Beethoven! A genius in the realm of passionate expression.

You can't avoid the emotional work of parenting. Whether you stuff your upset and try to be patient, or let your family see and hear it all, you're engaged in emotional work. You can try to keep on an even keel, but we humans don't function that well when we stuff lots of feelings. We can take those highly touted ten deep breaths and manage to keep an upset inside. But after awhile, we start itching for an excuse to show someone how we really feel, and eventually, we lose it. There aren't good conventional choices for handling this emotional work. There's just one thing for sure: whatever our choices, handle it we must.

What can happen to an ordinary family to put a deep stress-print on the parent-child relationship? To fill in a brief sketch of what parents face, here are a few real-life examples from just a handful of my relatives. When they were boys, my husband pushed his brother out of their moving car onto the Golden Gate Bridge. His mom had to stop mid-span, run back, and pluck her son up off the highway. My sister became profoundly mentally disabled, and after a year of decline, could not recognize us, or move her body at will. My brother came close to shooting a friend's eye out with a BB gun. My cousin got rheumatoid arthritis when she was twelve, and was confined to a wheelchair for many months. My uncle, an Air Force pilot, came back from the war in Southeast Asia too disturbed to be with his daughters, wife, or anyone else. He found no solace; he ended his life.

As you can imagine, every family member involved in these events was wracked with stress. For many of them, scars and grief still remain. And this is just a small sampling from a middle-class clan who wanted for nothing except emotional support.

I hardly know a parent that hasn't faced serious troubles at one time or another. We parents put one foot in front of the other, we keep a good face on at work and while we're out and around. But parenting can wear us down to the nub at any level of economic privilege.

Doing emotional work—finding a way to offload stress and lower the walls we've thrown up to protect ourselves—is not yet a common concept. When we're swept up by feelings and have no emotional support, we lose our compass. We're in a strange land. We don't feel good, we do things we regret, and we're too isolated or ashamed to tell anyone that we're struggling. A small minority of us have crawled, humbled, to a counselor or a support group of some kind. There, our privacy protected, we may have found ourselves choosing to do emotional work as we faced our situation. We may have learned that we weren't alone as we heard the stories of others grappling with similar circumstances. But most of us don't really even track the rumbling of our emotions. We just notice that the older our children get, the testier we become, and the less dear they seem. We tell ourselves that we're probably doing OK, but we spend a lot of energy skirting emotional land mines in order to keep peace in the home.

On the inside, every one of us is working hard. We have to handle our children's outbursts; we have to deal with our own. We want to help our child when he's been snubbed by a friend; we must cope with our own isolation. We want to help our children with their learning challenges; we have many things to learn about parenting, but where do we go? What can we do to recover when we feel depleted, or too ornery to be good company?

THERE IS A WAY FORWARD

Here's some welcome news: there are good and simple ways to handle the emotional rigors of parenting. You can bring more laughter and fun to your family. You can have the joy of seeing problems disappear because of *your* mothering, *your* fathering. There are tools that can help you.

When you use the Listening Tools we present, you'll have a new way to build your emotional stamina and plump up your support system. Instead of spending lots of energy trying to control your child's behavior, you can focus on building a strong connection with your child, and repair it when it frays. You'll be able to guide him without the traditional carrot or the well-worn stick. The limits you set will actually bring your child closer to you! You'll discover new aspects of your child's intelligence that you hadn't noticed before. And you'll put your head on your pillow at night, surer that you've met your child's core needs.

Your road won't be free of potholes and hairpin turns. Our society is riddled with enough trouble spots that you're sure to encounter some rough going. But with a clearer perspective, you and your child can get through the hard patches in better shape, with energy to spare.

Here's the framework for parenting that you deserve, and five simple Listening Tools that will bring you closer to your children, and to your own best self.

2
Connection Is The Key

Your child has a unique and wondrous mind. But to function well, her developing mind needs a sense of close connection with you as surely as she needs food, shelter, cleanliness, and sleep.

When your child feels close to you, her brain forms the neural pathways that allow her to learn, remember, and think. Just as her body needs good food to grow, her developing mind requires someone who will respond to her with interest and support. Every positive interaction helps her reach her full potential today, and for decades to come. When she senses you're on her side, she can learn, cooperate, and connect with others. In a nutshell, feeling closely connected helps your child *build* intelligence, and it helps her *use* the intelligence she already has.

- warmth
- respect
- eye contact
- listening

- trust
- cooperation
- respect

Child's neural pathways grow

Here's how your child's brain is structured and why connection is so vital to her wellbeing:

Her brain stem extends from the top of her spine upward toward the lower middle of her brain. Designed to be a sentinel and operations manager, it monitors your child's physical wellbeing. Governing reflexes, heart rate, breathing, and many other bodily functions, the brain stem reacts in a flash to any hint of a threat. When there's a sudden, loud noise, for example, your child's brain stem makes her startle and gets her heart racing. It does not participate in thinking. But your child's survival depends on the crucial job the brain stem does.

Her limbic system consists of several complex parts that form the social-emotional center of her being. Second to evolve, the limbic system allows children to build social relationships. Your child's limbic system sends signals that enable you to "read" her emotional state minute by minute. And, like an invisible radar beam, it checks all incoming data—sights, sounds, tastes, touch, and more—for information about her safety. It inquires, "Am I wanted? Do I belong? Will someone here be able to think about me?"

Body language is one of the limbic system's specialties. Eye contact, facial expression, tone of voice, posture, and movement all provide your child with information about the inner state of the people around her. When you or another caring adult signal, "I'm here. I like you. I'm available," your child's mind has a chance to feel the connection you offer. That satisfies her inborn need for inclusion and protection.

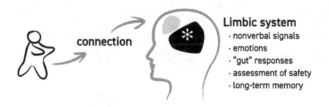

Children must have evolved this keen awareness of the inner states of others because their lives depended on it. Long before the dawn of civilization, a child's survival hinged on knowing which adult could meet her needs in an unpredictable environment. You have surely seen your child's preference for relaxed, connective adults in action. For instance, when Uncle Raymond comes to dinner and shoots questions at your young child in a booming voice, she's likely to run to your side and cling. Though Uncle Raymond means well, your child's limbic system receives just one news flash, "Warning! This adult isn't reading your signals! Back away!"

When your child feels connected and protected, her limbic system can do a very important job: it can coordinate communication between all parts of her brain. It opens access to her prefrontal cortex, so the reasoning center of her mind can hum. Connection "turns on the lights upstairs."

Your child's prefrontal cortex makes her uniquely human. Behind her forehead, it's part of the folded gray mass that is the most recent part of the human brain to evolve. Her prefrontal cortex is of interest to you because when it's engaged, *she can think*. She can reason. She has the attention she needs to experiment and learn. She has some control over her impulses, depending upon her age and stage of development. She can plan and then follow through; she can remember what you told her a few moments ago about not waking the baby, or needing to start her homework early tonight. And it's here that her judgment develops over time.

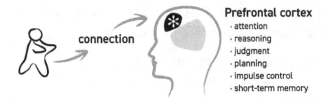

WHEN YOUR CHILD FEELS CONNECTED, SHE CAN THINK

When your child feels connected, she can understand that the cookies cooling on the counter are to take to Auntie Mae's, and she'll munch away on crackers and cheese instead. When your child feels connected, you can give the baby the first turn at a piggyback ride, and she's content to go second. When your child feels connected, she'll laugh as she slips and slides on roller skates for the first time. She'll persist, although it's not easy. When her need for connection is met, your child is a learner.

And as her sense of connection with you grows strong, she'll be able to carry it into her classroom, outside where the neighborhood kids play, and off to sleep-away camp, and keep right on learning and having fun.

BROKEN CONNECTION: THE INVISIBLE "OFF" SWITCH

Of course, we're talking about parenting here, so there are wrinkles! Through no fault of yours or anyone else's, your connection with your child will break often. When she feels threatened, frustrated, or when another feeling floods her system, she loses her sense of connection. Shazzam! Her prefrontal cortex shuts down. She literally can't think. It's an instantaneous process, and you've seen it happen hundreds of times.

- **You allow half an hour of TV before dinner**, because your child was an angel while you fed the baby. But after the TV show, she's balky. She refuses to help set the table and won't sit down for more than a minute. She starts a big fuss.

- **You go to the kitchen to fix dinner**, after your kids have played well with you nearby for a good while. Less than five minutes later, they are bickering loudly.

- **You take your child with you for a quick run to the market.** She's been content all morning. You hunt for your keys, feed the cat, talk on the phone, and make a stop for gas. By the time you're in the vegetable aisle, she's whiny, demanding, and fixated on getting Yummy Bears, something you never buy her.

Difficulties at moments like these spring from how our brains are constructed. They're designed to be in steady communication with others, and to function in a cooperative and nurturing environment. Things like a TV program and a parent leaving the room can fray a child's sense of being seen and wanted. And that long disconnection on the way to the market can throw a contented child entirely off-kilter.

· hurt feelings
· broken thinking

WHEN YOUR CHILD FEELS HURT, SHE CAN'T THINK

When your child's sense of connection with you or her caregiver breaks, she feels hurt immediately. As it must, her limbic system sends out an alarm: things aren't safe! In an instant, her prefrontal cortex—the center of reason, planning, impulse control, and attention—goes offline. When your child feels hurt and can't think, she's apt to do nutty things like pulling her sister's hair or breaking her pencil point in protest as she starts her homework.

Here are a few simple signs a child might give when she feels hurt and can't think:

- She can't hold your gaze for more than a second or two.

- She isn't cooperative.

- She looks impassive or unhappy.

- Her behavior appears stuck in a rut. She sucks her thumb, grabs from others, can't sleep although she's tired, asks for things that aren't allowed, rejects your help, hits or hurts others, or runs off to be alone. She clearly cannot feel your love.

These important signals tell us that our children need our help. It's time to reach out and help them back on track again, where they'd much rather be.

YOUR CHILD DOESN'T WANT TO ACT UP

When your child goes off track, she's struggling with a circumstance that's as disabling as a broken bone. A child with a broken leg can't walk or run until her leg has been set and healed. A child whose sense of connection has broken loses her impulse control and short-term memory. She can't reason. She doesn't *want* to act up. She's not trying to manipulate you into giving her what she's whining for. She'd much rather be sunny and cooperative, but her whole system goes haywire when she loses her sense of connection.

It's as if your child has an on/off switch somewhere inside. A thinking child can be generous; when she's off-track, she won't let anyone touch her belongings. A thinking child can be affectionate with her little sister; when she's off-track, her hug will be too tight or her kiss will turn into a bite. A thinking child can wait a bit for your attention; when she's off-track, she'll knock a sibling over to get to you first. When children can't think, they're desperate to connect, and their behavior brings us that news.

Every now and then, a child manages to actually state her needs in words before she loses her sense of connection. But even then, children aren't exactly polite. The daughter of a friend of mine was four years old when her little sister arrived. She was remarkably loving and thoughtful toward the new baby for several months. But finally one day, the connection she felt began to shred. She stood tall and yelled, "Mommy, put down that darn baby and pay attention to *me!*" Heading over the edge, she had the presence of mind to signal before her thinking flickered and went out.

Helping process
· move close
· stop off-track behavior
· listen
· offer connection

Healing process
· crying
· tantrums
· trembling
· perspiration
· laughter

YOUR CHILD INSTINCTIVELY KNOWS HOW TO RECOVER FROM HURT

Life is full of occasions that break a child's sense of connection, hurt her feelings, stop her thinking, and send her off track. Fortunately, your child was born with a sturdy emotional repair process. The feelings that have been stirred up in her need an avenue out, and she needs to feel your caring once again. Only one act will grant her permission to let her feelings out and convey that you really care: *listening*. Yes, listening can heal the hurt.

Simply halt, get close, and gently stop her nutty behavior. Don't rely on words—*your child can't respond to directions when she's unable to think!* Step in, gently but firmly, so she can't continue to kick the door, sweep books off the shelf, or get up and run from the homework table. Then put a gentle hand on her back, or get down next to her if she's lying on the floor and kicking. Listen to everything she says and shows. Absorb the meaning of her body language. She needs someone to understand her difficult feelings. As you listen, she will heal the feelings of hurt through crying, a tantrum, laughter, or the perspiration and trembling that foster recovery from fear.

She may go on for a while. In fact, the first few times you try listening instead of your usual discipline methods, you'll probably think, "Is she ever going to come back? This can't be right!" We are not used to seeing such passionate displays of emotion! But hang in there. All that passion has a purpose. These are the exact feelings that have been muddying her behavior! She'll persist because, although she's showing you how badly she feels, deeper inside, it's a big relief to shed corrosive tension. When your child has finished releasing her upset, she will feel your caring once again. She'll understand things better, behave more flexibly, and her sense of confidence will grow.

We don't know exactly how crying, tantrums, trembling, perspiring, and laughter relieve the emotional tension in a child's mind. The insight that these activities are normal, and part of an inborn healing process, is relatively new. Though we don't know *how* it works, we do know *that* it works. Whatever the neurons in her mind are doing, a crying child will regain her ability to think if she has a warm listener. And over time, situations that are difficult for her will become less so. As you listen to her feelings, you'll see your child change and grow. Her off-track behavior will become less frequent. She'll also become better at letting you know what she needs *before* she feels desperate.

Your child can't heal from hurt all by herself. Remember, she's first and foremost a social being, and you are her rock, her anchor. She needs your help to shake off the effects of hurt. So pour in your willingness to connect, while she pours out the feelings that prevent her from solving problems and having fun.

Here's a story to give you a feel for the results you'll enjoy when you offer love and listening, but no shushing, through your child's emotional moment.

———◇———

My grandson Reggie, four years old, had a play date with a boy from his preschool one Saturday. The boy didn't want to come to Reggie's, and Reggie didn't want him there either, but the father needed childcare, and their parents had agreed. I stayed with them quietly. They couldn't find a single thing they wanted to do together. I nudged them in one another's direction now and then, but no dice. They played separately in the same room, not even speaking to one another, for more than an hour.

Then the friend accidentally bumped into an elaborate marble track structure Reggie had built with his dad, and down it went. Reggie was devastated, and burst out crying. I brought him into my lap. He cried, "I will never, ever be able to build it again! It was so good! Now it's gone *forever!*" I said, "Yes, love, that's probably true," which made him cry even harder. I didn't want to rob him of his chance to grieve fully for his creation. His friend played quietly nearby, listening intently but not commenting. I said, "Ethan didn't mean to bump your structure. It was an accident. He didn't want it to fall."

Reggie cried hard for about twenty minutes. When he didn't feel like crying any longer, I asked them if they wanted a snack. They did. Then Reggie suggested we play hide and seek. The two of them ran through the house, giggling and whooping because I had such a "hard time" finding them. They were in synch with one another at last. They stuck together, jamming themselves into a small cupboard, then stuffing themselves behind a door. We played for quite a while. When Ethan's father finally came to get him, he begged, "Can I stay longer? I don't want to go home!" Reggie didn't want him to go, either.

———◇———

Crying and tantrums are not throwaway behaviors! Your child does the smartest thing possible when she enters a meltdown. She's blasting away emotional tension, in the effort to think again. And while she's crying, you have a direct line into her aching heart. Now is your moment! What you do when she's upset has ten times the love value of a cuddle or a pat on the back when times are good. She's longing for your help, even if she tells you, "Go away! I don't like you!" If you can listen to her feelings and offer your warmth, she'll be a very different person when she's done.

HURT FROM THE PAST CAN SEND YOUR CHILD OFF TRACK, TOO

But what about those times when your child suddenly goes wacky for no reason at all? For example, she's had a fun day but balks angrily when you want her to take a bath. Or she's perfectly content to play until the moment you start to talk with your wife. She jumps in and interrupts you both loudly. Isn't she just immature, or perhaps manipulative?

No, even very young children, when they feel safe and connected, can cooperate with bathing, or allow their parents to have a conversation. In these instances, stored hurt is probably the thorn in your child's side.

In infancy and toddlerhood, a child can't offload all her hurt feelings completely. So feelings from unresolved incidents remain in her emotional memory. She tries not to think about the hurts stored there, and most of the time they remain tucked away. But these stored feelings can surface at unexpected times. When she is in a situation that in some way resembles a moment of hurt in her past, bingo! Up they come! The sights, sounds, and the feel of a past upset flood her system once again. Emotion rules. For a while, your child can't reason, and seems to be unaware of your support.

For example, a single mother I know decided to help her six-year-old daughter overcome her fear of sleeping in her own bed, which was placed next to her mother's bed, just three feet away. Her child had always been afraid to sleep separately. After proposing they sleep in separate beds, the mom stayed close, and listened for a long time while her daughter sobbed and clung to her. She was still terrified after an hour of crying, so the mom slept with her as usual. The second night, her daughter's crying turned to active struggle and trembling. At one point, the girl screamed, "It hurts! It hurts!" When her mother asked her what hurt, she said, "The bee sting!" She had been stung on her leg that summer, so her mother took a look at that spot, but her daughter flailed with fear and said, "Not there! Here!" and frantically pointed to the top of her right hand. It was the very spot where, just hours after her birth, an inexperienced hospital technician had pricked her seven times before she managed to insert an IV the doctor had ordered. The idea of sleeping in her own bed had stirred big fears, perhaps stemming from that traumatic first day of her life. Her mother kept listening, anchoring her daughter with reassurance until her terror subsided. After that cry, and her mother's confident listening, she slept easily in her own bed. There was no further issue.

Fortunately, when your child can't think, you don't really need to know exactly what triggered her, or why. All you need to do is notice that she can't think, move in close, set limits if necessary, and listen. You'll learn how to do all that in the pages to come.

YOU CAN PARTNER WITH YOUR CHILD

Your power to communicate love for your child peaks when she begins to show you her feelings. In fact, emotional episodes allow you to *partner* with your child. There's a job for each of you.

- **Your job begins when you notice that she's off track.** Move in to stop any thoughtless behavior, and listen. Moving in as soon as you see that she's in trouble says, "I see you," and keeps her from resorting to more drastic behavior.

- **Her job is to offload her upset,** which she will do as soon as she feels your caring gaze.

- **Your job is to protect her and connect with her** as the feelings become intense. You may need to keep her from hurting herself or you if she needs to thrash or flail to release the pent-up tension.

- **Her job is to keep showing you all the hurt she feels.** Meanwhile, she'll absorb the healing connection you offer.

You don't have to control her. You don't have to teach her anything. You don't have to issue consequences for her behavior. She simply needs to offload that emotion so she can regain her ability to think. Your support protects her as she works. Listening is what she needs to heal and to recover. After the emotion trapped in that knot of feelings pours off, she will literally see things differently. She'll be able to connect. She'll be reasonable again. And she won't be quite so easily triggered in the future.

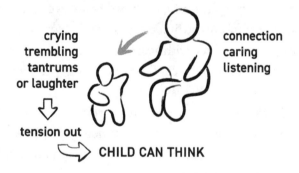

crying
trembling
tantrums
or laughter

⇩

tension out

connection
caring
listening

⇨ CHILD CAN THINK

YOUR CHILD'S HURT WAS INTENSE, AND SHE'LL SHOW YOU!

Your child has probably developed quite a backlog of upsets that haven't been heard. As you give her your warm support, it could look like things are heading in the wrong direction. She may thrash, arch, or scream as she is gripped by the feelings that have sent her off track. They are healing as you listen. Just stay there and support her, keeping her safe.

After you've anchored your child all the way through her outburst, she might relax in your arms for one last deep cry, or take a few shaky breaths, and simply stop. She'll feel relieved. If she doesn't fall fast asleep, she may contemplate you and the world around her for some moments. When your child yawns, begins to giggle, or asks for a glass of juice as if you'd just been chatting for the past half hour, you have both done your job. An excellent day is ahead.

LISTENING IS SIMPLE, BUT IT'S NOT EASY

By now, you may be thinking, "Forget it! I don't want to be anywhere near my child when she's a mess like that!" I realize that listening to your upset child that first time will take courage! I would only recommend something this challenging to a hardworking parent if it worked—and it does. We have seen it work for thousands of children in all types of families from many cultures. What is special about the Hand in Hand approach is that there's a Listening Tool for *you*. You can use a Listening Partnership, an exchange of listening between parents, as a source of support. You can create a place where *your* feelings are heard and respected. This will give you a real feel for your child's emotional life. And it will help you to actually enjoy shepherding your child through her emotional moments.

Once you've begun listening to your child's feelings, you can leave these problematic tools behind: scolding, lectures, demands, punishment, bribery, raising your voice, threats, consequences, star charts, and rewards for good behavior. You won't have to intimidate your child. You won't feel that you must control her every move. You will set limits, but you won't feel like the bad guy. You'll notice what a gift good limits are to your off-track child.

When you connect with Listening Tools, here's what will waft into your family: laughter, fun, cooperation, trust, love, creativity, and warmth. You'll get to see your child become surer of her goodness. You'll get to be surer of your own. Connected, close, and tucked in with one another is how we're built to live.

UNDERSTANDING YOUR CHILD'S SIGNALS FOR HELP

For a busy parent trying to get things done, a child's attempts at connection can feel like a deliberate effort to push your buttons. But when your child can't find a way to connect with a caring adult, she will keep signaling. A disconnected child can behave like the most stubborn, picky, whiny, ungrateful, aggressive, or overactive child on earth. What an individual parent can't see, though, is that children around the world send these exact same signals to their worn-out parents. The message is: "Emotional emergency! I don't feel connected!" It's sent in behavior, not words. If we translated your scrappy, unruly child's message into the phrases you'd prefer, the neatly printed note would say:

Dear Mom or Dad:

Thank you for receiving my note. I am trying hard to feel your love, but I just can't. It scares me to feel so far away. Would you please, at your earliest convenience, sit down and invite me to be with you? Can we have a little fun, or could you at least put your arm around me so I have half a chance of feeling your love? Please stop me nicely so I don't do nutty things—I really don't want to create problems. Your help will make things so much better.

I love you to infinity!

Your (temporarily) far-away child.

In fact, here's a note that one first-grader wrote to her parents:

"I love you when I'm mad, sad, angry, frustateit, happy, pround, and all the feelings. I love you even more than I mean. I love you when I say I hate you. And I mean it. I love you."

Although there's no translator available to help you when your child's behavior is driving you up the wall, this list might come in handy. These are signals that all children use to send up a flare for help.

THE "BROKEN COOKIE"

Sometimes a tiny thing, like seeing the corner fall off her cookie or losing one Lego in the heat register, catapults your child into tears or tantrums. This is probably the most common signal children give that they need your help and attention. This signal tells you, "I have so many feelings bottled up inside that I can't go on. Every little thing makes me unhappy. I need you to be with me while I get rid of this upset! It's making my life miserable."

When you witness a huge emotional flare ignited by a tiny issue, it's likely that much of the intensity is rooted in a difficult past experience. The broken cookie or lost Lego piece merely reminds your child of that earlier, harder time. What seems like much ado about nothing is actually a valuable opportunity to help your child heal. You can rebuild her sense of connection with you and make her less prone to difficult behavior in the future by offering connection and listening. If you anchor her through the storm, she'll recover her serenity.

THE "SPOILED OUTING"

This signal arises when you give extra time and attention to your child, or when a group of friends or relatives gathers. At some point during the special occasion, your child gets upset over some small thing. This signal says, "It feels so hopeful when we're having fun together. Now that we're close, let me tell you about this awful feeling I sometimes have. Help me with this, please!"

It's almost as if the security and fun of the moment flushes stale feelings out into the open with the power of a fire hose. Of course, this happens right when you're counting on your child to be cooperative and tuned in.

The Spoiled Outing is such a common occurrence that you can plan ahead for it. Birthday parties, family gatherings, holidays, and trips to special places will trigger a "spoiled outing" upset in almost every child. Your child is not ungrateful. She feels the good will around her, and her instincts tell her it's a great time to clean house!

"STOP ME!"

This is another classic. When you've been busy, worried, rushed, or spending time with others, your child's little boat drifts away from the anchor of your attention. She may have signaled for attention once or twice already. Perhaps you brushed her off, hoping trouble would go away; more likely, you had your hands full and couldn't respond.

So, desperate for connection, your child looks you straight in the eye and does something you've told her ten times not to do. She rips leaves off the plant in the living room, or throws a block at her sister. This signal says, "I'm feeling lost—it drives me nuts to see you right here next to me when I'm feeling so alone. Help me!"

When a child deliberately breaks the rules we've laid down, we parents often think she's out to defy or manipulate us. But getting your goat is not your child's goal. She's so driven to connect with you that she'd rather have you come to her angry than endure one more moment in isolation. Her mind needs a connection with you, pronto! So she finds a surefire way to bring you close.

WITHDRAWAL

Sometimes, a child will give up on asking for your help. She'll turn inward, and try to numb the ache of feeling alone or scared with a little ritual—sucking her thumb, twisting her hair, or clutching a blanket or action figure for dear life. This signal says, "I don't know what to do. I don't feel good. I'm going to shift into idle until someone comes to help me." There's not a lot of hubbub with this signal. But your child is losing precious time for learning and exploring. She's not ready to risk an active upset, but she's disconnected enough that she can't use her mind or body fully. If she's attached to a pacifier, she can't talk; while clutching a doll, she can't use one of her hands; if she's twisting her hair, she can't run, laugh, or explore. Her plea for help is silent, and it will continue until you come and connect.

AGGRESSION

When your child moves to hurt someone else or herself, her behavior says, "Connection: zero! Thinking: none! I have no idea why I'm lashing out, but I don't know how to stop!" A child trapped in aggressive behavior is frightened, and needs a warm but hands-on limit from a kind adult who can remember that she is good. Her sense of connection has simply run dry. Chapter 11, *Lifting Fear*, and Chapter 12, *Moving Beyond Aggression*, will show you how to use Listening Tools to shift your child from fear-based behavior to real connection and cooperation.

DISTRACTED PLAY

Sometimes, a child can become slightly electric when low-level feelings of fear are running through her. The only way she can keep up appearances is to flit from one activity to another, paying only superficial attention to what she's doing. She can't connect in play; there's no give and take with others. When any small challenge arises, she moves on to the next thing. When she's this flighty, she can't learn much. Her relationships aren't satisfying. She'll tend to be picky, bossy, or impulsive. Her behavior tells you, "I feel unsettled, and nothing I do makes me feel any better. I've got to keep moving because I don't know how to find safe harbor. Please help me!"

Your child is not to blame for any of these behaviors. They arise when she's hurting and can't think. Some children send up the same flare repeatedly; others shift from one signal to another as they try to attract the attention they need. None of these signals are fun for us to handle. We want to guide our children, but we find ourselves doing traditional things. We yell, hit, scold, shame, or give our children the cold shoulder, although these responses can't possibly help a child who feels adrift and alone.

Instead, with good tools and an understanding of the importance of connection, you can clear a path to warmth, fun, laughter, and sweeter times in your family. It takes work, but that's all it takes. Magic is not needed. You can learn to do it day by day. Connection is the key. Connection, and your strong will to love well.

PART II:
YOUR POWERFUL PARENTING TOOLBOX

Introduction

Each of the five Hand in Hand Listening Tools we present plays an important role in building wellbeing for your family. The tools work together to connect you with your children.

Special Time is a simple way to pour love and attention into your child. You set aside one-on-one time, and let your child choose what the two of you will do. She will use this time to show you what's important to her and reveal her struggles. Special Time lets your child feel seen. It deepens her trust in you, while giving you a window into her thinking. It builds the sense of safety that promotes cooperation. Special Time can help connect you and your child from her earliest years through her adolescence, young adulthood, and beyond. It's almost always the first Listening Tool to reach for when you're thinking, "I don't know what to do with this kid!"

Staylistening transmits your caring while your child feels hurt or afraid, and is expressing intense feelings. She pours out the hurt she feels; you listen, and pour in your quiet confidence that she'll recover. You protect her while she feels alone and undone. Listening to your child's upset doesn't mean approving of her feelings; it's your way of bathing her in your caring during her toughest moments. As her feelings pour out, an emotional burden will lift, and she'll be left with the deep imprint of your love and support in its place. Both you and she will learn that feelings of hurt will heal when someone listens and cares. Because most of us were not listened to in this way, Staylistening can be challenging for a parent. But this tool has the power to lift your child's spirits and transform bothersome behavior.

Setting Limits is crucial in your work as a parent. Your child needs and deserves a limit the minute her behavior starts to veer off track. A good limit gives your child the chance to offload the emotional tension that clouds her behavior, so she can return to the fun of learning and enjoying those around her. We'll help you recognize the early warning signals your child sends out, and show you how to set limits without harshness. There are even ways to bring a limit that will fill your child with laughter.

Playlistening is the art of eliciting laughter in play with your child, without tickling. A heartwarming, creative tool, it will strengthen your connection as you make time for fun and enjoyment. Laughter is a powerful antidote to stress. Your child's confidence will build as you learn to instigate playful role reversal and games full of friendly challenge and affection. Laughter will foster warmth in your family.

Finally, the **Listening Partnership** gives you a way to replenish your energy for parenting. An exchange of listening time with another parent can help you shed the stress that crops up when you live with young children. A Listening Partnership also gives you a haven for learning. You get a safe, private place to unfold your thoughts and feelings. How do you want your parenting to be different from the way you were raised? What gifts from your parents do you want to pass on? When you find yourself struggling with your child over a particular issue, how does your own past experience come into play? You'll also have the privilege of listening to another parent as they think, feel, and learn. You won't exchange advice, but you'll learn from one another every time you meet. As you listen and are listened to, you'll find it easier to enjoy your children, and to connect warmly with them during their troubled moments.

So there you have it!

Each tool is powerful in its own right, but no one tool is meant to be used alone. Setting limits—your use of parental power—is tempered with Special Time, which puts your child in the driver's seat for short chunks of time. Playlistening, the lighthearted side of parent-child interactions, helps to balance out the full-throated drama your child goes through as you Staylisten. Your Listening Partnership is a vital learning laboratory, as well as your sanctuary. There, you are respected and understood. Your every feeling is welcome, every experience is of interest, and every thought an important one.

With these five Hand in Hand Listening Tools, you can fully express your deep love for your kids and strengthen your family life. Enjoy!

3
Special Time

A sense of connection confers real powers on your child. It grants him the ability to think, to cooperate, to feel good about himself and the people around him. It opens up avenues to learning. And it helps him develop judgment over time. Want your child to be a good friend to others? Build his sense of connection. Want him to be brave? Nurture his sense of connection. Want him to be able to amuse himself part of the time? Plump up his sense of connection. Want him to know right from wrong? Keep restoring his sense of connection. He'll learn to catch himself before whomping on a friend in anger, or sneaking the guinea pig into his room and losing it there. Special Time, the first Listening Tool, will help you to keep this bond of connection strong.

In Special Time, you set aside some time—from three minutes to an hour—and your child tells you the recipe for reaching him. You say when and where you'll have time to connect. Your child tells you how. Special Time can be occasional or even a daily practice, depending on your family. Either way, as Dr. Lawrence J. Cohen says, it's meant to "fill your child's cup" with connection.

WHAT SETS SPECIAL TIME APART?

You may be thinking, "But I already do a lot of special time with my kids! I take them to the park on weekends, let them splash and play in the bath, sing with them. They get to run around a lot more than I did. We have a lot of fun times together." You're right! Those times are important.

But those times won't have the same effect as Special Time. You enjoy your children as they splash in the tub, but if the phone rings, you answer it. If your partner enters the bathroom to discuss the neighbor's noisy music, you converse. All day long, many things can and do distract you. In Special Time, you refuse to be distracted. You focus on just one child. You make arrangements for your other children, and the phone is off limits.

In Special Time, unlike normal life, your child runs the show. You do set the conditions: for example, Special Time will be for fifteen minutes, we can go inside or outside, but no car today, and we won't spend money. The rest is up to your child, and you'll see him become quite creative in directing things as the spotlight of your attention shines on him. You'll discover what tickles his fancy each time. On a day when you haven't got much patience, you can set up a short Special Time. On an easier day, you can be more generous.

There's always a start and an end to Special Time. Your child looks forward to the start of it. Many parents look forward to the end. A commitment to a limited period of time will give you greater tolerance for the interesting things your child chooses to do. For instance, say that your child somehow gets into chewing up soda crackers in the back yard and blowing the dry crumbs out of his mouth to make snow. Though you're a fastidious person, you can manage to chuckle and admire his originality. Wisely, you promised him just ten minutes, so you can almost enjoy seeing soda-cracker snow cover the grass. You pat yourself on the back—yes, he loves messes, but at least he's creative! And for ten minutes, you can handle it.

You could think of the majority of the time you spend with your child as the nourishing milk of parenting. Special Time is like the cream. It adds an important quality—emotional safety—to your relationship. But all cream would be too rich for both of you!

What can you accomplish with Special Time? You will soon find out. You'll read lots of examples in this book, but you and your child will develop your own path. Parents I know have used just five minutes of it to turn a clingy child at a party into one who can go play with the other children; to sate their child's fascination with matches, thus making their family life safer; to dispel their child's edginess at family gatherings; to help children release fears of many kinds; to help a child reconnect with a separated parent after long times apart; to help their child heal from trauma; to help a sibling adjust to the new baby; to provide an energy outlet for their aggressive child; and to dispel a child's fear of medical procedures. It's an almost infinitely flexible tool. You can begin to alleviate nearly any behavioral hitch that's got you baffled or irritated, using this Listening Tool.

Here's how one frustrated mother used Special Time to create much-needed change.

———◇———

I dreaded our mornings. They left an emotional scar on me every day. My girls did not want to be rushed, and the cooperation was nil. "Please brush your teeth," I would say. I was met with, "I am not brushing my teeth! I am not going to school!" I would say everything you are not supposed to say. "You will brush your teeth or else! You are going to school—and now—and I don't want to hear another word about it!" I could hear my mother's words and tone coming out of my mouth. I wanted to vomit. What was I doing?!

After trying every threat and punishment I could think of, I finally started using the Hand in Hand approach. We started getting up thirty minutes early so we could *play*! I mean, *really* play! We started with Special Time. My husband and I would trade off playing with each girl so each of them got a chance with each parent. We just did twenty minutes right after breakfast, before we asked them to do that infinite list of chores before they went to school. It *worked*! They actually brushed their teeth without my threats! They even made their beds without me helping. It was amazing. Just those few minutes with them "filled up their cup" with love and attention. Yes, it takes time and effort, but it is worth it! Twenty minutes in the mornings has given me hours of peace and love.

———◇———

This is a very simple tool. When you use it, you'll be rewarded with improved behavior and greater trust. Special Time accustoms your child to feeling well connected. It also attunes you to your child, so after a while you'll anticipate difficult moments more often, and learn to plan for them. You'll know you've arrived as a parent when your child notices that he's going off track and asks for Special Time so he can reconnect, instead of spiraling down into difficult behavior.

But aside from these practical benefits, this tool enriches your relationship. You'll get to know your child inside and out. He'll show you what he likes, what he loves, what he hates, and what frightens him through Special Time. He'll come up with his own unique graduate-level course in fun, and he'll make sure you get to sample kinds of play you've never thought of. Special Time with your child will set up traditions for the two of you that you'll love and chuckle about for many years to come.

Looking ahead, the connection grooves you develop with Special Time will stand you in good stead as your child enters adolescence. You'll be able to keep some of them well-oiled and active, like creating fancy hair-dos for your daughter, or massaging your son's back just the way he likes. But the Special Time activities your teen is no longer eager to do will still stand as beacons, pointing to the most hopeful times of his childhood, and orienting him to what his own children will need from him one day.

WHEN TO OFFER SPECIAL TIME

Special Time helps with these kinds of parenting situations:

- **The morning routine.** Some kids migrate from one distraction to another when it's time to get ready for school or daycare. Others balk. Special Time connects, so when you offer it before saying a word about what needs to get done, it can fuel your child's ability to think. And cooperate! Many parents tell us it's their go-to tool in the mornings, first thing.

- **Before other challenging times.** Before hated haircuts or shampoos. Before visiting Aunt Tilly, who is fussy about her house and isn't used to children. Before dinner. Before bedtime. Before a new baby arrives, and every day while your child adjusts to the new upstart. Before church, mosque, or temple; before Thanksgiving guests arrive; before walking into a grocery store stocked with eye-catching gum and candy. Special Time in advance isn't a surefire remedy, but after a few months of use, it will often serve to curb trouble.

- **To reconnect after school or daycare.** Instead of "What did you do today?" you can give your child a chance to *show* you how he is. Everything you need to know will spill out, once he feels connected.

- **Before it's time to do homework.** Special Time is a potent antidote to the rigors of school. It restores your child's sense that you're on his side.

- **To contain the activities your child loves, but you can't stand.** Special Time is a godsend for this! When your child is fascinated with cymbals made from the lids of pots and pans, you can set the timer for five minutes, pop in your earplugs, and hang in there. Special Time is a great tool if your child is into burying insects alive, is on a Barbie fashion jag, wants to practice his martial arts moves on you, or wants your help sorting through his Legos for the tiny piece he is missing. You can say, "No, not now," when you're running on fumes, but suggest a Special Time later when you figure you can be up for it.

- **When your child's behavior has gone off track.** When your child is full of complaints. When his behavior turns wild, when he's grabbing from others, or appears so starved for attention that he crawls all over you while you try to converse with a partner or friend. Special Time has a good track record in these situations. It helps your child feel seen and heard. It also tends to help you see your child in a more favorable light.

- **When your child is fearful.** For example, if school is starting in a month, and your child is afraid to go, you can do Special Time daily at his school. You may need to use other tools, as well, but Special Time can help create a sense of safety in any location or situation where your child tends to feel unsure.

- **When stress mounts in your family.** Hard times come to every family. One of your children falls ill; you lose your job; the family pet goes missing; a beloved grandparent or neighbor moves away. When tensions run high, the gift of Special Time can help you and your child focus on the positive, away from the stress that gnaws on your attention. This connection creates a strong lifeline for both of you when times are hard.

HOW TO DO SPECIAL TIME

Here are the features of Special Time. Each one is important. Together, they'll make for positive change in your family.

- **Name it.** Any name will do, but there has to be a name. "Special Time;" "Daddy-and-Noah Time;" "Kids Rule Time." Naming it emphasizes that the time is theirs, and you intend to pay full attention. It helps you focus, and sharpens your child's awareness that your attention is all his.

- **If possible, set a date and a time.** Then, keep your word. Anticipation helps make the time memorable. It also gives your child time to think about what he wants to do. But when life is a scramble, or when your child's behavior is spinning out of control, just announce, "Special Time!" and do it on the spur of the moment.

- **To begin, say, "It's your Special Time. I'll play anything you want to play!"** These words are hard for parents to say, but they're important. They open up broad vistas for your child. They also pry you out of the "I need to be in control" mindset. The break can be refreshing.

- **Set a timer.** Special Time must have a start and an end. A timer frames your attention. It also helps you out when your child chooses to do something you don't love. If you're not an exercise buff, for example, when your child takes you out to the sidewalk and races you to the telephone pole again and again, you'll absolutely love that timer!

- **To start, offer a short time—say, five or ten minutes.** Many parents find it surprisingly difficult to let their child lead them in play. Once you're in the groove and doing short Special Times regularly, you can try offering longer times. But don't offer more than an hour, *ever.* You'll get sleepy, you'll crave a cup of coffee, you'll need to pee, you'll be itching to get out of the Sorry! game, or you'll feel like one more minute of dressing Barbie in her furs and you'll pop! Better to offer a shorter time and lengthen it at the end if you choose, than to lose focus before it's over. Your Special Time stamina will build with practice, especially if you use Listening Partnerships to work on your feelings about the things your child chooses to do.

- **Expect good things to happen.** Expect to learn something new about your child. We tend to think we know our children inside and out: the truth is, we frequently pigeonhole them without realizing it. An expectant attitude—"I wonder what will happen today"—is a vital part of Special Time. Your child may not venture far from his well-trod play path today, but keep expecting to be surprised. Your mindset matters!

- **Enjoy your child.** Offer extra warmth, extra eye contact, and show interest in his choices, even if they're the same choices he's made every day for the past two weeks. Be patient if trust builds slowly.

- **End with affection.** You've just spent time with a marvelously intelligent young person. So close with a hug or a high five, and tell your child when the next Special Time will be.

This mother of eight shows how healing it can be to offer Special Time, even when it's highly inconvenient:

———◇———

I'd just come home from working an eight-hour shift. My hours at work recently changed from mornings to evenings, and this is so hard on my three youngest girls. By the time I get home they should be in bed, sound asleep. Not this evening! It was ten o'clock and the girls were up waiting for me. Shawneece, my nine-year-old, wanted to tell me about something that happened in her class today. Sharille, who is seven, has a hard time connecting, and when she is not feeling connected she will throw tantrums and is not nice to people, especially her sisters. It was way past my two-year-old's bedtime and she wanted to be held and loved. I was feeling tired, and needed to unwind from a long day. At this point I needed *help*. My partner gave me a bit of time to unwind, and then I went to the girls.

So at ten thirty, I asked Shawneece to be with the two-year-old, and I began Special Time with Sharille. She could not get a word out without doing this loud annoying laugh, and for the first time, I did not tell her to stop or quiet down. I listened. She told me a little about her day at school. She shared something that had happened with some of her classmates that had upset her. She cried. Then, she came to a part where she stopped crying and clearly said, "Mom, I don't like it when you aren't home. I miss you." And more tears came. I held her and told her I missed her so much, and that I come home to her as soon as I can. I told her I loved her, and that I was so happy we were together now. We held each other, and Sharille told me that she felt happy that we were together too.

This was the first time I was able to end Special Time with her without her crying about it being over. Then, as I transitioned to Special Time with Shawneece, her older sister, the most unusual thing happened! Sharille played with her baby sister while I had Special Time with Shawneece. There was no interruption. This was a first! Sharille *never* volunteers to play with her little sister! Shawneece had her time, then the older girls went to bed and I was able to do Special Time with the baby, Shalea. Sharille had the biggest breakthrough that evening, and it changed how the night went for all of them.

———◇———

THE DON'TS

Because we grownups aren't always good at following a child's lead, there are some pointers on what Special Time isn't. Hold yourself strictly to these guidelines, even if it's uncomfortable at first.

- **Don't give your child advice.** Don't teach; don't point out lessons you think might be important. For example, don't search for and point out the parts of your child's scribble that look like letters of the alphabet; don't ask him to count the snail shells he's collected. Let him have his own inner purpose as he plays.

- **Don't multitask.** No picking the lint off the carpet during your game of Crazy Eights. Don't carry the folded towels to the cupboard as your child leads you to his room. Don't mull over a problem at work while your daughter is creating a tea party for you. You're in the presence of a remarkable human being. Lint, laundry, and problems at work can wait.

- **Don't talk to others.** Phone off. Don't even *think* of texting! In Special Time, you honor a great love of yours. Do it with all your heart.

- **Don't modify your child's ideas unless his safety is at risk**, and then, try to find a work-around. If he wants to play soccer in the street like the big kids do on Sunday afternoons, just say, "Today's Tuesday. There are lots of cars. Want to walk over to the park instead?" If he wants to jump out his first-floor bedroom window into the tall weeds outside, put some washable blankets or a pile of towels down, and give him your hand. Find a safe way to make his dreams come true.

- **Don't take "personal time off" in the middle of Special Time.** Before you set the timer, take a trip to the bathroom; get a drink of water; or munch on half an apple so you're ready to roll. If you still feel a strong need to make yourself more comfortable after just a short bit of Special Time, it may mean your energy reserves are low. An exchange of listening time will help replenish your own sense of your importance.

- **Don't use Special Time as a reward.** When you see how your child comes to treasure Special Time, it will seem logical to say, "Honey, we can't do Special Time until you tidy up your room." But *don't*! Your child needs the sense of connection that Special Time builds. So offer it with no strings attached, like you offer fruit and water. Other Listening Tools will help you with the toys on the floor, and they'll work a heck of a lot better after Special Time.

A mother who works full time outside the home explains how a little Special Time can shift a child's behavior.

———◇———

My five-year-old son and I have a busy life. Unfortunately, as a single mom, I find myself rushing him through a bedtime routine after getting home late from our activities. Our deal was that he could play while I got his bath together, but after his bath he would always need to hurry to bed if he wanted a story. Well, upon arriving home, he would play, then complain that he wanted TV time, too. Then he would tell me that he wanted cereal before his bath and that he wasn't tired. The struggle got worse week by week.

Why wouldn't he listen to me? I realized that he had no time to connect with me before bedtime, with my rushing him around. I decided to get him home early and offer him Special Time. I told him I would set the timer for ten minutes so that we could do whatever he wanted. His eyes lit up. "Mama! I want you to throw me on the bed, then I want you and me to roll on the floor together!"

I set the timer and ran with him to the bedroom to throw him on the bed. For eight minutes, I joyfully tossed him on the bed, admiring his many different landings and the postures he took as he flew. He laughed and screamed, "Again, Mama!" After the ten-minute timer sounded, he realized that we hadn't rolled. I reminded him that Special Time was over. I said that I would love to roll for a while but that I might need to get up and start running his bath. He agreed and we rolled and laughed some more. After a couple minutes I excused myself and told him that he could play while I ran his bath.

I called him in for his bath and was surprised—the rest of the night went smoothly. He took his bath, came out when I asked, brushed his teeth and put his pajamas on by himself. We read a book and he went to sleep—warm, agreeable, and connected.

———◇———

And Special Time works well all the way into the teen years. One mother of a fourteen-year-old decided to give him his first Special Time for an hour right after church on Sunday. He wanted to go fishing off the city pier. So they went straight there when church was over. Although fishing was not this mom's favorite activity, she was game.

They bought some worms, and he said, "Mom, I want you to put the worm on the hook." She protested, saying she couldn't possibly put the worm on the hook. He knew he'd tweaked her, so he laughed and kept challenging her. Another fisherman there began to smile at the two of them, and made a brief comment in Spanish. Her son replied, also in Spanish, and the two of them shared a few jokes. They conversed awhile. The fisherman walked over and gave the mom a lesson, in Spanish, on how to put a worm on a hook. She squealed as she tried, and they all laughed. The mom watched her son in admiration. She said she had never heard him speak Spanish before, and the fact that he conversed so easily with this man changed her whole image of "her little boy." Finally, her son put his line in the water, and the two of them leaned on the railing, the boy fishing, his mom paying attention and listening in case he might want to talk.

After an hour, they packed up their gear, said goodbye to the fisherman they had befriended, and got into their car. On the way home, the son told his mom that he wanted permission to ride his bike to a park a few miles from their home, where some of his friends meet. She had always forbidden this, fearing for his safety. Today, she listened to him with a fresh perspective. Seeing him out on the pier, the master of a language she didn't know, and easily making friends in it, made her realize that perhaps her own judgment needed adjustment. So as they talked, she shared her concerns with him. She asked him to commit to a few safety guidelines, and he agreed. She gave him permission to ride to that park when he wanted.

When they got home, her son was elated, and he, too, had a new attitude. He cleaned up the kitchen without being asked, something he had never done. This mother said she would never see him as "her little boy" again. And she vowed to do Special Time again soon.

WHEN YOU USE SPECIAL TIME REGULARLY

When you give your child Special Time on a regular basis, he will show you more about himself, how he sees the world, and how he feels. You will probably see one or more of the following signs that your child is feeling safer with you.

- **You may be tested.** Your child may choose play that you find boring or irritating. He will be aware, at some level, that he is pushing you out of your comfort zone. But when you decide to play along, he'll be greatly encouraged. One good way to deal with your own reluctance is to protest in a comical way. When your child splashes water onto the kitchen floor, for example, you can gasp, throw your hands up, and say, "Yikes! It's raining in here! What's going on?" Your child will laugh because you're easing the tension, and the game will be on! The delight your child shows as you sputter and squawk will be well worth the two minutes of mop-up you have to do when the timer goes off. He may even decide to help you with that part. There is more about winning your child's laughter with your playful protest in Chapter 6, *Playlistening*.

- **Your child may explore new activities or new territory.** For instance, children love to use the safety of adult attention to test their physical powers. Your child may jump on the bed in every possible way, squeeze into the smallest hiding space he can find, walk much farther than he's ever walked before, or wade into a nearby mud puddle up to his knees. He'll use your permission to do intensive, whole-bodied learning.

- **Your child may raise important issues.** Your warm, relaxed attitude makes it safe enough to address experiences that didn't sit well with him. For example, if he recently got a painful shot at the doctor's, he may dig out the turkey baster and eagerly give you shot after pretend shot. Or if he was scolded at school, he may play "teacher" and lord it over you, sending you into Time Out. You can try playfully cringing or begging for mercy when he adopts the powerful role. Don't be too earnest—it's play, after all! If laughter erupts, he's busy resolving some tension.

- **Your child may show an increasing attachment to you.** You may notice some positive changes such as increased affection, hopefulness, and excitement about life, along with the sharing of thoughts and accomplishments. Your child may want even more of your healing attention. So—sorry to break this news—feelings of dependency or fears you thought he'd outgrown may reappear. You may be irritated, thinking that he has regressed. But this is what progress looks like! He feels safe enough now to ask for some help with his unfinished business.

- **Your child may become upset at the end of Special Time**, or shortly thereafter. Feeling safer with you means that bottled-up feelings rise to the surface more easily. Plan for this. If you've got a half hour of time to devote to him, you might want to offer him just ten minutes of Special Time. If he melts down, heartbroken that Special Time is over until tomorrow, love him with listening. Don't try to fix the problem. He actually needs this small disappointment in order to scrub long-held feelings out of his system. After you've listened several times, his emotional backlog won't be as great, and he'll be able to end Special Time without protest.

Over time, Special Time will teach you to read your child's body language and signals more accurately. Here's the kind of change one mother noticed as she made Special Time a part of her family's life:

—◇—

When I first started doing Special Time, I hated it—it seemed to be such a chore. Over time, though, I grew to enjoy Special Time with my girls.

I began to see the patterns in their off-track behavior. I could almost predict when trouble would happen, and I started to be able to tell why. I was becoming attuned to my kids in a way I never had been before. It was so beautiful.

For example, I noticed that when we went to an event where the kids were playing with other children and we were engaged with adults, my kids went off track when it was over. During these gatherings they would be playing happily and having a good time. Before doing Special Time, I couldn't understand why they would tantrum and whine afterward. I soon realized how disconnected they became from my husband and me at these events. It made sense that they felt detached from us, as we spent several hours mostly away from them. I realized that we were in the same place at the same time and seemingly "together," but we were not *together*.

So I began doing short Special Times before and after parties or outings that involved lots of other people. It made the biggest difference during our hours together after the events! It was so easy and simple, and yet it took me awhile to figure it out.

FINDING TIME FOR SPECIAL TIME

Time is a sore point with parents! Almost all of us feel pressured. But there's no one rule about how much Special Time to offer, or how to manage to do it when you have multiple children. If you can't figure out how in the world to fit it in, it will help to find a good listener. Talk about what's good in your life, and what's hard. Allow feelings to roll. Rant and curse, if you need to, about how stretched you are. It's hard to solve problems when you feel that no one understands the situation you face. Uninterrupted time to think and feel, while your listener offers warm attention, will make a difference. The insights that come to you will be yours—no book can offer you better thinking than what you come up with when someone listens! The oxygen mask drops for you first. Then, and only then, is it time to turn and help your child.

That said, some parents do five minutes of Special Time each morning, waking one child up early, while the others are asleep. Some do Special Time on Saturday or Sunday, when their partner can be with the other children. What I did as a single mom was to have a friend of both my sons come over once or twice a week after school. He would play with one son, and I'd do Special Time with the other. Then I'd take the second son, while the first played with the friend. After both my sons had had Special Time, they could play together well, so I'd give their friend the same amount of Special Time. This made him part of our family.

One two-job mom I know said to her kindergartner, "While I walk you to school, you can do anything you want! It's your Special Time." She would beam at him, and he came up with new ways to use her attention every day. The connection they felt grew, along with his cooperation. What an elegant solution to an extreme time crunch!

....

While scheduled Special Time is a key tool for building and maintaining a close connection with your child, it can also be used strategically throughout your parenting day to resolve specific issues. In Part III, *Solutions to Everyday Parenting Challenges*, you will read about parents who have used Special Time to help their children with separation, aggression, fear, sibling struggles, cooperation, and many related issues. Their stories will encourage you, but your experience will be unique. Your child has good things in store for you. So go ahead. Put down this book and give Special Time a try!

4
Staylistening

One of the things we parents want most is the power to make things better when our children have endured hard knocks. We want to help, truly help, when they're hurting. And we try. But the things we do don't always actually make the hurt go away. We hush our child and fix things up, but often, she remains glum. Or we may tell her there's nothing to be afraid of, but she can't help but continue to be cautious.

Very simply, Staylistening means listening all the way through your child's upset. You meet your crying child with an open heart, and stay with her until she recovers. Staylistening will give you the power to build your child's resilience. Your listening will help her bounce back after a hard knock: when the dog has shredded her new ladybug purse; when her friend says she wants to play with someone else today; when she falls off her bike and doesn't want to climb back on. Staylistening will also gradually deflate those tiresome daily disputes that eat away at your peace of mind.

When you Staylisten, you will move away from fixing things: instead, you will trust your child to recover and figure things out. You will move away from lecturing: you'll assist your child as she clears away her upset, so she can function better than before. You'll listen because it's connective, and lets your child know you care. You'll find that listening is a powerful remedy when your child cries, has a tantrum, or is frantic with fear.

When you Staylisten, you sail *with* your child through her emotionally stormy seas. Her little boat pitches and tosses; you climb in, and quietly keep your hand on the rudder. She feels lost; you murmur that safe harbor lies ahead. You stay nearby and keep her safe while she's overcome with upset. When she's cried things through or finished her tantrum, she'll realize that you've been there for her all along. She will relax, infused with a deep sense of belonging. You and she will have worked together to heal the feelings that tossed her off course.

And Staylistening will ease your mind about setting reasonable limits. It's an industrial-strength cleanup tool for those moments when you have said "no," but your child badly wants a "yes." It dissolves the toxic feelings that scream to her that you're not on her side, that you're not a good parent, that in fact, you are the worst parent ever.

WHAT SETS STAYLISTENING APART?

Understandably, parents often become annoyed by crying and use all kinds of strategies to hush their child up. In my family, the stock threat was, "If you don't stop your crying right now, I'll give you something to cry about!" The policy was dead straight: "No crying when I say no crying." It was backed by a spanking. Other parents might simply judge whether the reason for the crying seemed valid, and if not, a scolding would be in order.

On the more lenient end of the spectrum, parents try to rock, jiggle, or hold their child until the crying stops. Then there's the old standby: put her in Time Out. Or talk to her at length about why her crying doesn't make sense. Then there's one that's actually palatable to children: distract the child with something fun to do or sweet to eat. And finally, the most expensive option: replace the wanted, lost, or unsatisfactory item in question, and call it a day.

The problem is that none of these parenting tools works very well. With them, we struggle along, but there's a lot of "same old" that we go through with our children day after day. Over the years, we get worn down.

Staylistening is unique because you go *with* your child's natural instinct to cry, to throw tantrums, and to have screaming, fearful fits. Why? Because it helps the two of you connect so that she can think!

Once, in an introductory class for parents of toddlers, I introduced the tool of Staylistening. One mother responded, "I am so fed up with my child, I don't even want to go home tonight. I've had trouble with her for months! I get up in the morning, and she hates what I give her for breakfast. She won't get dressed. I'm late for work every day because she screams about everything. To get her into the car, I have to pry her fingers off the front gate. When I pick her up, it's the same thing. Whining and balking till bedtime. I'm not going to listen to her cry! I do that enough already." She did not look happy as she left the class.

She came back the next week, though, and said, "If you had told me last week that my daughter would be behaving like an angel, I would have laughed in your face. But I got the flu on Friday. I figured, 'Well, I'm home, and I don't have the energy to fight her all weekend, so I might as well try this listening stuff.' And I did. I stayed in my pajamas all weekend. Every time she got upset, I sat on the floor with her and listened to her. I was too sick to do anything else. She had five or six long cries with me Saturday and Sunday. Monday morning, she skipped in to breakfast, ate it all, got dressed, and couldn't wait to get into the car. She was still fine when I picked her up. This morning, same thing! Kisses and hugs! I am amazed!"

This single change—welcoming and supporting your child's big, showy feelings—can make an enormous difference for both you and your child. Your child will begin to sleep better, eat better, wait her turn, play better with her siblings, and overcome difficulties big and small. You need not resort to the old-school tools.

And in the long run, your child is more likely to reach adolescence still feeling close to you. She'll expand her world, but she'll want you to have a place in it. She'll have raged and stormed and blasted bad feelings out of her system many times, so she's less likely to have a chip on her shoulder, less inclined to be a risk-taker or a rebel.

Finally, when you Staylisten, you operate under a fresh definition of misbehavior. Hitting, hurting, grabbing, defiance, and sneaking candy from the cupboard all still qualify as behaviors that warrant limits. But crying, tantrums, and saying awful things in the midst of getting rid of negative feelings get a free ride out of the misbehavior bucket. They have a shiny new bucket of their own. It's labeled, "Healing Process. Just Add Listening." That's where you come in.

Many parents are amazed to find that listening to their children's passionate feelings doesn't promote misbehavior. Rather, it relieves the tension that *causes* misbehavior. In a sense, it allows your child to have an "emotional poop," a chance to eject the feelings left over from moments that hurt her feelings. Letting her clean out her pipes will build her resilience and help her feel more connected to you.

Although this approach is tolerant of emotional release, it's *not* permissive toward off-track behavior. You will learn to intervene quickly when your child shows that she can't think. You'll step in to calmly prevent her from doing unworkable things. That could mean putting your hand on your child's arm as she cocks it to throw something, or putting an arm around her tummy and pulling her toward you as she reaches to pull her sister's hair. These interventions are not punishment. You simply make the situation safe for all and then listen, so your child can notice her feelings and let them roll. A good limit, followed by Staylistening, helps her return to playing and functioning well once again. And over time, your child's backlog of held feelings empties, her confidence soars, and her intelligence shines.

WHEN TO STAYLISTEN

If you have a choice, try this Listening Tool for the first time when you and your child are in a safe space, with no onlookers nearby. Grownups are not known for their tolerance of crying children. You'll want the freedom to focus on your child, give her your full attention, and notice how *you* feel the first few times through.

Here are some times when Staylistening will come in handy:

- When your child cries about a bump or scrape.

- When a goodbye brings tears.

- When she cries about something she can't have.

- When she's trying to accomplish something, and suddenly erupts in a tantrum.

- When she bursts into tears out of fear.

- When she's tight and angry.

- When someone has hurt her feelings.

There are many more emotion-charged occasions when Staylistening will serve you and your child well, but I'm sure you get the picture.

Here's an assistant principal's story that shows how Staylistening can foster enormous change in a young person, even in a school setting. She works in a low-income urban community wracked by gang violence for generations.

For a year and a half, I'd been working with a junior high school student who had been sent to the office several times for minor behavior challenges. Each time, he shut down and talked about being a "bad" kid. I don't believe in such things, so I continuously assured him that I wanted him to do well and believed that he could.

Virtually every time he was sent to my office he would cry about something. One day I asked him what was really bothering him and, having established trust with Staylistening over time, he opened up about feeling like no one loved him. He cited his evidence. I listened to him and reassured him that he was valuable beyond his knowledge. I also met with his mother and listened to her. When I had the opportunity, I explained Special Time and encouraged her to try it, and she did. By March of last year there was a big change in the mother's energy. She had gained a positive attitude, and it spilled over to him.

After several Staylistening sessions with me and Special Time opportunities with his mother, he was able to realize he was loved and capable of doing well in school. This March, he was so proud when he told me he had raised his grade point average from a 1.9 to a 3.2. His attitude changed too. Instead of sucking his teeth and slumping his shoulders he began to stand up straight and smile. Occasionally he would also hug a teacher.

In June he found out he was getting a coveted end-of-year award, "Most Improved," assigned to only one student per grade.

It took a year and a half, but with a great deal of Staylistening from me, and with his mother engaging him in Special Time, we were able to develop trust and see a big difference. It made a lasting change in this young man, who now has a much brighter future.

HOW TO STAYLISTEN

Your goal will be to surround your child with warm attention and support while she feels deeply upset. She'll tell you when she's ready. She'll burst into tears or a tantrum, scream in fear, or writhe with fury. Anchor her while she's filled with emotion. Listen. Assume she is doing exactly what she needs to do to regain her ability to think. Your first few times, it may feel like this is the craziest idea you've ever tried. But focus on your child, and offer your caring. Her mind is good; her instincts are healthy! She'll show you how it works. Here, in more detail, is what to do:

- **Move close and offer eye contact.** If she turns away from you, keep listening, and after awhile, invite her to turn toward you again. Gently remind her of your presence. "I'm right here, sweetheart. Here comes a tiny kiss for your fingers." There's no need to insist. When her eyes do meet yours, if she's not finished, she'll cry harder. Seeing you is reassuring, and it intensifies the emotional healing taking place.

- **Settle in.** Staylistening often takes time. Big feelings come in chunks that take some time to dissolve. If you're new to listening to your child, most likely she's got a fair number of feelings to work through.

- **Use a gentle tone of voice**, even if she's telling you that you're the worst parent in the world. It's good to assume that you're just the right person to be by her side while she gets those awful feelings off her chest.

- **Listen. Say little.** "I'm sorry it's so hard," "I'm right here for you," or, "Sweetie, I see that you're upset," might be helpful, but listening is key. Kim John Payne, in *Simplicity Parenting*, says, "The more you say, the less you are listening." I agree. But if your child is thrashing, a low-key litany of verbal reassurance will anchor her as she fights unseen forces.

- **Gentle touch may be helpful.** Try it and see. Children differ in their preference for touch. If touch is helpful, it will probably intensify her feelings. It's not helpful if it stops her from crying or sends her into an angry battle. Your attention does not have to include touch or an embrace, although your child will gradually lean toward closeness with you as she clears emotion from her system.

  If your child is having a tantrum, it's usually best to move close without touching her, unless you need to guard her from hurting herself. Let her blow. She needs to move. You can hold her when she's done, if she likes. And if your child is working through fear, holding her will be a challenge. She may need to struggle or do battle with you.

- **Keep her safe. Keep yourself safe.** Sometimes, in the throes of deep fear, children get wild and have the impulse to do harm. Because you're listening, you'll become a prime target. Handling this kind of vigorous work is not easy. You can find useful information to guide you in the *What You Need to Know* sections of Chapter 11, *Lifting Fear*, and Chapter 12, *Moving Beyond Aggression*.

- **Let her decide when she's done.** Children's feelings have a size and a depth that you can't measure or predict. Some cries last three minutes, leaving your child bright and cogent. But especially at first, many of your child's upsets are likely to take a good while, as she catches up with the healing she's wanted to do since arriving in your arms.

Allowing your child to cry things all the way through is a bit like allowing your child to nap till she wakes. In both crying and napping, the mind is busy doing important internal work. Housekeeping, you could say. Things get tidied up nicely. Energy recharges. The mind sorts through information and puts it where it can be retrieved. And there's a pace to the process. That pace isn't under your child's conscious control, or yours. If you interrupt your child's sleep, you'll have a cranky, off-kilter young one who will remind you of your error for the rest of the day. It's the same with crying. If you can't listen all the way through, your child will be left with no way to release the rest of the difficult feelings her mind had hauled out for removal. There they sit, out in the open, infusing her behavior with signals that all is not well within.

However, it's OK to stop Staylistening, abruptly if you need to. In fact, it's *vital* to stop if you become upset. Just tell your child you can't listen any longer, and you'll listen again another time. Then set her up with a snack, a bath, or a favorite activity. She won't be at her best, but you need a break, and a chance to release feelings of your own. She'll soon figure out a way to kick-start the remainder of the healing that's needed.

How can you be sure that Staylistening isn't some kind of emotional coercion? Your child will certainly feel her worst while you listen to her upsets! If, at some point in her life, she felt threatened, panicked, trapped, helpless, abandoned, manipulated, or terrified, that's how she'll feel again as you provide the safety to work that troubling time through. How do you keep from doing unintentional harm?

There are four guidelines that will help ensure that the Staylistening you do is in fact a *partnership* between you and your child to get healing done.

- **Allow your child to choose the time and place.** She will either signal you when she can't think, inviting a limit from you that triggers the healing process, or she'll burst into tears or rage of her own accord. You respond with listening, until she can think again.

- **Maintain a healthy power balance** between you and your child by tempering Staylistening with roughly equal time using Special Time and Playlistening. These child-led tools hand the reins of the relationship back to your child.

- **Offload your own feelings regularly in a Listening Partnership.** This will deepen your understanding, move your own life forward, and help keep you from using Staylistening when you can't connect with an open heart. In particular, offload any temptation to use Staylistening as a punishment or a threat.

- **Stop Staylistening the minute you feel upset.** As the stories in Part III will show, parents who balance Staylistening with the use of the other four Listening Tools see unprecedented behavioral changes in their children. A four-year-old who couldn't stand up for himself corrects a much older child; a seven-year-old becomes generous with her baby sister; toddlers and preschoolers walk right up to the people or situations that had terrified them; a child who had a painful fall gets back on his bike and tries that big hill again; a fifth-grader aces a big memorization project that she was sure she couldn't do. Changes like these don't emanate from young people who feel dominated. They come from children who've been freed of tension, and bathed in quiet support.

IMPORTANT HURTS ARE HEALED THROUGH UPSETS ABOUT TINY ISSUES

You'll begin to relax with Staylistening when you've become accustomed to the fact that *our children pin their deepest feelings on tiny issues.* Remarkable, positive changes in a child's behavior can follow a long, deep cry about a toy lipstick that broke, or about her brother getting to sit in the blue booster seat.

Your child is triggered by tiny imperfections because hurt feelings can easily stun her, making emotional release impossible. For example, a four-year-old might become edgy while Daddy is away on a weeklong trip for work. Her behavior goes off track, but when she is asked, "Do you miss Daddy, sweetheart?" a blank look comes over her, and she says, "No." The truth is that she feels heartbroken, but she's too overwhelmed to cry about losing him. She's numb. It's too big a hurt to face head-on.

But then a friend comes to play and tries on her blue tutu without asking. The child bursts into tears. That faint hint of a loss—what if her friend keeps the tutu?—triggers the feelings she'd put on ice. Out they come, attached to the blue tutu! The deeper a child's hurt goes, the smaller the trigger for a good cry must be. She can stand to feel frantic about the possible loss of her tutu. But she can't bear to focus on her Daddy's absence.

We've all been taught that a good parent would step in and negotiate five-minute turns with the tutu to "fix" things. But Staylistening gives you an interesting option. A parent can support their child's instinct to heal, instead. Moving close, they can say gently, "Yes, she's wearing your tutu. I'm sure she'll give it back when she's done." Then their child can release the great sadness she carries. Not a word needs to be said about Daddy. We can trust our children's judgment about the issues they choose to hang their feelings on. For this child, an intense cry will prove that the tutu is the perfect trigger for much-needed emotional release and healing.

TENDERLY SUPPORT YOUR CHILD

When we were children, most of us weren't treated with kindness when we were upset. So here are some finer points to experiment with, in case you're coaxing your own tenderness along from small beginnings:

- **Gently touch on the painful details.** This is the opposite of trying to fix things, and it's deeply healing for your child. When you point gently toward the thing that hurts, with no hint of worry, your child will release a fresh wave of intense feeling. "You really wanted the teacup she took. Hmm, I see she still has it." "I do have to go soon. I will love you the whole time I'm gone." "I know this is hard." "Let's take a look at your knee now." "It's time to say goodbye." "Bruno got the blue bike." "We're out of orange juice." And in later years, "I know the party means a lot to you. I wish I could say yes." "He didn't even call you. That's hard." "You wanted this so badly. You had a good plan." Often, the simplest phrase—"I know," or "I'm right here"—will best convey your love.

- **Cite the safety of the present moment.** "Yes, she took the book you wanted. You can talk with her when you feel like it." "Your body knows how to heal." "You can have a cookie another day." "I can't let you grab like that. Stay here on my lap for now." "She didn't mean to hurt you." "I know you want it. It will be your turn when he's done." And in the teen years or beyond, simply let her know that you believe in her. "I think you can figure this out." "You are a good friend, no matter what they said today." "I think you can talk to her about this. You'll figure out how."

- **When she is resistant, allow her to cry fully *before* she complies.** Children often use the pretext of cleaning up, dressing themselves, going for a hike, doing their homework, or writing an essay as an opening into deep feelings of hurt, confusion, or helplessness. So unless the house is on fire, give your child the chance to cry hard while she tells you that she'll never, ever do what is required. Let her carry on until she feels done. Every now and then, calmly restate the next step, and ask her mildly if she's ready to take it. "Shall we take a step toward the car? It's time to go." "The table is cleared. It's time for homework." "The mitt was in Serena's hands. Are you ready to give it back?" Let your child cry hard about the *thought* of that next step. Show faith in her intelligence. Given the time she needs, she'll be able to comply in the end. Don't give in. Don't give up. Give her *you*. She'll connect, and her perspective will improve.

- **Staylisten right where the tears or tantrum began.** If you pick your child up and move her elsewhere right away, she'll be distracted and lose focus. When you can, listen to her right where she started for a good five minutes before moving her to ease the discomfort of others.

- **Bathe her in your quiet confidence.** Make mild, matter-of-fact statements from your heart. Your child feels vulnerable and upset, but she is not to be pitied. After all, she's on the mend! For example, tell your heartbroken child, "He'll be done with it in a while," after a friend has grabbed her ball. Say it with mild, relaxed confidence, as though you were saying, "The sky is blue." This will help your child cry hard, and get through her recovery in good time. Anchor her well by focusing on the fact that, in this very emotional moment, she has your attention, and that's all she really needs.

Below are things that some parents do when children cry that, in my experience, don't actually support a child to recover.

- **Don't name your child's feeling.** Credible research confirms that naming a child's feeling calms the child. To be more exact, it brings the emotional release process to a halt. Since most people believe that crying *is* the hurt, stopping a child's cry makes an adult feel like he has helped.

  But crying is not the hurt itself! The hurt jammed the child's thinking in the instant *before* she cried. Or, perhaps the hurt struck her years ago and still has not healed. The child may be crying because a tiny facsimile of that hurt clogged her thinking for the hundredth time.

  Crying is the *healing* process. Diverting a child away from crying with "I see you're feeling angry. You didn't want Grandpa to win at checkers," means that an opportunity is lost. The child's prefrontal cortex is called upon to understand what the grownup is saying, and she can no longer offload the feeling of hurt. That hurt will return to cause behavioral trouble tomorrow. So don't name the feeling. It's your *child's* feeling. It's *her* job to name it if she chooses. *Your* job is listening!

- **Don't question your child about what happened, unless her health is at stake.** Show interest, but stay mindful of the fact that, except in unusual circumstances, you don't need to know. You are there to listen and comprehend the *impact* of what happened to her. The details are exactly that—details. She will talk about them later if she needs to. Here's how it can work:

———◇———

My two-year-old daughter began crying one morning a short time after breakfast, and I had no idea what it was about. She cried steadily, wandering slowly from room to room. I followed her, said a few things, and just tried to stay with her. She would look at me now and then, but mostly, she looked sad and shed big tears. It was pretty clear that she wasn't sick or in pain, so I stayed with her almost two hours, until she finally felt better. We had a good day after that.

It happened the next day, as well. For another two hours, she cried and roamed the house. She had no words. But the rest of the day was fine. The third day, she had another long cry in the morning. But that day, when she finished she snuggled into my lap and asked, "Why does Daddy go to work?" It all finally made sense. He leaves after breakfast every day, and she just didn't understand it. After three days of crying, she could ask me about it. After that, she was OK in the mornings. She had worked something through.

——◇——

- **Don't take your child's anger personally.** As children cry, they shed uncomfortable thoughts and feelings. So sooner or later, every one of us will hear our child say something that sinks the heart. "You don't love me!" "I wish you weren't my Mommy!" "I hate you, Dad!" "My brother stinks. I want to kill him!"

  Hang on tight! Your child is doing what she must to get poisonous feelings out of her system. If you can stay supportive of her (there's no need to agree, of course), the oomph will go out of these terrible thoughts, and her bitterness will drain away. Try telling your child, "However you feel, I'll always love you," or "You don't have to love me right now. I understand," or, "I won't let you hurt Darryl, sweetie." She's not giving her final evaluation of you or anyone else. She'll be back in touch with how good you are just as soon as she's rid of those toxic feelings.

- **Don't scold your child.** Many of us were raised in such a climate of blame that we don't realize when we're scolding. These are the kinds of thoughts it's good to keep to ourselves: "That's not something to cry about!" "Don't you want to be a big boy?" "Good children don't say things like that!" "You had better control your temper, Missy!" Of course, we parents have the full right to *feel* any of these ways. In fact, many of the feelings we have about our kids can't be said aloud in polite company! But we undermine our children's wellbeing when we judge them harshly. Listening Partnerships are just the place for venting the heat we feel, far from our children's impressionable ears. We'll outline that Listening Tool in Chapter 7.

- **Don't discuss a child's cry or tantrum with her afterwards.** It's tedious. It's beside the point. There's nothing to be figured out. When a child has offloaded debilitating feelings, she's ready to enjoy the intelligence she just freed up. If you grill her after every emotional episode, she'll want to confide in you less and less. Listen well. Then trust her to sort things out while playing, sleeping, or downing a bowl of pasta. She'll know she wasn't supposed to grab from her brother. No lecture needed.

In fact, it might be helpful here to compare the workings of your child's emotional life to her digestive system. When she eats a banana, for example, her system extracts the nutrients, and not a thought goes into it! She is nourished, although not everything in that banana is digestible. Her body takes what it needs, and has a fine disposal system for the rest. Your child pees and poops the indigestible part away. Her elimination process is frequent and inconvenient for several years, and it's not the most pleasant stuff to deal with! But we parents make all kinds of allowances for these necessities.

Now consider your child's daily experience. You offer her the very best life you can provide. She learns. She thrives. But every day there are moments that jam her delicate system. The cat scratches her. Mommy is pregnant, tired, and bothered. The child next door calls her a name. At bedtime, her room feels scary. Each of these experiences carries an emotional charge. To keep thinking well, she needs to defuse that charge, so she can process those experiences and learn from them. And she's got a system for that! You play chase with her after dinner, and she laughs hard, releasing tension and stoking her sense that you cherish her. Then she loses a tiny Barbie shoe down the bathtub drain, and has a good cry. Voila! She has tidied up on the inside, and is ready for good day tomorrow.

When your child poops or pees, it doesn't worry you. And you certainly don't feel compelled to examine what goes into the diaper or toilet, figure out where it came from, and discuss why it's there. It's flush and go. You'll want to make your child's experience of releasing emotional tension that simple. She laughs, has a tantrum, cries, or trembles and writhes in fear. You anchor her; she finishes. It's time for some fun!

And finally, one last important point:

- **Don't urge your child, or anyone else, to cry.** Once you see what a good cry can do for your child's ability to think, you'll want to inform everyone, especially your child! But this is a bad idea. Saying things like, "Get those feelings out," or, "Go ahead and vent, it's good for you," or, "I think you need a good cry—this was a hard day for you," makes a child self-conscious about the emotional release process. It puts her emotional life under a microscope. *Your* microscope!

  The emotional release process *belongs to your child.* You can't command it or control it. The most useful thing you can do is to create the conditions under which she can feel your caring. This is what Listening Tools do—using them delivers your caring. So use Special Time and Playlistening, described in Chapter 6, to connect with her. Find other fun things to do together when you have time. Snuggle. Play. Romp. And perhaps most importantly, let off steam from the stress in your own life on a regular basis with a good listener. Put your focus on *caring*, and let *her* be in charge of crying.

After a good Staylistening, look for new insights, warmth, and creativity in your freshly relieved child.

STAYLISTENING TO HEAL YOUR CHILD'S GRIEF

The pointers and ideas we've given above all apply to a child releasing grief. The only thing left to say is that well-loved children with good lives tend to have quite a bit of grief to offload. Life is so new, and there is so much information to process. Crying away the hurt from little imperfect moments is an important job in childhood. Every time she launches an upset, she's using good judgment. She wants to think, and crying will help.

Here's how it can work:

———◇———

My seven-year-old daughter and five-year-old son have recently started at a new school. One day in their second week, my daughter came running out of class with a new friend, and asked if she could come over to play that afternoon at our house. I was happy to say "yes," so we started off toward home together. But my son said it wasn't fair. He said, "I don't have a friend to bring home and I wanted to bring a friend home too and I won't leave without one." I Staylistened, and he began to cry hard, repeating that he wanted a friend too, and didn't have one. I got down to his level, kept my eyes available for contact, and stayed close. He turned away and continued to cry hard facing the wall. I told him I was sorry it was hard for him right now and that I knew how much he wanted a friend. He had been very close to one boy in particular at his old school, and I really got the sense that he was grieving. I felt very compassionate toward him and it was easy to Staylisten and allow his tears.

After about five minutes, he turned into me and I held him in a close hug and then we looked into each other's eyes. He kept crying, telling me that he wanted a friend, too. I kept listening. After ten or fifteen minutes he was OK to walk home. He became cheerful and happily played nearby while I prepared food in the kitchen and the girls played together upstairs.

The next morning he asked, "Is it a school day or a weekend?" When I told him it was a school day he said, "Yippee!" which completely surprised me. That afternoon when I picked him up from school he had a new friend who came home with us to play! It felt like a wonderful outcome, and I was grateful for the practice I have had with the tool of Staylistening.

———◇———

STAYLISTENING TO RELIEVE YOUR CHILD'S FRUSTRATION

Tantrums aren't a pretty sight, but you'll come to value them, once you see how a tantrum can boost your child's ability to think and learn. It may be difficult to Staylisten at first. But once you manage, I think you'll be impressed with a tantrum's positive power!

It's important to note what tantrums are not. A true tantrum doesn't drive a child to try to hurt anyone. A tantrum is more like a string of fire-crackers going off than a bullet meant to hurt.

Tantrums release frustration. They come on suddenly. A frustrated child is noisy, her body heats up, and she's full of fiery emotion. All she wants to do is expend that hot energy *now*! Frustration arises because your child is an eager learner, and her ideas of what she wants to do will some-times outpace what she *can* do. She'll want to walk long before she takes a step, and she'll want to talk long before she says her first word. She has to learn by trial and error for days, weeks, perhaps even months, in order to master a skill she's pinned her heart on. And because she has to try and fail many times, frustration can make her feel like jumping out of her skin. She loses her ability to think. If, as is commonly done, you forbid her to have a tantrum, she'll have to abandon her learning project then and there because every time she returns to it, that same feeling will bristle and shut down her thinking once more.

But a good tantrum solves the problem. When frustration hits she'll jump up and down, push up against some immoveable object, or throw herself onto the ground and writhe. There might be tears and perspiration. She might go on for five to fifteen minutes—it's unusual for a tantrum to go much longer. When she's done, she'll relax. And when she returns to try her task again, she'll get a little farther. Some tasks will spark a series of tantrums, because your child's expectations are high and her skills build slowly. However many tantrums she needs, Staylistening is your best move to support her as a learner.

It's usually better *not* to take your child into your arms if she's begun a tantrum. She needs to move! Come close, offer warm eye contact, and pick her up only if safety is an issue, or if you need to move her to a more private spot. She doesn't need much verbal reassurance. She knows what she needs to do and how to do it. The balm of your steady listening will help her come through feeling whole and smart.

Children's tantrums often erupt when they're on the cusp of a devel-opmental leap. Prime times for the healing power of a tantrum are just before a child crawls or walks; just before she talks; just before she learns a new skill like tying her shoes, riding a bike, or reading; and just before or during the early months of entering daycare or school. Tantrums are richly protective of your child's intelligence. They lubricate the learning process when it jams.

This mother tells how a tantrum moved her daughter forward:

—◇—

My six-year-old twin girls and I were home together one hot summer afternoon, and were looking for something to do. I thought paper crafting would be fun, so I looked up information about making long strings of paper dolls and snowflakes. Why snowflakes? Any cool thought when it's over 108° outside helps.

I traced pictures of boys or girls onto paper, and my daughters would cut them out. We were having a decent time, but after a short while, my daughter was very frustrated. She gets frustrated when she can't learn something as fast as she would like. Often she gives up entirely, and calls herself stupid. It pains me to watch this bright child give up. I had done some listening time to deal with my own feelings about this, and that was about to pay off.

Cutting the paper dolls wasn't easy, as we had to cut through eight layers of paper. She wanted to do it herself without help, but she couldn't with her kid scissors and small hands. She was so frustrated that she threw the paper doll onto the table and said, "I quit!"

I saw the learning pattern show up, and so instead of trying to make her feel better by comforting her or doing it for her, I stayed calm and waited. She fell on the floor and had a tantrum, yelling, crying and showing me how helpless she felt. I Staylistened for ten to fifteen minutes.

As quickly as she began, she stopped. I watched her settle down, and though I was convinced that she would feel better, I didn't think she'd go back to the craft after being so upset.

I was wrong. She came back to the table, asked for the scissors, and went back to cutting the dolls. Not only did she finish that set of paper dolls, she continued making dolls for an hour, and by the time she was done, she'd made a girl, boy, mom, dad and two other strings of paper dolls. I was amazed. And relieved!

She was so proud of herself and her ability to make the dolls after all. And I learned something important. These tools work as promised. I felt empowered to help her. I finally had a way to reach for her when she was shutting down: just listen.

———◇———

Allowing a big feeling of hurt to roll right out, as this mom did, is one of the ways Staylistening will preserve your patience. You'll be done with trying to please a frustrated or unhappy child, a nearly impossible task. Instead, you'll simply pay attention and support her while she offloads her upset and clears her mind. This is an efficient use of your energy, and it will spark your child's instinct to heal.

I hope it's a relief to know that it's smart of your child to throw a tantrum. She wants to learn, and she knows exactly how to jump-start the recovery process when her hope and patience have hit bottom.

STAYLISTENING TO HEAL YOUR CHILD'S FEAR

If your child is screaming, trembling, and perspiring, is wrecking things, or is driven to try to hit, scratch, or hurt someone, she is ready to heal from fear. Fear is a gripping, sticky emotion that rocks a child to her core. When fear is triggered, she feels that her very existence is threatened, and she'll either run away or turn and fight anyone who dares to come close. Although tricky to handle, the release of fear is a natural part of the emotional healing process, too. Fear makes its exit through perspiration and body heat (or, in the case of raw terror, cold and clammy skin), trembling, screaming and yelling, writhing, flailing, panic, or struggling.

While working through fear, a child will usually shut her eyes tight and cry out loudly, but you won't see many tears. When children are afraid for their lives, they are too frightened to grieve. Their attention is riveted on survival. But when you've supported your child through this deeply emotional process, the feeling of fear will finally pass, and she may then lean into you, fully relaxed and aware at last that you have protected her all along. She'll sob in relief as she absorbs your caring. Then she may fall asleep, or brighten up, look around, find some little thing to laugh about, and continue her day, chipper and hopeful.

You, on the other hand, will feel like you've been through the wringer! When your child feels deeply threatened, it sets off the biggest internal alarms a parent has. It takes courage to hold on to the perspective that your child's feelings are leftovers from some trouble that is long gone. You'll need listening time regularly if you've got a child who is signaling that it's high time to help her with fear. Please turn to the *What You Need to Know* sections of Chapter 11, *Lifting Fear*, and Chapter 12, *Moving Beyond Aggression*, for a summary of parents' experience in helping their children recover from fear.

....

When used with patience and warmth, Staylistening will help you build the foundation for an enjoyable family life. You'll see the powerful healing effect of your listening and caring. It's important to balance your use of Staylistening with the other Listening Tools, so that limits, laughter, and one-on-one time become part of your life with your child as well. You'll find that with time, the example you set with Staylistening will lead your child to treat others with warmth and respect. The healing wrought by this Listening Tool will amaze you.

5
Setting Limits

Children need limits! Limits keep them safe, and point them toward respectful relationships, good fun, and learning. Imagine your child's dental health, cleanliness, diet, sleep schedule, playroom floor, and the state of his friendships without well-chosen limits on his strong wishes! "No" is sometimes the kindest word, and it's often an absolutely necessary word. A good "no" can move your child forward, and save lots of wear and tear on you. To be clear, Hand in Hand Parenting is *not* a permissive approach to parenting. It is, however, a respectful one.

There are times, more often than you might notice, that you set a limit for your child and there's no issue at all. The times you do notice are the times when your child's behavior puts you in a tough spot. He goes off track, and although you want to treat him well, your mild interventions don't improve things. So you issue a warning, but he can't think, so he doesn't comply. Before too long, there's a scene. He feels attacked, you feel angry, and you swat, yell, or put him in his room and keep your distance for a while till you both calm down. There must be a better way!

And there is. There's a way to set limits for your child *and* furnish the love he needs, before you've reached your boiling point. When you follow "no" with listening, your child's judgment will actually improve over time. You can work *with* him to heal the hurt feelings that were bothering him. Limiting your child's wacky behavior invites release of the feelings that have riled him up. And, relieved of that hurt, he won't be quite so easily derailed tomorrow. The biggest surprise for parents when they first set limits this way is that it brings their child closer to them!

Pairing limits with listening isn't wishy-washy. It doesn't let your child off the hook. Your child will detest the limits you set just as much as always. But because you listen to how he feels, that hatred will drain away. Because you listen, your child's perspective will readjust. He'll come to realize that, although you've said "no," you *care* about him. That's all he really needs.

WHAT SETS SETTING LIMITS APART?

Most approaches to discipline assume that the adult has the intelligence and judgment, and that the child must be trained. He's seen as essentially uncivilized. It's the child's job to obey quickly; it's the parent's job to meet uncivil acts with negative responses. Many modern parents have a somewhat more generous outlook on their children's nature and intelligence. Still, their patience runs out, too. By the time our children reach middle school, we parents are weary. We're at the cusp of a challenging stage of parenting, but thousands of struggles over limits have sapped our energy, with no clear progress to show for it all.

It's time to change the assumptions about our children's intelligence. You will avoid a tremendous amount of work and confusion if you assume that your child has in inborn sense of love, a strong desire to cooperate, and a keen sense of justice. Our children know right from wrong—often, they detect our tones of disrespect or anger before we do! Uncooperative or unloving behavior isn't part of a child's "uncivilized nature." It is behavior that's fueled by disconnection and hurt feelings.

When you make this more generous assumption, a whole lot of work falls away. Instead of teaching your child right from wrong, worried that he might not "get it," you can pay more attention to connecting with him. Focusing on connection will help him use his intelligence more of the time. When he can't be cooperative, bring a limit and listen to his feelings. Then, your child will return to himself, relaxed and attuned again.

For example, instead of policing turns or devising penalties for not sharing well, you can assume that your children know how to get along. When one grabs a treasured item from the other, simply put your hand on the prize and say, "She had it. I think you'll need to give it back." Then, keep your hand on the treasure, and let your child explode about why it's his turn to play with it, and how stupid you are. "I know you really want it, but you need to give it back," is all you need to say while he has a good cry or a tantrum. After you've listened to his feelings, he'll return to his right mind, give the toy back, and proceed to play more flexibly. No lecture, no moral judgment coming down on his head, no negotiation or diplomacy needed. And no coercion. You don't force a thing. You just prevent further action, and listen until he can think. He'll get there. It takes time, but you're spared fruitless lectures and worry. You've got good children. They know how to get along. It just takes some time to peel the emotional tension away. When it's gone, they'll know what to do.

Pairing this kind of limit setting with careful listening opens a gateway to better times and happier children. Your child's misbehavior is a clear signal that his genius has gone offline. The kindest thing you can do for him is to stop the misbehavior and listen. Out will come the emotional tension. In will go your caring. That will set things right.

When we use reward-and-punishment schemes with our children, they come to understand that we're manipulating their behavior, and they learn to work the systems we set up. When punishment is frequent, they numb themselves to it, or they flat-out rebel. Setting limits, then moving in to listen to a child's feelings is a method free of harshness, and free of bribes and threats. It calls forth the best in your child and you.

I am certain that, on occasion, every parent who uses the Hand in Hand approach offers rewards or gives a Time Out when they're frazzled. But when our heads are on straight, we go with "connect, bring the limit, and listen." We do it because it works well.

There's one more feature of Setting Limits the Hand in Hand way that is unique. We encourage you to set limits *playfully*. It's a powerful tool for defusing power struggles, and a way to delight and reassure your child that, though you've set the limit, you care about him. We'll explain more about this in Chapter 6, *Playlistening*.

WHEN TO SET A LIMIT

Your child tells you very clearly when it's time to set a limit. When you don't read the signal, he'll send another, and if still you can't respond, he'll send signals that he's *sure* will trigger you. Your child wasn't designed to tolerate an irrational state of mind. So when he feels disconnected and hurt, he'd rather have you come at him with irritation than not have you come at all. He needs your attention that badly.

While his thinking mind is flooded with upset, he can't love you or anyone else. He can't remember that you're on his side. Not much computes. However, he is keenly aware of your emotional state, and of how you feel about him. That does register, and it goes deep.

Here are a few signs that often precede truly difficult behavior warranting limits. They give you advance warning that your child is feeling disconnected:

- He can't maintain relaxed eye contact with you.

- He doesn't want to be touched.

- He is not open to change.

- He won't include others in play, or will only play with certain children.

- His attention is stuck on playthings, and he won't connect with anyone.

- He wants things a particular way. Any variation upsets him.

- He is listless, unfocused, or preoccupied with a repetitive activity like twirling his hair, sucking his thumb, or holding onto a comfort item.

A child who feels disconnected can't think, so he has little flexibility. Earnestly trying to get him to do things differently provokes protest and unhappy feelings. At the end of Chapter 2, you'll find a short list of six other common behavioral flares that indicate disconnection. Of course, because children are inventive, there are hundreds more. I hope it reassures you to know that children everywhere do the same nutty stuff your child does when they're off track.

Here's an example of a behavioral signal that could easily have been ignored. Reading it accurately led to a real breakthrough.

———◇———

A mom and her three-and-a-half-year-old son arrived for their first visit to a Special Time class we offered. His mom had been troubled by his increasingly aggressive behavior. I greeted them with a friendly, quiet smile.

After some time, he came in and played for a bit with his mom, then made another exit out the door. She had asked him to take off his shoes, as the other children had done. He took one shoe off and put it down, but he threw his other shoe into the classroom. It didn't land near any of us. Although nobody was hurt, he was sending a signal. He needed a limit.

I brought his shoe to him, and, squatting, said quietly, "I can't let you throw your shoe into the room." He burst into tears and began screaming. His mom sat down next to him, and he dove into her lap. He cried, writhed, perspired, and proceeded to hate where he was. He begged again and again to go home.

His mom knew a little about Staylistening, so she remained calm. She listened and murmured, "No, we are fine here. I'm right with you. We'll go home when it's over." He cried a long time, beside himself with the desire to go home. I stayed with them, also murmuring now and then, "You're safe here. You'll go home for sure. Just not yet."

Another instructor kept the play going for the others while he cried and sweated, with his mom's and my full attention. When the class was almost over, he finally wiped his tears, asked for some water, then explored the room with his mom. They played a bit with pillows. When it was time to go, he met my gaze and said a warm goodbye. I got down at his level and told him I had liked being with him. Then, he turned to his mom and said, "Mommy, now I think I have two homes. One is at home, and the other one is here." His mom let me know that his behavior was much improved that week.

——◇——

Simply bringing his shoe back to this child served as an opening to an upset he was eager to shed. He didn't need to be punished! With our clear message that we could see his difficulty, he was able to show us how badly he was feeling. He cried hard until he could think, and saw that he was, in fact, safe right where he was. Then his world expanded in a big and wonderful way. Using your own sense of off-kilter behavior, you'll become an expert at spotting your child's signals for help, so you can step in with a limit before the other shoe drops.

HOW TO LISTEN, LIMIT, LISTEN

You'll want to set limits as a *way of connecting*, not as punishment or payback, and not as proof that you are in charge. To be successful at setting limits, you don't have to be at your glowing best, but things won't work well if you're consumed with upset. Chapter 13, *Connecting When You're at Wits' End*, includes some ideas you can try in those moments when you can't think. But we've found over time that trading listening time with another parent gives you the best chance to bring about promising results as you set limits. Your child needs emotional release to be at his best, and you deserve this kind of support as well!

I like to think about setting limits in three connective steps: *Listen, Limit, Listen.*

Step 1. Listen and think. We often think of setting limits as a means of enforcing rules. Conventional wisdom has it that children, like puppies, need parents to be clear and consistent with them. But children are not puppies! Their intelligence is vast. You will want to think alongside your child and foster *his* judgment, rather than "train" him to obey. It's much more reassuring to your child to learn from a parent who thinks well about each situation as it arises, rather than from one who insists that rules always be followed. Your good judgment and caring are what give your child his sense of security.

We parents do need to have standards and policies about important things like bedtime, cleanliness, and treating one another well. But life with children has its twists and turns, so there will occasionally be good reasons for you to say "No" to something that's usually allowed, and "Yes" to something that's usually off limits. A bit of flexibility now and then won't spoil your child. We've found that parenting flows more sweetly when we think of ourselves as first responders who think on the spot, rather than as enforcers.

This perspective will free you to take in the details of each new experience, and share your thinking with your child. It will also teach your child to think critically, and to respect your thinking. If the rule is "No dessert during the week," but your neighbor comes by with a plate of freshly baked cookies, maybe it's OK to say "Yes" to dessert. This doesn't mean that evenings become a free-for-all at the cookie jar. It means that you thought it made sense to enjoy warm cookies together that particular night. So first off, scan the scene. Is someone's safety at stake? If not, you can afford to take a moment to decide whether or not a limit makes sense.

Learning to be flexible during your child's emotional moments takes time because we can't often differentiate between our own driving emotions and our child's. The more you bring your limit-setting concerns to your Listening Partnership, the faster you'll master the skill. Let your listening partner in on how limits were set for you as a child. Rail about how you would have been treated if you had behaved like your child. Explore why you feel compulsive about setting limits, or why the thought of setting even one limit scares you. As you offload your feelings, you will notice that figuring out if and when a limit is necessary gets easier and easier.

When your child's behavior seems out of whack, stop what you're doing, listen, and think. Get down at his eye level, showing interest. No scolding, no barking, no warnings! You might inquire why he's yelling, or why he *has* to have the blue shirt that's in the wash right now. Once in a while, we parents think our child is off track when he's not, and listening first gives him the benefit of the doubt.

In a very short time, you can probably figure out what's going on.

- **Does your child need information or assistance?** For instance, if your child is upset because he can't find his other sock, you can suggest a few places to look. If your children start a chase game, but the baby is sleeping, you can help them move their game outside. Just give the situation a little nudge in a better direction.

- **Do your expectations need to shift?** Your child might seem off-track because your expectations don't suit his age or abilities. If, for example, you expect your three-year-old to be quiet and stand next to you for half an hour at the Department of Motor Vehicles, you are bound to be disappointed. He's three and quivering with life! Or, if your son has had a string of difficult years in school, you can't expect him to sit and do an hour of homework by himself every night like the other seventh-graders. He can build academic muscle, but his confidence is low. He'll need extra support to do it. Consult with someone who knows children well if your child is often unable to meet your expectations. You may be able to get useful information and a fresh perspective.

- **Are you running on empty?** Sometimes, your children will do things active kids thrive on—playing chase through the apartment, giggling together after lights out, yelling "Hi" out the backseat window to drivers on the road—and it drives you nuts! It may be good healthy fun, but it's too much to handle when your day has been hard. Preserving your equilibrium is a good reason to set a limit. But be honest about it. Let your child know there's nothing wrong with the activity he has chosen, but that it won't work right now because of *your* needs.

- **Is your child off track?** You know the signs. You'll read him better and better as you use Listening Tools. Often, you can figure out what's going on in a flash. If your child is angrily yelling and running through the house, grabbing things away from others, or refusing to get down from his sister's top bunk when asked, and you're not raging with upset, it's simple. It's time for a limit!

Step 2. *Bring* the limit. There's no need for harshness. Instead of yelling, issuing an order, or scolding your child for bad behavior, simply put yourself between your child and the nutty thing he's doing. Instead of the town crier, you're going to be the *action hero* as you set limits.

Most parents say or yell the limit. "Stop pulling Sissie's hair!" or "Don't you dare throw that shoe!" But standing there and talking brings only frustration because your child can't process anything you say. He can't control his own behavior. If he could, he wouldn't be pulling hair or throwing shoes.

Instead, *bring* the limit. Move in. Make swift but respectful physical contact. For example, put your hand over your child's, and slowly pry his fingers from Sissie's hair. Or put your hand on his arm so he can't hurl the shoe. If the shoe has already flown, you might gently grasp his wrists so he can't throw another one. Slice through his misbehavior with a physical limit and as little emotional static as possible.

Here's a story of a parent who set a limit on buying things. It's a great example of how a child's issue melts away when you give him your attention, rather than the item he's fixed his longings on.

———◇———

We were all excited that runners would be carrying the Olympic torch past our house. The day of the run, my six-year-old son was all keyed up and eager to get out onto the road. We found a good spot atop a wall. Finally, the torchbearer ran by as we clapped and waved. My children wanted to run along after the torch for a bit, so I followed them. Then, my son asked me repeatedly for some Olympic merchandise that other children were waving and wearing—green ribbons on sticks, and fake gold medals. I had bought the children each a flag to wave, and didn't have the money or inclination to buy more.

So I set a limit. I got down to his eye level and kindly said, "No, we're not buying any more Olympic things now." At this point, we were in a mall. My son had jammed himself against the doorway of a sports shop filled with Olympic items.

He got angry and said he would bite me if I didn't buy something for him. I was surprised by his vehemence but said I wouldn't let him hurt me. He tried to kick out at me so I gently held his leg and repeated that I wouldn't let him hurt me. He said I *had* to buy him something. I gently said I wasn't going to buy any other Olympic things today. His anger turned into tears. He said, "I want something I can keep forever!" I really heard him on this. I could empathize with his feelings of excitement, and then, perhaps, disappointment, as it was all over so quickly. I was consciously practicing bringing a loving limit, trusting that it would be useful to him longer term than a piece of Olympic junk. He cried and I stayed with him, listening. In time, he was ready to go and his mood turned cheerful.

That evening, I had to go to a class, and said goodbye to him with a warm hug and a kiss. He followed me downstairs and wanted to give me another hug, blew me lots of kisses, and waved as I left. In my son's warm, affectionate goodbye I felt the connection between us, built by setting the limit and holding it lovingly.

———◇———

When bringing a limit, act first; talk second. For example, pull a kicking, hitting child onto your lap, away from his target, before you say a word. Or, if one of your children calls "First!" for the favored booster seat in the car, but the other one scrambles in and claims it, just put your hand on his knee and tug gently. "It's time to get out. Your sister called it." You don't have to pull him out; you don't have to promise him first dibs next trip. Just keep tugging now and then so he can cry hard enough to eventually remember his generous nature.

Once you've brought a limit, relax and pay attention. Your child couldn't feel the pain that was bothering him while he was busy being an off-track kid. Once you bring your limit and show your child that you can listen, he has a much better chance of finally shedding the tension that drove him. He might squirm, scream, or run away as he tries to escape the emotional furies he carries inside. Stay with him. He needs your kindness and attention.

From all we've seen, punishment is counterproductive when you're bringing a healthy limit. The minute you threaten a child, swat him, or isolate him in time out, you've added a fresh hurt—a fear, an attack, or moments of isolation—to the hurt that has jammed his thinking. His rational mind isn't functioning, so whatever lesson you intended is lost on your child. He was hurting when he went off track, and punishment will confuse him further. Your child didn't want to go off track, and he desperately wants to be back in connection with you! He needs *you* to stop his nutty behavior, then reach for him as soon as you can.

Step 3. Listen. This is the crown jewel of the three steps. Once you have brought the limit, listening to your child's upset will allow him to recover from whatever hurt him. The information in Chapter 4, *Staylistening*, and Chapter 6, *Playlistening*, can be your guide.

Don't expect your child to return to a better perspective quickly. If he has flipped out because his sister marked up his drawing paper, be glad for this opportunity to let him offload feelings. Your limit—keeping him two feet from her so he can't pound on her in fury—and all the sweating and crying he does while you Staylisten, can save the two of them from many future altercations.

It seems to me that children sometimes use a small upset to test the waters. You'll set a seemingly ordinary limit, unaware that your child has an industrial-sized upset stashed away. He'll move into working on that bigger issue if you handle those first five or ten minutes of his cry thoughtfully.

One mother shares her experience with this:

———◇———

It was well beyond bedtime, but my daughter was still awake. Again. She'd had some trouble falling asleep for a few weeks. I suspected fears were affecting her sleep, and I was getting more listening time for myself so I could dig in and work with her on this emotional project.

We'd gotten back a few days before from a weekend at a relative's place. While there, we'd bought her a light brown teddy bear at a thrift store. She'd named it Goldie. We have a rule: things bought when we're with this relative stay there till we return. She had really wanted to bring Goldie home, but I held firm.

Once home, she couldn't sleep without Goldie. Now, this child is not at all deprived in the stuffed animal department; in fact, we're overflowing with stuffed animals. This was a big ah-ha! moment for me. In the past, I would have thought she was crying about what she *said* she was crying about. I would have tried to comfort her as best I could. This night was different. I realized that she was not crying about Goldie at all.

Goldie was a (drum roll, please) *pretext*. She was crying about the things that were keeping her up at night. Duh! Now that the light bulb was on in my head, I sat with her and Staylistened. She cried deep heaving sobs. I told her Goldie was safe, and would be there at her next visit. She cried more.

Although I'd braced myself for a good, long Staylistening session, she was done in five minutes. Then she settled down and quickly fell asleep. She slept through the night, and I haven't heard one peep about Goldie in the days since. She's going to sleep easily, too. I'm still a bit surprised about how easy it was. And should she miss Goldie again, I will know exactly what to do.

———◇———

SET LIMITS *BEFORE* YOU ARE UPSET

The most common mistake we make in setting limits is to hope against hope that the upset we see brewing right in front of us will go away. Ignoring a mound of evidence, we tend to hope that our kids won't kick each other under the table tonight, like they have nightly for the past six weeks! We tense up in advance of dinner, expect a miracle, and feel terribly discouraged and angry when their kicking begins.

Setting limits well is at least 50 percent planning! When you connect with your child at the first whiff of upset, you'll be warmer and more flexible, and so will your child. A few minutes of cuddling, hanging out, or horsing around the minute things start to head south can change the whole day. He would much rather be in touch with you than on his way to battle. But to pull off this smooth move, you'll have to lay plans to meet the problems that crop up regularly with limits before your child signals you more than once.

TRY SETTING LIMITS PLAYFULLY!

Humor is an uplifting strategy to use in setting limits, if your child isn't too upset. Kids love nothing better than a good laugh, and using humor to pry them out of their behavioral ruts can lift your whole family's spirits. For example, as you physically herd your pre-teen daughter out of the bathroom, you could say, "Ahhh, there's my sweet girl! You do look lovely! Your bathroom bouncer has arrived. Moving right along! Hallway mirror, here we come. Chug-a-chug!" To which your daughter will roll her eyes and say, "You're the weirdest parent I know!" but she'll move on, perhaps giving you some playful resistance, and benefitting from the laughter that results. The affection in your voice will reach her heart.

"The Vigorous Snuggle" is another way to set limits with humor. It plays on the tendencies of parents to issue consequences for misbehavior. Your child does something off-limits, and instead of making a federal case of it, you issue a mock threat. It works best when you're gleefully eager to catch your young "offender."

Here's a mother who used this strategy with her daughter's fussiness on a special day. She didn't ever get to the snuggle part, but the laughter was just what her children needed to turn their day around.

—◇—

My husband and I took our three kids, ages eleven, ten, and seven, for a hike on Mother's Day. My girls love to hike barefoot. I told my youngest that was fine, but that she should bring her shoes in my backpack. When my older daughter couldn't find her shoes, I said that was fine, she didn't need to bring any along. After we'd hiked awhile, my youngest learned that her older sister didn't have to bring shoes along, and she was really upset. She kept fussing that it wasn't fair. I said she was right, it wasn't, and that I was sorry. But since she wasn't even carrying them and didn't have to put them on, it didn't matter. That reasonable approach didn't work, and she kept fussing. I was annoyed that my Mother's Day hike was going sour.

Then I remembered Listening Tools! With an exaggeratedly authoritative voice, I said, "Oh yes. Of course you had to bring your shoes and your sister wasn't allowed to. That's because I am the Mean Queen, and I set different rules for every person on the hike." My daughter looked up, definitely interested. "Yes, your sister was not allowed to bring any shoes at all. If she had, she would be in big trouble. And you... well, you had to bring shoes but you are not allowed to wear them no matter what. And your brother, well he has to wear his shoes for at least half the hike and then he can take them off but he may not put them on again." She was hooked. She asked me, "What about Daddy?"

"Oh, him? Well, he may not take off his shoes under any circumstances, or he will face the wrath of the Mean Queen."

Well, that turned the whole hike around. They spent the rest of the time breaking the Mean Queen's rules, and every time they did, I chased them but never actually caught them. At one point, after I chased my son, who had disobediently put his shoes back on, I looked back and saw my seven-year-old wearing my husband's big shoes. Oh, was that queen angry with all of her subjects! A bit later, I took a "nap" while the girls took off my shoes and hid them. Boy, was I mad again! There were lots and lots of giggles and squeals all afternoon. We all felt really close afterwards. I think it was so successful because the Mean Queen routine, with those absurd and arbitrary rules, was playing around with issues of fairness, which was what my daughter was upset about in the first place.

------◇------

When you set limits playfully, your child will want to test that limit over and over, so he can enjoy being stopped in a playful way. You'll learn to smoosh, chase, pounce, pummel, give raspberries, issue grandiose threats, and do all kinds of horsing around in response to off-track behavior. The message you give is, "I know you're good, no matter what darned thing you're up to! Here I come!" It's a message children thrive on.

Conventional wisdom would tell you that setting limits playfully would encourage more misbehavior, not less. What we find is that when children feel themselves drifting away, or when they need reassurance that you care, they'll playfully do things that warrant a Vigorous Snuggle. It might look like misbehavior to others, but in the love-language you and your child will develop, it's an invitation to play and connect. When your child's hunger for playful limits is greater than you can satisfy, set a non-playful limit. Corral him and stay with him until he can think of something else to do. If he needs to cry, he will, and that will connect you.

MOVE YOUR CHILD FORWARD BY SETTING EXPECTATIONS

When your child has been stuck in a difficult behavior for quite some time, you'll need to set a fresh expectation to pry him out of his rut. Setting expectations is not rocket science, but success will come only when you have invested time in building a warm connection with your child. If he is going to trust you with the big feelings that confine him to that rut, he'll need to feel some real support from your corner!

Here are a few pointers to help you set expectations well. Feel free to try them out in simple situations first, like asking your child to bring his plate to the sink after eating, or asking him to shelve his toys after play.

- **Work on *your* feelings about the expectation you want to set.** After all, if you have to announce an expectation, then your child has probably failed to meet it many times. And each one of these failures has kicked up feelings for you. You'll be of better help to him if you offload some of your frustration first. A good listener can help you, and we describe how in Chapter 7, *The Listening Partnership.*

- **Share your expectation in advance.** It's best to see setting a new expectation as a *project* with ups and downs for both of you. Your child needs help, but he may need more than one chance to bang up against your expectation and have his necessary upsets. So give him plenty of notice. Cast your expectation in a positive light. "Next week, I'm going to ask you to put away your toys at the end of the day. You might not like it, but I'll help you with that. And then, it will be your regular job, just like doing the shopping is my regular job."

- **Use Listening Tools to connect.** You could try doing a bit of Special Time before the moment when you're going to expect sparkling behavior. Or use the tool of Playlistening described in Chapter 6. With it, you could let your child play out his reluctance, and secure laughter as you respond in a humorous way. For example, if your child runs away when it's time to pick up his blocks, you could scoop him up in your arms and bring him back, saying, "Don't you *love* your blocks? Aren't they beautiful? Don't you want to pick one up and hold it and put it on this lovely shelf?" He'll run away again, but he'll laugh and laugh as you bring him back and sing the praises of making a stack with his beautiful blocks. Special Time and Playlistening will help connect your child to you, and send the message that your request is not so urgent that you've forgotten you love him. After some laughter, you can return to your more serious expectation, and take the next step.

- **When you're well connected, set your expectation.** Then Staylisten. In this case, you might say cheerfully, "It's time to put your blocks away," hoping he can have a good cry about it. If he bolts, you could catch him and pull him into your lap, saying, "Today, you need to put your blocks away. I'll stay with you if it's hard." Stay with your child, letting him writhe and complain, until he can find a way to get to tears or sweaty struggle. Don't force him to even touch a block. Just help keep him focused on the feelings at hand. "Here are the blocks." "There's the empty shelf." "It's just a little job. It won't take very long." "When you're ready, I'll help you." Directing his attention to the task at hand will keep the feelings flowing. Listen. Now and then, ask gently, "Are you ready?" Sooner or later, he will be. A child who has had a well-supported cry can enjoy doing the expected job, and perhaps even be creative in how he does it. Feeling connected changes everything. Here's a story of setting expectations in order to move a child forward.

———◇———

My nine-year-old son takes piano lessons, and used to be happy to play for his friends. However, for the last half year, he disliked practicing at home and he wasn't making much progress.

One day, my son's piano teacher nudged us to work on practicing more at home. On our way home from the lesson, I started lecturing my son. He went quiet and clearly felt ashamed. I caught myself. It felt wrong to lecture like this. It took a lot to bite my tongue, but I apologized and shut my mouth until we got home, which allowed me to regain relative calm.

At home, I asked my son if it was OK for us to talk about piano lessons. He reluctantly agreed. This time, I tried my best to keep from saying, "If you can't practice, you should stop taking lessons," which was what my mom would say to me when I was small. I sat down next to him, looked him in the eye, and asked as calmly as I could what I could do to help him practice every day. My son started complaining about how his younger brother was bothering him or how it was unfair that his brother could play while he had to practice. I listened and resisted the urge to say things like, "That's not true!"

I asked him gently again, "What help do you need? I am sure you can do it." This made my son really upset, and he answered, "You can just shut up and be quiet! Go away!"

I responded, "I really want to figure out a way to help you practice. I am sure you can practice." I held my ground, but at the same time kept wondering if I was still motivated by my upset, or was now offering him real support at last. I chose an attitude of listening and giving confidence to him rather than lecturing and expecting him to change. I thought, "He knows what he is supposed to do, and actually likes to do, but he just can't for some reason."

My son was soon crying. He cried hard, saying it was unfair and all my fault. I kept on Staylistening. He cried sitting down next to the piano keyboard with me at his side. After about fifteen minutes, I needed to take care of other things and he wasn't crying hard any more, so I told him I was going to have to move on, and got up. To my surprise, he started practicing piano on his own soon after I left his side. I couldn't believe it.

Since that evening, he has practiced piano almost every day, sometimes starting on his own, other times with my encouragement, which had never worked before. Piano practice did not feel like a dreaded chore any more. Something was lighter. I could tell that my son was playing because he liked it and he wanted to. Seeing this changed the way I think about music, too. I stopped saying, "It's time to practice your piano," and started saying, "I want to hear your music. Can you play?" I can see that I was able to help him to work through whatever was in the way of him enjoying music practice.

————◆————

Our children are primed for love, respect, and justice. The thoughtful limits we set, and the listening we do afterwards, give them exactly what they need. But this approach to setting limits takes time, especially at first, because children's emotional memories are usually cluttered with feelings that have had little outlet. You may have to postpone some items on your to-do list while you work with your child to whittle down the backlog. But the time you spend listening and setting limits will yield freedom from trouble in the future. Your child will become closer to you, freer of hurt, and more soundly secure.

....

It's fine to wade into Listen, Limit, Listen slowly. Be proud of every success. Small steps are important steps. And in Part III, *Solutions to Everyday Parenting Challenges*, you'll read about a great variety of situations where parents with stress levels similar to yours have linked limits and listening with remarkable success.

6
Playlistening

Play is the safe cradle in which our children experiment, express themselves, and explore their world. Whatever the activity, your child is playing when her actions are spontaneous, she controls her role, and there's no pressure to reach a goal. Play is its own reward, and is deeply satisfying to your child. It is no trivial pursuit, however. It builds your child's intellect, judgment, strength, coordination, and character. In fact, play is so vital to children's development that the United Nations Commission on Human Rights has declared it an inalienable right.

All play nurtures our children, but Playlistening carries a special kind of power. It enhances your child's confidence and strengthens her connection with you and others. Playlistening is a tool that can help your child recover from challenging experiences, and face situations that once scared her. All this, while having fun!

The two hallmarks of Playlistening are laughter and your child's sense that she's in charge. Any time your child is full of unforced giggles and her appetite for fun is big, she's making gains. During safe, connected play, every laugh lets her release low-level tension. Every laugh moves her closer to freedom from fears and worries. She'll become braver, more creative, and more experimental as you find ways to keep the giggles coming. Children love Playlistening! And you'll find that it's a creative outlet for you, too, as you rediscover your own knack for play.

Let's say your daughter laughs when she climbs on your back and you jiggle her gently. To Playlisten, keep her laughter going with just enough motion to elicit more giggles. Pour affection and interest into your voice to add a connective tone to the play. Offer eye contact, share the giggles, and read her body language for clues about how the play is going. This is the "listening" aspect of Playlistening. Let her decide how and when this little game should change. She might want to climb down, put her stuffed animals on your back, and laugh as you jiggle them off. Or she might want to put a blanket over you, call you a turtle, and try standing on your back in all her glory. She'll have good ideas for continuing the laughter and fun: you'll love seeing her spirits rise.

Here's a taste of what Playlistening is like, from a mom who helped her daughter with some troublesome behavior that cropped up after preschool.

—◇—

A few weeks into her first year of preschool, I began to see a lot of tension in my daughter when I came to pick her up at the end of the day. She didn't want to leave, and it would take a long time to get her out the door. She also avoided saying goodbye to her friends and her teacher.

One day when I came to get her, she started biting her arm. That alarmed me. I worried about her hurting herself and I also had feelings about what other people would think of her and of me. By the time we got to the car, I remembered that I could take my feelings to my listening partner and work on them there. This allowed me to think clearly again, and remember to try a playful approach.

As I was putting her into her car seat, she was still biting her arm, so I pretended to have a nibble and playfully said, "Yum! That tastes like strawberries!" She began to giggle. I then nibbled at her other arm and pretended it tasted like chocolate. She was laughing and laughing. I nibbled at her fingers, and she offered me her leg, asking, "What does this taste like?" As we played like this for a few minutes, she continued to laugh along with me. She also stopped biting her arm.

At home, when I came to get her out of her car seat, she looked at me with a twinkle in her eye and put her arm in her mouth, inviting me to keep the game going. I nibbled at her arm, taking it from her mouth, and continued on with the game, saying how delicious she was. When we came inside, she ran to her dad and told him how delicious she was, and what flavors her arms were. He caught on to the game and picked her up, carrying her to the dining table. He placed her on the table and said, "Yum! I'm having you for dinner!" She laughed and laughed as he pretended to eat her up.

She was much happier the following day when I picked her up from preschool. When I arrived, she ran away and hid from me, and I pretended I couldn't find her. Then, she jumped out at me. I offered playful connection, and she now had a way to laugh off some of the tension from her day.

— ◇ —

WHAT SETS PLAYLISTENING APART

We parents have a tough time moving our children out of their frightened or prickly moments. We get frustrated when they just won't budge. Even when we devise rewards, lecture them, or set up unpleasant consequences, we come away with a bad taste in our mouths, and so do they. Then their issues crop up again because their underlying feelings stay glued in place.

Playlistening gives you an elegant strategy: you can help your child *release* some of that tension by initiating play. You don't, and can't, force her, of course—coercion is the antithesis of play. But you can try some humor, mix it with affection and a dash of imagination, and see where it takes you. One laugh, and you've lightened the tone for everyone. And because laughter connects us, Playlistening can be as restorative for you as it is for your child.

This tool is a godsend for parents of more than one child, and for working with children in a group. Playlistening can work with one child, two children, or ten. For instance, when one child excludes another in a group, you can help them all by offering your affection and then taking the less powerful role. "Oh, I have some hugs for you all. Smooshy hugs! Lots of hugs! Who's going to get my first hug?" Then, throwing your arms wide with an expectant grin, you start a slow chase through the house, or around the play yard. You might manage to tug on a sweater here or grab a shirttail there, but you play clumsily, so they all escape. You might heighten their laughter by giving a big hug to the sofa or the playground slide by mistake. As you play the warm and goofy foe, the children are brought together on the same side. You let them playfully exclude *you*! The laughter they share will begin to bond them, and move them away from targeting one of their own.

Playlistening helps children build cooperative relationships, and it can take the sting out of being instructed, guided, directed, and taught by adults day in and day out. For example, my grandson played on a baseball team of seven- to nine-year-old boys. Their coach was warm and patient with the boys during practice, but as coach, it was his job to give them lots of direction and instructions. At the end of every practice and game, he'd hold a team meeting, and then reverse their roles. He'd say, "OK, team, it's time to get the coach!" He would run off to the outfield, dodging and darting, with the boys giving chase. Eventually they'd tackle him and all pile on, making gleefully sure he couldn't get up. That's Playlistening. It lightened their practices and bonded their team.

Once you've built a strong relationship with your child, you can use Playlistening to lift specific fears and smooth bumpy relationships. For example, you can build your child's confidence before visiting the doctor or dentist, plump up her connections with relatives who don't visit often, and lighten the burdens presented by siblings, chores, homework, and even foods that don't hit her A-list. These and other practical uses for Playlistening are illustrated in Part III, *Solutions to Everyday Parenting Challenges*.

This parent figured out how to create a Playlistening outlet for behavior that was spoiling a family evening. She made a fifteen-minute investment, and reaped a remarkably smooth evening for all.

———◇———

At a family gathering there were too many kids and too many expectations of polite behavior. The kids, my son in particular, were falling apart.

My son and I took a break in another room and had a bad manners festival. We burped, blew bad breath at each other, made farting noises, and just laughed and laughed. A couple of cousins joined us and we had a fabulous time for about fifteen minutes before having to head back to the dining room for dinner.

The kids were so lighthearted and cooperative! They had excellent manners throughout the meal. The bonus was building a secret alliance in which we all shared an inside joke.

———◇———

And finally, Playlistening gives you an uplifting way to set limits. We grownups tend to get stuck in the "bad guy" role when our children go off track. We get sick of our own tone of voice, and it's easy to forget that our children are good people. Playlistening is your ticket out of those ruts. It takes a bit of time to set limits playfully, but as you do, you'll build your connection with your child, and the results will often be rewarding.

For example, when my grandson was in fourth grade, he often made fun of his younger sister. As soon as they arrived for a visit, he would mock her. At the very first comment, I'd head right over and wrestle him to the ground. I'd pretend to be incensed, and say, "Come here, you! I heard what you said! That's your beautiful sister you're talking about! That gets you some bonks on the butt!" Because I wasn't really upset, and we have built a tradition of roughhousing, he could laugh as I playfully pummeled him. He'd give me a good wrestle, then look at me with a twinkle and mock her again, as bait to get me to come after him once more. The words he used didn't sting. It was easy to see that, whatever the words, he meant, "Show me you want me!" And I did. After five or ten minutes of tussling and laughter, he'd figure out something else he wanted to do, and could play well with his sister. We'll explain more about playful limit setting soon.

In short, Playlistening is a way to build trust and closeness, an antidote to fear, and a refreshing way to set limits. Best of all, it brings good fun into your family.

WHEN TO OFFER PLAYLISTENING

This tool is almost infinitely flexible! Here are some of the occasions that will go better when you stir up a little Playlistening:

- When a child is shy.

- When a child is whiny.

- When two children are having a dispute.

- At the beginning of a play date or family gathering.

- With any child who behaves aggressively.

- With a child who is sucking her thumb or a pacifier.

- When a child is calling names.

- When a child struggles with a learning task.

- When a child is fearful.

It's a tool that works for children of all ages, as long as the adult is relatively free of irritation and willing to use a bit of imagination.

HOW TO BEGIN PLAYLISTENING

Your child has spent most of her short life far less informed and capable than you, although she's certainly not less intelligent. She has to make a hundred miscalculations each day as she masters new skills and encounters new situations. She also has to cope with lots of instruction from you and other adults. Under these conditions, a child can't help but feel inadequate some of the time. Playlistening is your confidence-repair tool. When you take on the less powerful role in a humorous way, she has the chance to be the swift, the sure, and the powerful. Her whole being will light up as tension releases in laughter.

You play the befuddled one; she is in the know. You do things backwards; she gets it right. You try hard and fail; she wins, and then wins again! You make a show of expecting wonderful things to happen, but those things go "wrong" as she pulls little tricks on you. With every giggle, the burden of trying so hard and being so small will lift. Laughter and your good humor will fill her sails.

For example, if your child giggles when a pea falls from your spoon at dinner, scoop up another spoonful of peas and say, in cartoon character fashion, "Hey, you rascally peas, stay on my spoon!" Then, spill some again. Be the picture of surprise. If your child laughs, spend the next several minutes trying hard to feed yourself. Lecture your peas. Fail and flail. And reap the benefits of her delight at seeing a grownup that can't quite manage a fork or a spoon.

Another key to sparking laughter is to set up a slight but safe physical challenge for your child. When she survives it, laughter bursts forth! For example, you might lie on the floor, giving your child an airplane ride on your raised feet. You say, "Whoa! Bumpy air ahead! Here it comes!" and bounce her up and down a bit as she "flies." You make it safe by announcing that the bumps are coming. If she laughs, the challenge is just right for her. Perhaps after several rounds of laughter you can ask her if she wants the bumpy air to come as a surprise. If so, she's gained some confidence and is on to a bigger challenge.

When you play like this, you create brief, faux "survival dramas." You stir up a bit of the unexpected, couched in affection. You set up challenges of just the right size, so any fear your child was holding releases in giggles. *Do refrain from tickling*, though, because tickling is a mechanical goad for laughter. Since the balance of power is not in your child's favor, being tickled probably won't build her confidence or help her release stored tension.

Over time, your child will gain physical confidence, along with strength and coordination. She learns her body's capabilities, and stretches herself. Meanwhile, the physical closeness she gets in Playlistening reassures every cell in her body that she is wanted and loved. Lawrence J. Cohen and Anthony De Benedet, MD, have written a wonderful illustrated book on physical play, *The Art of Roughhousing*, which will help you and your child get started if physical play is new to you.

You'll find that Playlistening works better and better as you lay in a foundation of regular Special Time with your child. If your first attempts at sparking laughter fall flat, don't worry. Just go back to waiting for your child's spontaneous laughter, and see what you can do to extend it on the spot.

Here are a few more pointers.

- **Invite physical contact and adopt an affectionate tone.** Most of the contact we make with children is gentle or practical in nature: combing their hair, buttoning their shirts, kissing them goodbye on the cheek. When a loving parent affectionately and actively pursues his child, lots of laughter often breaks out. Nuzzling, enthusiastic cuddling, rolling together on the floor, romping, pillow or rolled-up sock fights, and wrestling all are deeply reassuring for children, and great fun.

- **Be sure not to overwhelm or overpower your child.** You can offer a playful challenge if your child feels confident enough to handle it and continues to laugh. But every time you do, fall back for a few seconds to give your child the chance to take the reins of play again. With a baby or toddler, you can simply lie on your back on the floor and make a few surprised noises as she bounces her bottom on your tummy. When throwing pillows with an older child, make a comic show of your might, but see that your pillow lands a good three feet from her at first. Work up over time to direct thumps. With a confident child, laughter may come when you put up a good fight and score a few points before you lose. Each child's tolerance for physical challenge is different, so promote laughter at the distance and pace that works best for your child.

  If you are too forceful, your child will laugh frantically, screech, or look at you with wide, frightened eyes. Try not to push her to this edge. When you notice signs of fear, bumble. Get down on your knees to see if you can spark more laughter that way. Your goal is to let her laugh in delight and triumph. Nearly always, it's best for your child to come out the winner.

- **Don't let your own issues intrude.** Sometimes we parents will tend to direct play toward issues our child did not raise, or away from activities we simply don't like. For example, perhaps your child asks to be chased. The play is lively and full of giggles for a while. Then you begin to say, "I'm Tyrannosaurus Rex! And I'm hungry!" You smack your lips and make scary sounds, but soon, your child is staring at you with a frightened look. Oops! The dinosaur was your idea, and it made the play unsafe. Back to the chase your child designed!

- **If play doesn't come easily for you, listening time will help.**
You'll learn more about how you can free yourself from worry,
irritation, and boredom in Chapter 7, *The Listening Partnership*.
Talk with your listening partner about how play was for you as a
child. What happened when you asked your parents to play with
you? What do you like about playing with your child? What can't
you stand? Why do you think you have those aversions? What
kind of talk goes on in your mind when you try to play? These
topics will help you air your fears and dislikes, and find the cor-
ners where your playful side can begin to show.

USE PLAYLISTENING TO ADDRESS CHALLENGING ISSUES

When they're scared, children adopt lots of repetitive, isolating behaviors that stump the adults around them. Let's take a quick look at some
ways that Playlistening can ease these kinds of hurt.

- **Help your child while she's sucking her thumb or a pacifier**
by doing some playful nuzzling. You might nibble on her hair
a bit, then become enthusiastic about how good it tastes. Or
you might bounce some kisses up her leg, across her head, and
down the other leg. Sometimes, all it takes is a few giggles to
help a child engage without something in her mouth.

- **Help your whining child** by nudging her out of that rut in much
the same way. If she's moaning, "I wanna coookkkiiiieeee....,"
do something eager and off-the-wall, like saying, "And I want a
nibble of your ear!" Then, bounce your kisses up her leg, up her
arm, and play-nibble her ear with happy munching sounds. Or
you could pick her up, throw her over your shoulders like a sack
of potatoes, and march around the house, chanting, "We want
a cookie! We want a cookie!" When an older child balks and
whines you can, with a friendly air, drape yourself all over her,
saying that you, too, want to take a few minutes' break. Then,
pretend to have an extraordinary case of the hiccups. Do anything to make physical contact, create gentle surprise, and be
silly. Your warm, happy-go-lucky tone will carry the day. And
your own creativity, once you fire it up, will delight you both.

- **Help your child with her fears.** If your child hides in your skirt when she's introduced to strangers, busily wrap her up well in it, and then paw all over her as you speak to your friend. "Rebecca's in here somewhere!" If your child won't try new foods, play the picky eater yourself. Poke at your peas with your fork, and make a disgusted face. Ask, "Should I touch one? They're wrinkly! Ewww!" She'll catch on, and order you to touch them right now. Make every disgusted grimace you can think of. Put a pea in your mouth and (gasp!) spit it out. Stretch this out for as long as she's able to laugh. You'll probably have to do this many times— children who are super-sensitive to taste and texture don't shed that sensitivity quickly. But it's fun, and it relieves her of the burden of being the only one who rejects food. That's worth a lot! To address other specific fears, just play that you're the one who's scared.

- **Help your child, or others, with the impulse to call names.** This is a tough one for grownups. We tend to feel indignant, like there's a flaw in the character of any child who would call names. But almost every child has tried out name-calling by the time she's three. The urge comes from times when she or other children were called names. The behavior pattern sticks because no one helped your child offload the fear she felt as it happened. A fascination with name-calling grows from the seed of that fear. See the *Bad Words from Good Kids* section of Chapter 12, *Moving Beyond Aggression*, for some playful ways to reduce your child's urge to call names.

- **Try Playlistening when you're locked in a power struggle with your child.** If your child hates to put on her snowsuit, don't trudge into battle. Take the less powerful role instead. When it's time to bundle her up, become "confused" and put her jacket over your head, then ask her, amazed, why it suddenly became so dark. If there's laughter, go further. Busily dress the armchair with it, snaps and all, before you realize that's not quite right, either.

Or if your child hates shampoos, you can lather up your hands with shampoo and earnestly soap up the waterspout in the tub, saying, "Now, doesn't this feel good? Nice, soft suds! And they smell so good! Ahhhh!" Then, look at the sudsy spout, look back at your child, and cry, "Wait one darn minute here! That's not Tessie's hair! What happened?" Your child's laughter is likely to be rolling well. Then soap her foot, her elbow, and finally her belly button in your further attempts to give her a fine shampoo. Again and again, she's "in the know," while you play her busy but dim-witted parent.

Your child's laughter signals the release of tension from previous interactions that weren't so jolly—the times you were frustrated, the times you two battled over every little thing. Each crummy moment left traces of tension; as you Playlisten, your child's laughter dissolves it and strengthens her.

PLAYLISTENING OFTEN PROVIDES ACCESS TO DEEPER FEELINGS

After a child has laughed a lot, she feels quite safe and loved. At this point, she will often find a way to bring up deeper feelings. She may become upset, sad, or frustrated, usually about a minor thing. For instance, she'll want her red sweater, which is in the wash, or she'll need a pencil with the right kind of eraser, and no pencil you have will satisfy her. She is ready to release long-held feelings that don't make sense any more but won't go away.

She is, in a sense, asking you to set a limit. Don't placate her or try to talk sense into her. She needs this opportunity to tantrum or cry vigorously. These are the times that try parents' souls—so much emotion about an insignificant issue! But this outburst is a blessing. It allows her to blast away a heavy burden. When you've listened, she'll feel relaxed, refreshed, and much closer to you than before.

SOME CHILDREN WARM SLOWLY TO PLAYLISTENING,
MANY BURST INTO TEARS IN THE MIDDLE OF IT

A timid child may only welcome Playlistening after several months of Special Time and bits of laughter in tamer play. And little insults—an accidental bop on the wrist, or a sister who plays a game "the wrong way"—can spark big upsets. A smaller child or one who has faced difficulties in life often feels like the victim in this scenario. Don't blame or scold others in the family, even if they were a bit too rough. Your child is healing those spots where her confidence is not yet up to snuff. You can reassure her that she is loved, listen, and resume play when the storm has passed. Your ten-derhearted child will gradually build resilience with repeated chances to cry.

I've watched this process with many a child, including my grand-daughter, who is two-and-a-half years younger than her brother. She has had hundreds of cries over the years, sparked by being accidentally (or not-so-accidentally) munched and crunched in play. Her brother also has received good listening when we've brought a limit to keep him from nee-dling her. Now, at ages eleven and fourteen, they laugh, play, and wrestle long and hard without incident. She is much smaller, but is a full match for him in strength. She is fearless, and he's not far behind. Hundreds of other families report similar marvels—their girls become strong and their boys don't lose their gentle side when physical Playlistening and Staylis-tening have been part of their lives.

YOU CAN SET LIMITS WITH PLAYLISTENING

Children will test limits when they are tense and feeling disconnect-ed. Often, you can use Playlistening to dissolve this tension by delivering enough affection to remind your child that she belongs and is loved.

To get started, you'll need to invent some playful, light-as-a-feather tones with which to say "No." The trouble is, few of us ever heard "No" said playfully, and we can't imagine how to say "No" without the tones of threat and harshness mixed in. Try experimenting with the pitch of your voice, your words, and some exaggerations of a grown-up, serious "No" to see if you can discover your talent in this department. I like to use a mild, musical, "Na, na, na-aah," or a high-pitched, pipsqueak voice for, "Uh-oh! You're in trouble now!" said with great affection. You could try a big, bil-lowy "Noooo," given like you're pinning the Medal of Honor on your child. There's a friendly, "I'm going to catch you" tone you can use when you say, "I saw that! You're into the cookies again!" which will start a chase through your house, crumbs flying, that's worthy of a Roadrunner cartoon. You can issue pretend threats—"I'm going to put frogs in the shirt of anybody who touches those cookies just out of the oven! *Frogs!*" Invent your own!

When you combine a "No" with vigorous, affectionate contact or a chase that ends with affection and nuzzling, we call it the Vigorous Snuggle. With it, you tackle the isolation that sends your child off track. Your child tries to get away with the forbidden thing she wants to do; she laughs away tension as you hold the limit. For example, as your child reaches for her brother's prized robot, you swoop down, scoop her into your arms, and run jauntily into the next room. She laughs, wriggles away, and heads for the robot again. You catch her many times, with flair; she laughs and feels your affection. She doesn't get the robot; she gets *you.*

Often, after such a playtime, a child can cry heartily in your arms about some small thing. This relieves the deeper feeling of need that has glued her desire onto something she must not have. She'll be relaxed and cooperative when her laughter and tears have restored her better judgment.

Playful Parenting, by Lawrence J. Cohen, will show you how you can, in fact, center your parenting around Playlistening. He offers a multitude of ideas about connecting with our children through play. It's one of the most warmly practical books on parenting I know.

Playlistening will greatly encourage your child. She wants a close relationship with you. She's looking for oodles of fun. She hopes you'll be thrilled with her—her thinking, her experiments, her very being. Playlistening is just what she's been waiting for, so she'll want to partner with you to get laughter going often.

To some parents, the things children will do to try to initiate Playlistening—jumping on your back, shooting you with a Nerf gun—might seem to border on disrespect. Traditionally, respect is thought to require a gulf between parent and child, with the child treating her parent with great deference. But this gulf doesn't serve a child well. Yes, parents know more facts than children. Yes, parents have some skills and judgment that can't be perfected in childhood. Yes, children need guidance daily. But when grownups act like they're superior and their children are inferior, it doesn't support a child's confidence, and it doesn't credit a child with the vast intelligence and healthy instincts she possesses from the very start. You can be playful one minute, and set a needed limit the next. We've noticed that in families that focus on connection and listening, children respect and love their parents without commands to do so. They also try to initiate play often!

We win our children's hearts when we get down on our hands and knees and play. We can bond with our kids through watermelon-seed-spitting contests and squirt-gun battles. Laughter narrows the gulf between parent and child, but it won't erode your child's respect for you. On the contrary. As one Hand in Hand-raised teen told his folks before he left home for his first year of college, "You know, Mom, it has been so different with you and Dad, compared to most parents. It has never been about the grades or the rules. You and Dad took the time to build a relationship with me and my sister. What we have is special."

....

In Part III, *Solutions to Everyday Parenting Challenges*, you'll find lots of examples of common fears and behavioral difficulties that can be tackled with Playlistening. They'll give you a feel for the power you have to help your child using your sense of humor, affection, and the healing power of laughter.

7
The Listening Partnership

Parenting isn't easy! Some days start with one child sitting defiantly on the floor, refusing to put on his shoes while the other huffs away, ignoring the garbage she's been asked to take out. We're bristling before breakfast is over, and things tumble downhill from there. When we're upset, the fun drains out of parenting. Even our sense that our children are dear to us disappears. Every single one of us grapples with tough days as we do our best to be good parents.

A Listening Partnership is built to tackle the inevitable stress that's a byproduct of parenting. It's a straightforward tool: you exchange listening with a parent of your choice. You decide what you want to say. You express your feelings about the situations that irk you day after day. The other parent listens with warmth and respect. They don't give advice—*you* know your own life and children best. Their aim is to help you offload tension. Then, you listen in return. It's simple and cost-free.

As you and your listening partner come to rely on one another's attention and respect, trust will build. And positive change will follow. You'll see these signs that emotional burdens are lifting:

- **Talking**, thinking, and reviewing your experience as you absorb the warm attention of a listener will release mild tension.

- **Laughter** will help the two of you connect and brush away fears.

- **Crying** will provide an outlet for your grief, and give you more slack for fresh insights.

- **Trembling and perspiring** as you tell about hard times will get you past your fears.

- **Tantrums** will help blast away frustration, so it's easier to try and try again.

- **Yawns** may occur as your body begins to relax, and will signal that your system is shifting from "on guard" to "A-OK" status.

You've seen your children release their feelings of hurt and tension in all these ways. They're naturals! The minute something challenging happens, they dive right in to expel the tension. With a Listening Partnership, it's your turn. You'll find that listening and being listened to will refuel your energy for parenting. Refreshed, it will be easier to connect with your child. Solutions to the problems that weigh on your mind will come along.

Here's how it can work:

———◇———

This story is all about poop. My son had toilet trained at age two. He continued on wonderfully until turning three. Then, bang! He started pooping and peeing in his pants. It was surprising and incredibly frustrating. Infuriating, in fact. Why had he started doing this *now*? We knew he knew where to go—specifically, not in his pants! And yet he continued to do it. No matter what we tried, on it went, month after month.

My husband and I were getting more and more upset about it, and this was obviously being passed on to our son as further tension. I discussed it with a number of close friends, and tried everything I could think of. Nothing changed.

I finally admitted I needed some listening time around the issue. What was it about his poopy pants that drove me nuts? Oh, yeah, that's right—that little issue of having my own poopy undies rubbed in my face when I was five years old and was going through a bad patch of pooping in my pants myself. My mom had been infuriated too, and she had rubbed poop in my face in exasperation. It was a mortifying, painful, and embarrassing memory, but one I had to re-experience to heal from. I cried and raged about it with my listening partner.

Then, pretty much instantly, I relaxed when I responded to my son's poops landing in his pants instead of the toilet. "Oh, you've pooped in your pants? No problem! Mommy can clean it up. Let's try for the toilet next time OK?" Sweet. And you know, the issue cleared itself up in less than a month.

———◇———

In listening to thousands of parents over several decades, I've seen that when a parent can offload tension, things get better. What seemed impossible eases; their children begin to relax. Parents have used Listening Partnerships to overcome their inability to play; their habit of correcting their child at every turn; their fear of their child's strong feelings; their anger; their paralysis when faced with conflict; their exhaustion; their inability to ask for help; their sense that they just can't stand their child; their difficulties setting limits; frequent yelling; their sense of distance from other loved ones; and more. Listening Partnerships have helped parents lift any number of fears. Parents have then opened ways for their children to get along, helped their super-competitive children relax, brought fun into their families, set limits comfortably, and helped their children with learning difficulties, school, and much more.

On a broader scale, parents have used Listening Partnerships to rebuild their lives after a job loss or divorce; to successfully lobby for needed change in their children's daycare centers, preschools, schools, and neighborhoods; and to be their child's advocate through long sagas with medical treatment.

WHAT SETS A LISTENING PARTNERSHIP APART?

There's nothing like a Listening Partnership out there! It's the parent support tool that helps us bring our best selves to our children and each other, day in and day out. No special qualifications are needed to set one up.

A good listening partner doesn't have to know what the other person should do; all you need to know is that your partner is worthy of your focused attention. You don't need to understand your partner's situation fully; you simply offer them warmth and respect while they sort things through. You can call on one another night or day, but you each decide how available you want to be, and respect that boundary. Three minutes each way can be amazingly useful, with an hour each way probably the longest you would ever spend. The relationship can be brief or last for decades. A listening partner can become a very close confidant, but you'll never be expected to send them a birthday card, invite them for Thanksgiving dinner, or babysit their children when they're sick. Although you may share your deepest thoughts and feelings, you don't owe your partner a thing. It's a relationship for the purpose of listening: that's all.

Here is how a Listening Partnership helped one mother soar over a relationship hurdle with her pre-teen daughter:

—◇—

I was having a really hard time with my twelve-year-old. She and I could not see eye-to-eye at all. My listening partner invited me to talk about what it was like for me when I was twelve. That's the age I was when my Mom left us, and we were very poor. I had so much work I had to do! I cried many times about the shock and the very hard times we had. No wonder seeing my daughter have so much more than I had brings up a lot of feelings! In my listening time, I could say, "How *dare* you say that you don't have anything! I had *nothing*!" and cry and cry.

I think that really helped me, because now when we're together, we have a lot of fun. She and I have playful ways to connect. I'm no longer screaming, "Why aren't you cleaning your room? Why are you complaining? You have everything!"

Her life is so different than mine was at her age, and it wasn't her fault that I didn't have all the stuff that she has now. All I can do is wish the best for her, and hope that she will use what she has wisely. The most important thing is that the connection between us is there. We go for walks; I get along with her so much better now than when I wasn't working on my feelings about when I was twelve years old.

—◇—

WHEN TO USE A LISTENING PARTNERSHIP

Any time you feel stressed, a Listening Partnership can help. The problem can seem relatively minor—for example, your daughter is complaining about her soccer practices. She doesn't want to go. Should you allow her to quit? What might be going on? She won't talk about it. How can you learn more? Or, the problem can feel overwhelming—you have no savings, a demanding job, a wife and young child, and your mother has become ill. She needs help, but your wife wants you to spend more time at home. Things are strained. How can you address the many needs all around you? A Listening Partnership can bring increased clarity—*your* clarity—to any family issue.

There are two ways to make this tool work. You start by setting up a Listening Partnership regularly to develop your skills, review how things are going, and learn to offload the stress of parenting instead of letting it pile up. Then, when you've developed trust and some skill with a listener or two, you can use a Listening Partnership on the spur of the moment. The two of you can agree to call or text one another, requesting Listening Time when you otherwise might explode at your children or others close to you. Whether you use a Listening Partnership regularly or add a "red button" feature to your relationship, you agree to an equal exchange. You'll always give listening time in return, if not at that very moment.

Here's an example of a mom who used her Listening Partnership to explore her earliest experience, which eased daily burdens in surprising ways.

———◇———

I had been exchanging listening time regularly with another mother for about a year when we decided to set up some additional time each week, separate from our regular time, to focus on telling the story of our lives. We wanted to spend time on the things in our lives that had shaped some habitual responses and persistent difficulties.

I noticed that this separate time allowed me to have feelings about some very early challenges I had experienced. As a newborn I spent a couple of weeks in an incubator in the neonatal intensive care unit. I was born early, was underweight, had jaundice, and struggled with feeding in those early weeks. So my first experiences in life involved not feeling well and, I think, feeling overwhelmed by external stimuli, including people. I do not have explicit memories of this time, but as I talked about what I thought it must have been like, many of the feelings I had were the ones that often crop up for me when I am overworked, or spend a lot of time with other people.

As I shed these feelings, I noticed that I felt less exhausted. I was not so drained by spending time with my friends. I had always thought of myself as a pretty strong introvert, because spending time with others felt like it required a lot of energy. This started to gradually shift. I enjoyed myself for longer periods of time with others, and I didn't need as much time to myself afterward to recuperate.

Telling my life story, from the beginning, with an interested listener and no time pressure, has already been such an amazing experience, and I haven't even finished the work I want to do on my time in the hospital yet!

———◇———

And many parents call on their Listening Partners for five minutes of tension release several times a week. This can turn your day around; and it's just as rewarding to make that kind of difference for another parent you've come to care about. Here's a mother who used the trust she'd built to help her turn her holiday around:

———◇———

It was New Year's morning. Our family had plans to head up to the mountains to spend two days in the snow. My husband yelled at me for making noise before he'd gotten up. I had quite a reaction: I was trembling and scared—it must have reminded me of my parents' yelling and arguing when I was a child.

I reassured our son that everything was going to be OK, calmed down, then told my husband I didn't want to be in the car with him if he was going to be angry. I had never stood up like this before, and I was now more upset than ever. I went to the cottage out back, and threw a mighty tantrum there. I cried and hit the wall. Then I called my Listening Partner, who didn't answer. I left her a three-minute message, full of everything I was angry about, complete with expletives that aren't in my normal vocabulary. I knew she would listen.

When I hung up, my anger had evaporated, and I sobbed on the floor. I could feel the hurt and frustration underneath. After several minutes, my head cleared, and I understood why I'd been so angry. I recognized that this was part of a larger project that wasn't all going to get fixed today. Yet I felt relieved.

Giving myself some listening time saved our trip. I was able to let go of my emotions enough to relax. I relaxed about our departure time. I didn't feel the need to pressure my husband or son. We ended up having a good drive, and a great weekend. I'm so glad I made that three-minute phone call.

———◇———

HOW TO DO A LISTENING PARTNERSHIP

FIND A LISTENING PARTNER

Listening Partnerships are simple to do. You choose someone you'd like to exchange listening with. Pick someone you trust, or someone you think will be a good listener. You don't have to know them well; all that's required is that they have an interest in parenting well. Good choices might be a friend, another parent interested in Hand in Hand Parenting (see our Resources section for how to connect), a parent from your child's school or daycare center, or a colleague at work. Then ask them if they'd like to try a new way of supporting each other in parenting.

There's one additional proviso: it's not usually a good idea to choose your husband, wife, parent, sibling, boss, or subordinate to be your first Listening Partner, unless you have an unusually stress-free relationship. For a Listening Partnership to work, each person needs to be able to listen to the other without getting personally tangled in their concerns, and without giving or asking for advice.

Because "Let's try a listening exchange" is not your everyday proposal, the person you ask will feel cautious about trying this. You'll probably feel that way yourself! You could suggest that the two of you test-drive the idea two or three times before you each decide whether you're interested in more.

MAKE LISTENING YOUR FOCUS

I think you'll find that the quality of your Listening Partnership will be richer if you don't treat it like a friendship. Let it be what it is, a listening exchange between two dedicated parents, without additional obligations. Your relationship will revolve around the listening you exchange, your dedication to parenting, and the trust you've built. Don't clutter it with teatime or Girl Scout cookie sales—just get down to listening. Where else can you develop this chance to offload the stress of parenting?

Of course, if you and your listening partner have a friendship already, there's no need to suspend it. But it may work best if, in listening time, you stick with topics that don't relate to areas of contention between you. And don't expect your listening partner to listen to your upsets about him or her. Take those topics to a listener less involved in your life.

FIND A PLACE TO MEET

If parents listen in person, most get together in their bedrooms, attics, basements, or some other little, out-of-the-way place that offers privacy. You could also meet in a spare office at work, or in your car when the weather is decent. For most people, meeting outdoors for listening time leads to feeling hazy and unable to focus on shedding emotion. There's something about a sheltered, enclosed space that allows us to *feel* our stories as we tell them.

Wherever you meet, bring a handkerchief or tissues, and a timer of some kind. That's all you need.

FOLLOW THESE SIMPLE GUIDELINES

Here are the guidelines you'll both follow as you listen.

- Listen with warmth and respect. Offer your complete attention.

- Trust that your attention will make a difference.

- Trust in your partner's intelligence.

- Don't advise or judge.

- Keep what your partner says strictly confidential.

GET STARTED

Set up a convenient time for the two of you to get together in person, by videoconference, or over the phone. Meeting in person can be far richer and warmer, but phone or videoconferencing also works remarkably well for many parents. Agree on the amount of time you'll take, divide it equally, and decide who's the first listener. Set a timer, and get comfortable.

One of you begins by listening with warmth and respect. The other gets to talk and think about parenting, or any other subject that feels important. When you're the listener, keep your mind on the other person:

both *how* they are as they talk, and *what* they are telling you. Be alert for the presence of emotion. At first, it will be difficult to keep your mind on *them*. You'll want to solve the problem. You'll have a similar story. You might have a cousin who works where they work, and you'll wonder if they've met. Just note these distractions, then move your mind back to *who* they are, *how* they are, and to whether any wisps of emotion are visible as they talk. Is there a chuckle? What thought brought it? What detail of their story made tears well up? Notice these things silently, and be pleased they are sharing themselves with you.

When the agreed-upon time is up, help your partner break away from their whirl of concerns, so they can listen well to you. Do this by asking a little "refresher question" that brings your partner's attention to matter-of-fact, emotionally neutral things. Stay away from topics they talked about in their turn. Here are a few samples:

Describe the oldest pair of shoes you own.

Tell me three things you know about earthworms.

Create a sentence using these words—"sailboat," "balloon," "zebra."

Tell me a few cities that begin with the letter "M."

You get the idea. Avoid math questions, an area of stress for many of us. Accept any answer. If you happen to ask a question that triggers negative thoughts for them, follow with a different question. Your goal is to bring their mind away from troubles, so they can listen well.

Now trade roles. It's the listener's turn to talk. We recommend that you and your listening partner use your first several listening times to each tell the story of your lives. Start with the very first memory you have. You won't necessarily know how old you were in these early memories, but tell the details you recall. If you don't have memories of your early life, tell the facts you've been told, and your best guesses about how infancy and early childhood went for you. Get to the things you actually do remember when you can. See if feelings emerge as you tell your story.

These first few times, you'll be getting used to listening and being listened to. You'll review your life—what has happened, the details you remember, and the feelings you recall. That's all. You are building an understanding of one another, and the connection between you.

That said, if your mind is absolutely riveted on your current parenting challenges, talk about them. I advise parents to begin each listening time by saying one thing that's going well for them: one little moment they enjoyed in the past week. We do plenty of fretting, so it's good to take a moment to notice what's been easy or fun, even if it takes time to think of something!

To be clear: this won't be chitchat. The two of you agree to *listen*. Your rapt attention will amplify your partner's ability to notice his or her thoughts and feelings. Although you may not notice any change in your partner then and there, they are likely to feel your attention for days to come. And you are likely to feel theirs. This simple inpouring of focused warmth and attention signals the limbic system that we're not alone. As Daniel J. Siegel, MD, puts it, you'll each begin to "feel felt." This turns out to be a very strong aid to human awareness, and to our ability to bounce back from hard times.

KEEP EVERYTHING YOUR PARTNER SAYS CONFIDENTIAL

Keeping what's said completely confidential is the only way a Listening Partnership can work long term. If, as you offload frustration, you say the awful things that run through your mind, you have to be able to trust that you won't be quoted in gossip circles! And it's important that listening partners never joke or tease the other about what has been shared. It's even best that you don't inquire about how the things your partner talked about turned out when you see them next, although you're dying to know. Let your partner decide what they want to bring up. Your goal is to help them release emotional tension on the topic of their choice, not to stay informed on every twist and turn in their saga.

SUPPORT EMOTIONAL RELEASE

As listener, don't focus on whether the person you're listening to is coming up with solutions, or having positive or negative feelings. Their feelings will come and go, and solutions will occur to them at random moments. Your role is to see what you can do to *help them release tension* through talking, laughter, trembling, perspiration, tantrums, crying, or, oddly enough, yawning. Note the thoughts and memories that bring them close to releasing feelings. These show both your partner and you a path toward emotional release. And that will bring better times in parenting.

Talking is a mild form of tension release. Often, it's the necessary prelude to showing emotion and releasing it more fully. So when it's your turn, talk away. Let your mind go where it will. There's no need to tell a coherent story, stay on one subject, or fill your listener in so they can follow your train of thought. You are talking to ease your own mind, not to entertain your listener. You can also stop talking any time you wish, and simply notice your feelings. This can sometimes aid the release of tension. If it helps, you can make noise or move around. Stay loose! If you try hard to be organized and coherent, as though you were in school, you're less likely to be able to offload tension.

Laughter is contagious, and it releases both fear and embarrassment. If you come upon a thought that makes you laugh, don't rush on. Explore. Perhaps related thoughts or details will evoke more chuckles. Your listening partner might smile or laugh along with you. When you're the listener and your partner laughs, it's fine to respond by joining in if it helps them continue. You can even ask them to repeat the phrase that got them started: "She said *what?*" or "*Cheerios* in his pants?" Your goal is to give the person permission to thoroughly enjoy and extend their laughter.

Perspiration and trembling release our fears. This may strike you as strange, but you've probably experienced it. Have you ever been in an accident, then trembled almost uncontrollably as soon as you could tell you were safe? Or have your sweat glands worked overtime as you stood up to speak in front of a group? Did your hands tremble? Were your knees shaky? If so, you've offloaded fear.

When you talk about the things that worry you, you may relive some of the fear then and there. Your listening partner can remind you that you're remembering and releasing fear. To accelerate the healing process, move your body. You might stand up, move your shoulders, give your hands a shake, pound on a pillow, make a roller-coaster-type whoop, or make noise and stomp. Moving things from talking to assertive action, especially in the standing position, can often induce the release of shivers, perspiration, or tears. In any case, it's a refreshing alternative to quietly describing one's fears, which can leave you feeling numb.

Crying releases grief. Sometimes our tears just trickle out, other times we alternate between stifling tears and shedding them. Eventually, we learn to let go and sob. We can prolong crying by focusing on the vivid details or specific thoughts that intensify the feeling.

Anger is a sign that a big wad of grief and fear is encased in a hard outer shell. The tender feelings won't release because an angry person feels alone, mistrustful, and unloved. Because anger keeps others at a distance, a person who feels angry has trouble getting to the core of the hurt that waits to be expressed and healed.

To work free of anger, a person first needs to talk about how they feel, what triggers them, and how this anger became a hot-button issue for them. They need permission to express anger, full out, to see if this allows them to release their grief and fear. You might encourage your partner to say and show the heat they feel with gestures and crude language, or by hitting a sofa or cushion. This may let them finally cry, tremble, or perspire away the feelings that lie buried beneath the angry stance.

However, if your partner tends to let their anger nip and bite the people around them, you might need to help them with an alternate suggestion. Encourage them to say what a vulnerable, hurt child might say before mistrust has set in. For example, "Help me. I'm scared," or "Don't you care about me?" or "Why are you doing this to me?" This may give your partner access to the hurt feelings they had to bury long ago.

Yawns can pop up during listening time; a small percentage of people yawn often when they feel safe. Some adults even yawn in the midst of crying. This isn't a sign of boredom or lack of oxygen. Yawns actually release physical tension. They signal that the body is relaxing and repairing itself, and emotions will flow more easily.

ADDITIONAL STRATEGIES FOR LISTENING PARTNERS

When you're the listener, you will mostly listen with respect and warmth. But you will be actively thinking about your partner, and there are some additional initiatives you can take now and then to help open the door to emotional release. And when it's your turn to talk, but emotional release isn't coming easily, you can try them out for yourself when the time seems right.

Appreciate your partner. It's easy for parents to forget how good they are and how hard they try! So you might offer a brief, concrete appreciation to counter a negative feeling your partner is caught in. Just a few words will do. "You're so brave," for the parent who is worrying about bringing up a concern with her child's teacher, for example. It's also a good idea to exchange an appreciation at the end of each time together, without referring to the feelings your partner worked on.

Reassure your partner. You might remind your partner that he is a good person; his children are good through and through; he has a good mind; and he has always done his best. These simple truths may help counter the feelings of failure that stifle tears, laughter, and fresh thinking.

Encourage your partner to take pride in himself. When a parent looks pleased, stands proudly, and says positive things about himself and his children, feelings can bubble up for release, often beginning with laughter. Taking pride in ourselves and our children is a helpful way to combat the inner put-downs our minds toss at us all day long.

Encourage your partner to talk about his memories of love and acceptance. For example, if a mother is furious at her preteen daughter, you might direct her to talk about the thoughts and the words of love she used when her daughter was a baby, and to imagine speaking to her daughter in that vein. If a father is deeply worried about being reunited with a child he hasn't seen in three years, you might ask him to remember good times before they were separated, or to try telling his child that he loves him, and anything else he wants his child to know.

These ideas, which point a parent's attention toward the positive, can work like a shovel on hard soil. You can try them when feelings are packed down tightly. Demonstrating or remembering love, caring, confidence, power, and even playfulness can loosen feelings of hopelessness, fear, and isolation, so they can release at last.

TAKE A BREAK FROM TRYING TO SOLVE THE PROBLEM

We encourage parents to free themselves from the task of finding solutions in their Listening Partnerships! It's hard to find fresh insight as you poke around in this week's briar patch of who did what to whom. Move your attention to how you *feel* about the situation, and trust your mind to find good strategies later. It can also be helpful to reflect on how you feel about past situations that remind you of the one that has you stumped.

Here are several questions you can ask yourself or your listening partner that will point back to where the troubled feelings may have originated. Focus on releasing feelings you uncover, and on having your say about the wrongs you remember.

- What does this situation remind me of?

- What's the earliest time in my life I felt this way?

- Who does this person remind me of?

- When I was my child's age now, what was happening in *my* life?

- How would my parents have treated me if I did what my child is doing now?

- What does this situation make me *feel* like doing or saying?

- When's a time when I *didn't* feel this way?

- What are my worst fears? Have things like that happened before?

- What's the last time things went *well* for me in this area of concern?

Exploring the feelings from the past, instead of recounting current frustrations and worries, has led many a parent to the emotional release needed to connect better with their children, and offer real help to them.

AVOID THESE HABITS THAT SOMETIMES PASS FOR LISTENING

There are a few practices, sometimes touted as "listening," that will erode the safety of your Listening Partnership. They are intended to help, but the effect will be otherwise. Set up a signal between you and your listening partner—say, a tap on the knee—so you can let one another know, should one of you make a misstep.

Don't psychologize: "Oh, it sounds like you have a lot of anger left over from your relationship with your mother." Instead, inquire: "What would you have said to your mother back then, if you'd had good support?"

Don't summarize what your partner said to you: "Oh, I think I heard you say that you are too upset with your twins to set any limits at all right now. Is that right?" Instead, help your partner to unfold his story: "Tell me more. What runs through your mind when they fight?"

Don't advise: "Oh, *I* know what to do with kids who are picky eaters! Here's what worked really well with my nephew..." Instead, focus on finding a way to help your partner release feelings, which will lead to his own good thinking.

Please remember that the most powerful agent of change will be the trust you build with your listening partner. So concentrate on listening. Develop a warm and respectful relationship. The fancier footwork can follow. We offer a link to fuller information about being a listener, and using a listener, in our Resources section.

That's all you need to know to get started! You don't have to memorize this chapter, just glance at the main points now and then as you get some experience under your belt. Your life will go better with more support, so think, call upon your pioneering spirit, pick up your phone, and reach out to give this a try!

AT TIMES, A LICENSED THERAPIST MAY BE HELPFUL

There are times when a Listening Partnership may not be the best tool for the tensions you need help with. A licensed therapist is a good alternative if you are bowled over by an unexpected circumstance and are too upset to listen in return, or when you have something highly confidential to work on. Find someone you respect. You'll want a therapist who will support you to act with integrity, release the pent-up emotion, and figure things out in your own good way.

....

You deserve good support for your work as a parent! With these understandings and a little gumption, you can broaden your network of caring relationships. The energy you reap will enrich your life and benefit your whole family.

8
Emotional Projects

After you've used Listening Tools for a few months, you'll notice that one good cry or a laughter-filled Playlistening time isn't always enough to permanently change your child's behavior. Laughter or a good upset may relieve her temporarily, but that same tension rolls in again like the tide with a pattern of behavior that just won't quit. For example, your child has a meltdown about getting dressed, morning after morning. After you set a limit and Staylisten, she becomes cheerful and connected, but the next day is just as difficult.

This happens when your child is caught by a hurt that's deeply rooted. It eats at her sense of safety. The feeling of threat usually has one or two recurring triggers, ordinary situations that she just can't abide. Common ones are transitions from play to mealtime, using a car seat, entering a group of children already playing together, or going to sleep at night. One cry or some active Playlistening can release a chunk of stored emotion each time, but if the hurt goes deep, that chunk might dissolve just a small portion of the hurt she's working through. The issue will recur because she has opened the door to a long-term recovery project—an *emotional project*. She'll need to revisit it many times in order to shake free of its effect on her behavior.

Here are more signs that your child has an emotional project ready to be tackled:

- People are tempted to label your child. One trait stands out in their minds—and in her behavior.

- Her feelings are intense. She's often fearful.

- When you listen, she vents feelings for quite a while.

- Your child expresses the same feeling time after time—"It's not fair!" or "I can't do it!" or "You aren't the boss of me!" or "I *need* you!"

- When you Staylisten all the way through, her behavior clears nicely.

- As you Staylisten often and fully, the time between episodes lengthens.

The repeated release of emotion is her ticket out of the rut. By using one or two pretexts often—say, fears wake her screaming in the night or she's painfully shy around other children—she can get the hundred chances she needs to slowly but surely drain that hurt, and feel more at ease.

WHAT SETS AN EMOTIONAL PROJECT APART?

The concept of emotional projects is a powerful one because it allows you to trust your child's judgment in situations that would otherwise drive you nuts with worry or frustration. It's an idea that recognizes the innate wisdom of your child's meltdowns. She's not "immature," "manipulative," or "out to get you" when she flies into a tantrum after getting a drop of water on her pajamas at bedtime, *again*. She's working methodically—nightly—on the panic she feels when something doesn't line up perfectly with her expectations. And if you anchor her through another meltdown tonight, she'll become a bit more tolerant when she's playing with friends tomorrow, and things don't go quite the way she had in mind. She'll be less likely to lash out, less likely to run away, saying she doesn't want to play with them anymore. Her emotional project will lead her, and you, to a more relaxed life overall.

I've seen many children's personalities change over time as they worked their way through a big emotional project. Timid children can become confident, aggressive children can become open and tolerant, and possessive children can become fond of sharing their toys and games with others. In my experience, what we think of as a child's "personality" or "temperament" can actually be a behavioral reaction to situations that weren't easy on that child. You'll be helped greatly if you understand that an emotional project can take from a month to as long as three years. Your willingness to stick by your child as she works through her big issue will repair her confidence, and provide an unshakable realization that she is loved and supported.

WHEN TO BEGIN AN EMOTIONAL PROJECT

Because emotional projects require patience, commitment, and a fair bit of listening work, their success depends upon you being in good emotional shape. You can't help your child to feel safer in the world when you're frazzled! Your listening time and energy will be repaid many times over as your child makes gains and her life evens out. But seeing how frightened or how deeply sad she feels will kick up big feelings for you. And you may need to shift your expectations of her, anticipate difficult moments, protect her from the criticism of others, and temporarily excuse her from situations that overwhelm her.

Your first step is to bring all your feelings about taking on the emotional project to a listening partner. Are you scared you child will hurt you while she thrashes through her fears? Worried she'll never get beyond this behavior? Embarrassed that she's acting this way at all? Do her upsets create a distance between the two of you that feels like it can't be bridged? The first step to getting things on better footing is to notice feelings like these. There is no right or wrong way to feel, but being aware of how you feel puts you in a more powerful position when you go about the business of helping her heal.

Your listening partner can support you to release your feelings about your child's behavior, whatever they may be. You can protest each and every one of the unfair conditions you're laboring under. You can curse and carry on. It *is* unfair that you're so stressed! It is an outrage that your child needs so much, and you are so worn. You have capacities you can't yet feel, but you'll tap into them only if you receive the benefit of some loving attention and unconditional support yourself.

It's time to start tackling your child's emotional project when you know your listening partner is on your side, feelings are flowing, and you're beginning to feel refreshed after each Listening Partnership.

HOW TO MANAGE AN EMOTIONAL PROJECT

Step 1. Increase the reassurance you give your child, and lower her stress. This is a two-pronged strategy. Temporarily, you'll want to increase the Special Time and Playlistening you do with your child. She needs the feel of your attention, the fun of play with you, and the warmth that laughter provides. You might want to do Special Time in the morning, again after school or daycare, and then Playlistening after dinner to spark laughter, physical contact, and affection. See what other kinds of reassurance you can devise. Daily snuggles while reading books together, lying with your child before sleep, and ten-minute WrestleMania free-for-alls once or twice a day for children who tend to be aggressive, can help you pour in the message, "You're safe. I'm here. I want you!" All are powerful antidotes to stored hurt.

Couple these confidence-building moves with a bit of strategic coddling. Do what you can to lower the number of times in a day your child is stopped in her tracks by fear or upset. That may mean some inconvenience for you. If she's anxious, for example, you might consider fostering out your two big, easily agitated dogs for a few months. Their frequent, sudden barking can't help but set off fear responses in your child, and add to her sense of lurking danger. If your child is in agony over goodbyes at daycare, you might want to shift her to fewer mornings each week for a month or two, or make the time to do the long, tearful separation work in the mornings that will help her shed her fears. If your second-grader is having dreams that provoke screaming and tears, you might let her sleep with you for a week or two to calm her system, before listening to her fears as you propose to have her sleep on her own again. You get the idea: pour on support for a while. You can bring back an expectation or a limit later, when she feels connected enough to do the emotional work well.

One single mom I know had a nine-year-old son who balked at getting dressed every morning before school. Their mornings were acrimonious every single school day. So she told herself that she would add reassurance for two weeks, to try to turn things around. She planned to give him Special Time before dinner each day, and in the mornings, she would dress him with as much love and affection as she would dress a toddler. She wanted to create a warm connection in the exact place it was missing in their mornings.

The very first morning of her program, she saw and felt a remarkable change. They had giggled while she cooed over him as she dressed him that morning, and they'd had a sweet conversation over breakfast. Both felt real happiness as they left for school and work. After the second week of morning affection like this, I suggested that she give him a small task, like putting on his own socks, as a tiny trigger for whatever big feelings he had about dressing himself. She told me she would do that in a few more weeks—she didn't want to stop dressing him yet! They were enjoying this little ritual, and because of it, their relationship was now stronger. Since she'd begun, her son had cried twice with her about issues with his Dad, and had shed feelings he had never shared with her before. His issues with dressing himself faded as his ability to shed big feelings increased.

Step 2. Make Listening Partnerships part of your routine. To balance the extra attention and work you're doing, add Listening Partnership time so your energies won't flag after a week. You were working hard *before* you decided to take this project on, and *now* look at you! So tank up on emotional support.

Step 3. Anticipate difficulty, and plan for it. Planning for hard moments ahead of time is a key way to keep from losing it with our children. If your daughter creates a storm around going to school, wake her up earlier to begin your whole routine. Then when her upsets erupt, you've got the time to offer caring and Staylistening. If your twins are in a stage where they squabble ten times a day, visit your parents for much shorter stays, so you don't fry their patience and yell at your children. If your child gets defensive when her friend comes over to play, set up a Playlistening game of tag, or set them up as a team in a sock war against you for the first fifteen minutes of the playtime. Lose, colorfully and comically. This will get them working together, and may make the remainder of the playtime work better. And if one of them runs into trouble with the other anyhow, they're more likely to cry fully about it, rather than having to pull hair or shove or grab.

Step 4. Set limits and Staylisten. When you've upped your child's sense of safety with the steps above, the limits you set will give her the opportunities she needs to shed big feelings repeatedly. If your child can't be close to her baby brother without giving him a hurtful squeeze, then warmly appreciate her love, but hold her by the tummy so she can't embrace him fully. If your younger two can't play together without hurting one another while you make the dinner, you'll need to bring one of them into the kitchen with you each evening, listening to them if necessary as you separate them. Do what you must to keep each child safe, and listen to the feelings as you go. When you are proactive about ensuring safety with firm but kindly limits, your children will drain feelings at a good rate, and start enjoying life more fully again.

HOW LONG DOES AN EMOTIONAL PROJECT TAKE?

Unfortunately, there's no dipstick that will measure the depth of your child's feelings about her sticky issue. Some emotional projects are short and clear-cut, like this project on frustration:

———◇———

My daughter is twenty months old, and she wants to do things *herself*. There are so many things she wants but is not able to do, so she's feeling a lot of frustration. Previously, I tried to get her to stop crying, or to cajole her out of it. Now I'm trying to just be there for her, knowing that good things are happening even though it looks like she's at her wits' end. I've been able to stay there with her much longer than before.

One thing that frustrates her lately is putting on my shoes, or her own shoes. She finds shoes and tries to buckle them and unbuckle them, but she can't get them completely on. I've thought, "Maybe she just wants them *on!*" But if I move in to put them on her feet, she is even *more* upset than if I let her struggle, crying and trying. And I can't head her away from the shoes. She *wants* to work at putting them on. I think she really wants to be in charge of learning to do her shoes, and tantrums are part of being in charge. They can't be that uncomfortable for her, because she keeps going back to this place again and again. This is a hard, hard stage, but she's getting through it, I know.

———◇———

This emotional project on sleep was taxing, but it was nearly over in just a week:

———◇———

Getting our two-year-old son to sleep was wearing us down. It was taking us almost two hours every night, and my wife had to lie by his side until he finally slept. And he would always choose Mommy to sleep with him if she was around. When my wife had no energy to put him to sleep, we would pretend that she was not at home and he only had Dad to put him to bed.

On the first night, we prepared ourselves for a lot of emotion from our son. We read him bedtime stories, kissed and cuddled, and then told him that we would be right outside the door. We sat by the door so that he could see us. As we expected, he kept climbing out of bed and wanted Mommy to sleep next to him. He began to cry when she set the limit that he needed to go back to bed. As he began to get more desperate, he started to hit his head against the wall and cried. We moved in and cradled his head to keep him safe. We could hear his fear. We Staylistened. He was kicking and yelling out big cries. We continued to do all we could to keep him safe and to help him shed his feelings. After two hours he finally fell asleep.

The following night, I put him down to bed, but we did not pretend that my wife was out. When she said good night and left, our son climbed out of bed and ran to the door. He kept asking me to open it. I moved in close and got down on my knees next to him. I told him it was time for bed. He started stomping his feet as his cries got more anxious and desperate. He began screaming reasons why he needed the door open. He even felt desperate to get his teeth brushed! His cries were loud and filled with fear and panic. After about thirty minutes, I pulled him into my lap. His eyes were shut tight. His cries were deep. He kept burying his head into my chest. After listening to him for another hour, I called for my wife to come in, and she held him. We continued Staylistening on his bed for another thirty minutes, and then he finally went to sleep.

These nights were full of feelings for both of us. We both used our Listening Partnerships to help us with our fears and the sadness we felt, seeing him so very desperate and scared.

On the third night, my wife tucked him in, and we sat outside his door. He climbed out of bed, and we tucked him back in. After to-ing and fro-ing for a bit he started crying, and we Staylistened. This time, his cries felt different. No longer was there panic or a desperate tone. His cries felt more healing. We both stayed by his side. My wife held him, and each time his cries eased off, she would tell him that it was time for bed and that she would be sitting outside. This would start his cries again. And then came the breakthrough. This time, he managed to cry it all through. He brightened up, started chatting with us, and giggled for a bit. Then, my wife and I left the room. Our son rolled onto his side and went to sleep. This took an hour and a half.

The following night we had a bit of to-ing and fro-ing before he could release big feelings. We repeated the events of the previous night. When he was done crying he reconnected with us, gave us both a kiss and a hug and went to sleep. This only took us an hour.

Now, after a week of Setting Limits and Staylistening at bedtime, our son is a totally different boy even during the day. He is more confident and independent. He is more social with the other children at the childcare center—even the childcare worker noticed a change. Before we began this bedtime project, he usually cried for Mommy or Daddy after his nap. Since we helped him with bedtime, this has stopped as well. Our son now plays on his own more often and for a longer time without needing our attention. He is definitely chattier, and he's asking a lot more questions!

This project has been rewarding for us and for him. There were a lot of feelings for us all to work through, and we did!

———◇———

Some emotional projects take much longer to resolve. That doesn't sound like good news, I know, but you won't be laboring away without a hint of success. Children tend to show subtle hints of progress every time they laugh, tantrum, or cry. Occasionally, you'll see a significant behavior change after just one or two big emotional episodes. Daniel's story is an example of subtle hints, gradual progress, and one big final breakthrough.

———◇———

Daniel attended the parent cooperative preschool I directed. He was three the year he began, and he was a quiet boy. He loved drumming, though, and had a favorite drum he would frequently play with. One day, one of the children snatched his drum, and a teacher noticed that he sat there blankly. He didn't protest, nor did he get up and find something else he wanted to do. She got down next to him and asked him whether he liked what had happened. He looked at her, said nothing, and began to cry. She listened, and posed the question again. He cried for a good long time, but never managed to say a word.

We decided to keep an eye out for other such interactions, and found that he simply couldn't stick up for himself under any circumstance. So we began helping him with an emotional project: saying what he wanted, and standing up for himself.

It took him many long cries before he could say what he didn't like, but he finally did it. Progress! After that, when an interaction went badly, a teacher would propose that he stand up, or if he was standing, that he take one step toward the child who had offended him. We wanted to help him gain the ability to take action. He couldn't move toward a child to talk to them for several more long cries. But eventually, when he had worked off enough helplessness, he did stand. He did take a step or two. Of course, the offending child was long gone by then, but that didn't matter. We weren't trying to get an apology or enforce sharing. What mattered was that he was working his way out of paralysis when injustice occurred.

Then we said, "I'll go with you to talk to him," and he had several more long cries before he could be that forward. We didn't insist on any one outcome. We pointed out the next step and encouraged him gently. "You can talk to her," or "Arianna is your friend. You can walk over to her." His helpless feelings went deep, so this project took many months with a cry or two each week. We'd listen for ten to twenty minutes each time, then thank him for his courage in thinking about the next step, and ask him what he wanted to play. He rarely finished one of these cries, because we had other children to tend to. He kept the gains he made, but progress didn't come quickly.

Once he could stand up and take a step or two, the progression of expectations that were held out for him was this: "Let's go over to him," and when he could do that, "What do you want to say to him?" But we soon broke that down into smaller steps, "Can you tell him, 'I didn't like that?'" or, "Can you tell her, 'I want it back?'" or, "Do you want to say, 'Don't do that again?'" Each time, he would stand there and cry for a good long time. Often, the other child would walk away, which we permitted. We would encourage him to follow, and then more feelings of helplessness would roll off in tears. As his work on these feelings progressed, he became a more active child in our program. He laughed more, played harder, and even began to play jokes on teachers now and then. And he turned four years old.

Finally, on one of the last days of the school year, a fifth-grader from an adjacent classroom tossed an apple core into our room. Daniel saw this, and said to me, "He shouldn't do that!" I said, "Yep! What do you want to do about it?" He said, "I want to talk to him." I asked if he wanted me to go with him, and he said yes. He picked up the apple core, and together, we went to the child's classroom, a place neither of us had been before. Daniel opened the door, spotted the boy, walked up to him, and said, "You shouldn't throw this into our room." He handed the student the apple core, turned around, and went back out. I was three feet behind him, had made no suggestions, and forced absolutely nothing. His emotional project was over! At four years old, he was unafraid to stick up for what he thought was right with a complete stranger in a completely new place!

—◇—

Children of all ages let us know that big feelings have wrapped them in a straightjacket of frustration, fear, or grief. They go from waking once in the night to waking every hour, or from one upset a day about sharing to one every fifteen minutes. Times of transition often spark an emotional project: upsets just before a child starts to talk; blasting off frustration at the cusp of toddlerhood; mastering the challenges of sharing, ownership, and taking turns in preschool; dealing with learning difficulties in elementary school; working on "Am I OK?" during preteen and early teen years; and struggling through separation fears and myriad feelings about parents during each of these stages. If we parents can recognize emotional projects, we can then take the necessary steps to help our children work through them.

WE WORK THROUGH EMOTIONAL PROJECTS TOO

We parents have lots in common with our children; we too can find ourselves knee-deep in an emotional project. We get touchy about our children's safety, we can't stand how they fight, we feel so alone that we stop reaching out, and we tighten up and work harder until our health starts to unravel. When you've got a good Listening Partnership going, and the feelings you're working on are very similar week to week, it's possible that you're in the midst of your own emotional project. The feelings you have are triggered by current conditions, but in fact, they are relics of your past.

It takes two crowbars—emotional release and positive action—to lift our minds and hearts out of emotional ruts that have deepened over time. Lasting change will not come from simply forcing yourself to take positive action. Nor will change come from venting about challenges without taking positive action. We must both release painful feelings *and* take positive action to hoist ourselves out of rigid behavior.

Here's how one parent took on her own emotional project, her struggle with yelling:

———◇———

Who doesn't want to be a calm parent? I sure do! My daughter is six. We adopted her three-and-a-half years ago. Just before I lose my patience and yell at her, an internal voice whispers, "Call a friend! Get some listening time, now!" I hear it. Then I seem to panic and think, "I can't... no way," and down I tumble. One night, I roared at my daughter with full force, scaring both of us. I knew I could have kept things from going that far, if only I'd had the courage to pick up the phone. But for me, the thought of calling someone for help brings up massive fear.

So I used listening time to explore my fear of asking for help from a friend or listening partner. My listening partner asked me gently, "What happened when you asked for help in the past?" I remembered feeling like I was condemned for needing help. Then my listening partner asked, "What is the worst thing that could happen if you rang someone in that moment of need?" I answered, "It seems so trivial, but the worst thing would be if they said they couldn't take my call right now." I cried as I thought about that possibility, and after awhile I realized, well, darn! Why not tell my fear to a friend, and then ask for what I want? I later spoke to a couple of friends and my listening partner, and all of them agreed to be available to me on a moment's notice. I sensed that this was my very own emotional project.

Not long after, my daughter and I were alone and facing a long weekend together. My husband was away for work. I felt disconnected and distant. I realized I was teetering. And then she yelled, really yelled, right in my face! I yelled her words back to her, and just as loud. Right in her face! I fled from the room and all I could think was, "I can't do this! I can't do this mom thing!" And there was the whisper—"Phone a friend."

My daughter was crying and banging on the door I was locked behind. I came out, squatted down, and said as gently as I could muster, "Darling,

I need to get some help. I don't want to be yelling at you. I am going to phone a friend. I am going to my room for ten minutes." Then I sat on my bed, staring at my phone. Did I dare? I wrote a text, "Could you spare me ten minutes?" I swallowed my fear and pressed "Send."

"Aagh! Now I have done it," I thought, "No backing out now," and I felt panic rising. Almost instantly my listening partner replied, "Shall I call you?" The moment I heard her voice I started to cry a deep, guttural cry. "I'm here," she said warmly. I cried some more and shared a little. "I am sorry it's so hard for you right now," I heard her say. I felt her warmth, acceptance, and understanding. I cried some more. After five minutes, I could hear my daughter outside the bedroom door, so I brought the call to a close. But, wow! It was such a relief to cry, to not have to figure anything out, to let the emotion have expression. It was all that was needed.

I did it! I felt lighter, less stressed, and able to return to my daughter. That brief five minutes with my listening partner opened my heart; I found empathy for my daughter. It made all the difference to our weekend. I'll be doing it again, and I look forward to an opportunity to reciprocate.

———◇———

An emotional project might sound like a lot of work at first. But your project will progress one hour at a time. And launching one is far better than the alternative. Consider how disheartening it is to pretzel yourself around the sharp edges of an issue that comes up again and again. Using ordinary "discipline," you have to distance yourself from your child each time he flares. The history of negative feelings between you grows.

Using Listening Tools, you'll move *toward* your struggling child, step by step, to repair his sense of connection. You'll organize some support for yourself first. Then, when you have a good outlet for your own upsets, you'll create a plan of action that will communicate your caring and bring the best of you to your child during challenging times.

Thousands of parents are changing their lives and lifting their children's persistent troubles by focusing on *support and connection*, so that lasting solutions spring from their thinking and efforts.

....

As you move into Section III, *Solutions to Everyday Parenting Challenges,* you'll notice the stories that involve emotional projects. Read through them, get inspired, and decide which project you're going to take on first! And in the Resources section you'll find a list of services Hand in Hand Parenting offers to help you build your own support system.

PART III
SOLUTIONS TO EVERYDAY PARENTING CHALLENGES

Introduction

In this section, we bring you stories from a good number of parents who've faced situations that are probably familiar to you. These parents used Listening Tools to connect with their children, and find the help they themselves needed so they could think more clearly about how to deliver their love. We don't recommend you do exactly the same things they did—no two families are alike. But their stories can inspire you. Though your story will be different, we're confident your child wants to connect with you, and that you can find a way to make it happen.

We've chosen four areas most parents struggle with, and broken each of them down into challenges parents face daily. We show how the five Listening Tools can be used to resolve upsets and bring parents and their children closer. Each parent's story is followed by a brief commentary to help you understand why the particular Listening Tools worked. You'll notice the intelligence of the parents and their children, even in the midst of hard times. Such brilliance lies within you and your child, too. Look for it. Listen. Experiment.

9
Building Cooperation

WHAT YOU NEED TO KNOW

We're often terribly frustrated when we try to get our children to cooperate. On this issue, there seem to be two camps. Many of us get so fed up with our inability to control our kids that we give up. We just pick up the toys or clear the table ourselves, but resentment builds over time, creating distance between ourselves and our children. We feel inadequate. And our lack of confidence makes our children's world feel shakier. Those of us in the second camp get so triggered by lack of cooperation that we yell, shame, blame, or punish until the deed is done by force. Here, too, we feel badly. Anger and frustration reign. Our children can't help but internalize the message that they are not good enough, which hinders their ability to learn and make friends.

In seeking cooperation, we must think of our children as *partners in a relationship*. Paying attention to connection before asking a child to cooperate is like greeting a neighbor and chatting a bit before mentioning that the fence between your yards needs repair. You honor the relationship, since it is the foundation for any positive action to follow.

For example, a mother once came to me, furious at her two young children for not emptying their backpacks and putting their lunch boxes in the kitchen after school. She had tried "everything," and they just wouldn't listen. Instead, they would walk into the house, drop their things by the front door, and run to the living room to play. This mom could feel her frustration rising every afternoon at the anticipation of the standoff she knew was coming.

I pointed out that they'd been away from her all day long, doing what their teachers wanted. So rather than greeting them with a demand, it might work better to simply join them in play for ten minutes or so. Then she could try asking them to empty their backpacks. And it worked! This was a fine example of a parent setting herself up for success by connecting first. When children feel connected to their parents and truly seen, cooperation comes naturally. Rather than ruffling up your feathers and preparing for a showdown with an uncooperative child, here's how to use our Listening Tools to build the cooperation you long for.

FOSTERING A CLIMATE OF COOPERATION

What we know:

- Your child wants to cooperate.

- When your child feels close and connected, he can choose to cooperate.

- If your child feels threatened or unsafe, he is not able to cooperate.

We parents often feel urgent about getting things done right now, a feeling that tends to arise when we feel burdened and alone. We want to *feel* better, so we try to get the kids to sit down to lunch *now*, or get the bedroom cleaned up *now*, or get them piled into the car *now*. And there *are* times to force cooperation immediately. When your child is darting out onto a busy street, you've got to scoop him up right away, no matter how insulted he may feel! But otherwise, to win cooperation, you need to allow a bit of time for connection between the two of you.

To build a climate of cooperation, you will want to create a balance between your generous yesses and the gift of no. When your yes is a warm one, the bond between you grows. Special Time is one good way to say "Yes" to your child. As you allow him to show you his interests, your generous attitude will rub off on him. Special Time lets you limit your "Yes" with a timer, and limit how often you can offer it, so you don't have to worry about being dominated by your child's whims. On a good day, most of us can manage to love what our child loves for five or ten minutes. This provides the foundation for cooperation. Over time, your child will become more likely to be generous with you and with others, because he has your full-strength "Yes" behind him on a regular basis.

Here's how one mom turned things around with the "Yes" of Special Time:

———◇———

I'd been having ongoing trouble getting my girls ready for school in the mornings. My temper would flare every day because my kids wouldn't cooperate. So I got some Listening Time to clear my head and decided that I needed to squeeze in some Special Time with them.

One morning, one of my girls got up at five forty-five, earlier than usual. She seemed well rested, and the coast was clear so I offered her five minutes of Special Time. She wanted to color, one of her favorite pastimes. We got out the special markers, and I spent five minutes following her instructions, drawing designs for her to color in. When the timer went off, we finished the last one, cleaned up, and she went off to get dressed for school. We had fun together. I felt encouraged and connected, and she looked happy.

Then I went to wake up my other girl and offered her Special Time first thing. She was wrapped in a blanket. Quietly, I asked if she wanted to be my baby. She did. So I pulled her onto my lap and we cuddled. I sang her our special lullabies, looked into her eyes, cradled her long body in my arms, and showed her my delight.

It was a very small investment, time-wise, but it sure paid off! The rest of the morning went smoothly. At breakfast, they both ate instead of dallying. They quickly got their socks and shoes on. Instead of looking all around the house for the perfect toy to bring to the car, they got their backpacks, climbed in, and off we went. I even got them to school on time! No yelling, no threats. It was such a sweet morning!

———◇———

When you've made a good connection and your child still won't cooperate, Setting Limits and Staylistening are the tools that will help you deliver the gift of "No." With them, you can help your child work through the upsets that make him balk, so he can then reconnect. Let's take Setting Limits first.

Imagine that your two-year-old has dumped the entire box of blocks onto the rug while you were preparing dinner. He's having a blast banging them together and discovering the sounds they make, but it's now time to clean up and come eat.

You call from the kitchen to put the blocks away, but the banging continues. Rather than calling him a second and a third time, you head into the living room to connect. You admire him as he plays you a song that is unlikely to win a Grammy, but beautiful in that two-year-old block-banging kind of way. Then you say lightly, "OK, time to put the blocks away." Because he is so smitten with himself and his music, he doesn't stop. So you kneel down on the rug, place your hand gently on his hands so he can't keep banging, and say lovingly, "Dinner time. Time to put the blocks away."

At this point, an upset may very well bubble up. If you make warm eye contact and listen, rather than lecture or cajole, he will soon find the safety he needs to scream or cry. Though the others around you may not understand, the situation has improved. All you need to do is to keep holding the limit and offering your warmth. When his crying tapers down, you ask again, "Son, can you put the blocks away yet?" He will release feelings until he can reconnect with you and regain his ability to reason.

Your child's reaction is likely to seem huge, compared to the small request you're making, but you can assume he's clearing out tension from other days and other limits. When he's done, the two of you can take turns tossing the blocks back into their box, showing him that you enjoy cooperating, too.

Playlistening also works wonders in helping a child cooperate. Imagine that your five-year-old son refuses to brush his teeth, but he's just finished a sugary dessert. You decide that tonight, dental care is a must. Instead of repeating your demand over and over, consider doing something that will make him laugh.

"What? You don't want to brush your teeth? OK. Why don't you brush your elbow instead?" You get a strange sideways glance. "Or, I know! How about your nose?" Now you hear a little chuckle. He sees that a game is developing.

"How about my butt crack!" he blurts out as he launches into a big belly laugh. He's five, and butt cracks are a topic of great interest.

"Gross!" you say. But you grab his toothbrush and, playing along, you pretend to brush his butt crack.

You get the idea. After a few minutes of laughter, mild wrestling, and additional outrageous ideas, you say, "Okay, kiddo, now let's do your teeth.

But wait! Let's wash your toothbrush off. You don't want elbow grease and butt yuck in your mouth!" And then you brush his teeth, or he does, and you head off to tuck him into bed. There are body-brushing parents in many countries now who have successfully turned their evening routines from screaming stand-offs into silly play. Their children's teeth are, for the most part, clean, and everyone goes to bed feeling close and connected.

If you set limits warmly, then follow with Staylistening or Playlistening, it will help your child connect with you and clear out feelings that prevent him from cooperating. He'll see you as a partner who can help with his struggles. It's true that these strategies require both time and warmth. But there's a sweet payoff. When you put your caring forward, make reasonable requests, and balance the limits you set with regular Special Time, you'll see a shift in your child. You'll notice that his sense of connection becomes sturdier. Fewer emotional moments will stem from issues around cooperation.

The following examples will show you how parents have used Listening Tools to win their children's cooperation. These aren't formulas to follow precisely. Rather, they are stories that will encourage you to find your own ways to connect and allow your child to offload tension. More cooperative and connective times await you.

Cooperation: Morning Routines

WHEN THE STRUGGLE IS OUR OWN

TOOL: LISTENING PARTNERSHIP

Once my son turned five, he was ready to go to school. As the school year progressed, he began a habit of calling out to me in the mornings, saying he couldn't dry himself when he got out of the shower. This became frustrating, as I needed to get everyone out by a certain time, and I knew that he was good at drying himself and getting dressed.

One day, in a Listening Partnership, I talked about my frustration and the feelings that were coming up for me each morning. I remembered that, at this same age, I also wanted my parents to come dry me after showering. I remembered wanting to feel their closeness, that they made it fun, and that my older brother had called me a big baby. I had the chance to cry about this, and realized that my son needed the connection with me. I am now able to approach mornings with a whole new understanding and patience.

HOW IT WORKED

This parent realized that her morning frustration harkened back to early hurts of her own. After releasing those old hurts to a loving listener, she discovered a newfound patience with her son, and their relationship grew stronger.

Continually doing for a child something he's able to do on his own can hold him back, but sometimes requests like this one are simple calls for connection—calls worth answering. If a limit needs to be set, it usually works better to lay a foundation of play and connection first, as our next story shows.

GETTING DRESSED

TOOLS:  PLAYLISTENING    SETTING LIMITS   STAYLISTENING

When my son was four, he went through a period of great resistance to getting dressed. Over a few weeks I tried all sorts of play to loosen the tension. I'd make his clothes talk to him and hide from him, try to put them on myself, pretend to not know how to help him get dressed, and more. Despite my efforts, getting dressed remained a daily struggle.

Finally, one day I told him it was time to put his clothes on. When he tried to run away I pulled him onto my lap and said again, "It's time to get dressed now." He started to cry and thrash. I kept him with me, holding his arms so he couldn't hit or scratch, and listened. When he started to let up I'd tell him that it was time to put his clothes on, and then listen while he cried some more.

After what felt like a very long time he stopped struggling, sat up in my lap, looked right at me and asked if I would still recognize him when he grows up. I reassured him that I'd always know him and always love him, even if he looked different. It was like a switch had been flipped. After offloading that fear, getting dressed was no longer an issue.

HOW IT WORKED

This parent was smart to try to help her son through his resistance by Playlistening. But sometimes Playlistening is simply "Step One." It builds closeness between you and your child, signals that you're not desperate to see a certain behavior, and relaxes him. It opens the doors to feelings but not enough to prompt the deep healing the child needs. In these cases, a child often needs "Step Two," a firm but loving limit. With that clear message of "No," he's able to process his upset and return to a cooperative state.

Rather than let her son run from her and from the feelings upsetting him, this mom set a limit by holding him in her lap. She had already determined that he was stuck in his helplessness. If she had let him go, the struggles over getting dressed likely would have continued. By holding him close and repeating the limit, "It's time to put your clothes on," she created a safe setting for him to show her his fears. What this parent discovered was a surprise. It was also their ticket out of a long-standing struggle.

GETTING OUT OF THE HOUSE

TOOL: STAYLISTENING

I noticed that my five-year-old son had a really difficult time getting up in the mornings and preparing for school. Granted, I don't actually like to hurry through my morning either.

I did my best to make the routine of getting out of the house fun. One morning, no matter how creative I got, he refused to leave his bed. When I finally got him out of bed he dragged his feet to the kitchen, but kept playing instead of moving toward the table to eat. I offered to hold his toy for him so he could eat, and as I reached for the toy my nail brushed his arm. "Ouch! Why did you do that?" He threw himself on the floor in anger, telling me that I had scratched him on purpose. "No, honey, that was an accident," I replied calmly. He got louder as he started to argue with me.

I immediately noticed that he was no longer rational, and figured that he just needed to be angry about the scratch, so I listened warmly, placing my hand on his back and offering him my gaze. "I'm sorry I scratched you, sweetie," I told him as he looked at me, crying. After a short time, he let me know that the reason he was so upset was that he really didn't want to go to school. He didn't feel listened to, and felt alone there. I just listened.

When he was done crying, he walked over to eat. Then he put his clothes on for school. We brushed our teeth. "Maybe it will be a good day," my son said. He put on his jacket and backpack, and we headed out to the car.

HOW IT WORKED

It is very common for a child to use an accidental bump or scratch as a pretext to cry or rage about something completely unrelated. This parent was brilliant to recognize what was going on! Instead of getting upset with him about his "disproportionate reaction" to her touch, she simply listened to it. The reward was an actual explanation of why mornings were so hard for him. After crying about his struggles at school, this boy was able to find his optimistic attitude, and head happily out to the car.

Cooperation: Mealtime

HANDWASHING

TOOLS: SETTING LIMITS    STAYLISTENING

My five-year-old son has had a rough time beginning kindergarten. He came from a small preschool, but now he is in public school with a lot of kids in his class and few teachers. He has come home in a strange mood every day. I work full time, so we get back together again around dinnertime.

On one particular day, he was in good spirits when I picked him up, but I sensed that something was amiss. I asked him how his day was, and his face dropped a little. "Fine," he said. We got home, and he followed me into the kitchen. "Wash your hands, Boo, we are gonna eat dinner in five minutes," I said playfully.

"I don't like washing my hands. I'm not gonna wash my hands!" he said and started playing. I stopped what I was doing, walked over to him, and looked him in the eye. "We are going to wash our hands now, Boo. We can't eat with dirty hands," I said, guiding his shoulders toward the sink. "No!" His voice was strong but shaky as he tried to squirm away. I went back and put my arm around him again, reminding him that we were washing his hands. When I got him to the sink, he began to complain about the soap. "I don't like to use soap when I wash my hands!" Considering that he has never protested about either of these two things, I began to wonder what was behind it.

"We are going to use a little soap, too," I said, wrapping my body warmly around the back of his, and helping him wash. He started crying, "I don't like soap! I don't like soap!" I turned him around, looked in his eyes, and listened. "Today wasn't a good day," he said as he continued to cry. "Would you like to tell me about it?" I asked warmly, still maintaining eye contact. He told me how many times he had been hit by other kids at school, and that they had made fun of him. I held him as he cried hard about his horrible day, and we sat until he came out of his cry and was able to change the subject without resistance. Afterwards, I noticed he felt lighter and in better spirits, and to my surprise, without me asking, he washed his hands and sat down for dinner.

HOW IT WORKED

Refusal to do something ordinary, like washing hands before a meal, is usually a sign that a child is struggling and needs connection. This parent brought a limit lovingly and then Staylistened to the feelings that arose in her son. When he said he'd had a difficult day at school, she encouraged him to tell her more. She guided him toward his hard feelings so that he could cry them out with her love beaming at him.

Had this parent simply entered into a power struggle about handwashing, her son would have missed the opportunity to heal from the hurts that had set in that day. Instead, his mood improved, he washed his hands, and he went to the dinner table without prompting.

A NEW FOOD BECOMES YUMMY

TOOLS:  SPECIAL TIME    PLAYLISTENING

While our son was away, my husband and I had the chance to give our three-year-old daughter some Special Time with both of us together. She really relished this. At first, she wrestled us and we fell dramatically. We played, "That's *my* child," where we stole her from each other. Then she had us line up and pretend to be reindeer pulling a sleigh. She was riding the daddy reindeer and bossing us around. She told us she was the baby reindeer and snuggled between us while we nuzzled and stroked her. We played with her for half an hour, really pouring on our love and letting her be in charge. She took up the space beautifully and received it all. She then got to go swimming one-on-one with her dad. When she came home I had made a supper she would usually have turned her nose up at. She ate a lot! She even said, "This is yummy quinoa," though quinoa is a food she has always refused. She was so cooperative and sweet that evening. She even picked up cards her brother had strewn all over the floor and went to bed without any fuss.

HOW IT WORKED

Sometimes, connection is all it takes to help a child out of a rigid behavior. Here, after lots of Special Time and Playlistening, a child who would normally balk at a plate of quinoa not only ate it, but did so with pleasure. To top it off, she was cooperative and easygoing all evening.

HELPING A PICKY EATER

TOOLS: 🚦 SETTING LIMITS 💗 STAYLISTENING

My son, four, had always been a picky eater. In the months leading up to his fourth birthday, he got pickier and pickier. Foods that he'd been open to, like eggs and salmon, were falling off the list. We were essentially down to plain starches.

I decided to try setting a limit with him at the next opportunity. I had been reluctant to push food on him, because I'd also been a picky eater as a child, and had hated being forced to eat certain foods. So I vowed not to force him but instead to set a limit and an expectation.

Two days later, I was given an opportunity. My son followed me into the kitchen as I began to prepare dinner, and he was restless. He began asking for a snack. I replied that it was time for dinner, and I wanted him to eat something healthy with protein, like beans or an egg. He was very upset by this and began to cry and protest. I repeated with optimism and confidence that I would prepare eggs and beans for dinner, and offered him both as a choice again. The crying continued. He was on the kitchen floor, rolling and repeating that he didn't want eggs. I listened.

After fifteen minutes of working through his frustrations, he quieted down, turned to the cookbooks on the nearby shelves and began to leaf through the pictures and ask questions about them. I reminded him that I was going to prepare the eggs, and he didn't seem concerned. When I put his plate on the table, he got up from the floor, sat down in his chair, and happily ate his dinner. In the last two weeks, he has been eating heartily at dinner. We're not to broccoli yet, though I am optimistic.

HOW IT WORKED

This mother used her experience being a picky eater as a child in concert with Hand in Hand tools to resolve a tricky situation. She didn't force her son to eat, something she recalled hating as a child. Instead, she continued to present her expectation that he eat something healthy. She Staylistened through his tears and tantrum. In just fifteen minutes, her son was sitting at the table, content to eat his healthy meal.

While fifteen minutes can feel like an eternity when your child is upset, it sure beats day after day of the same picky eater struggles. Those few minutes of Staylistening enabled this boy to continue enjoying his dinners for many days to follow.

BIG FEELINGS AT MEALTIME

TOOLS:  SETTING LIMITS STAYLISTENING

Our family went on an all-day trip this weekend, and we all had a great time. On the way home, my son took a short nap in the car, but woke up grumpy and irritable. When it was time to come to the table for dinner, he said he wasn't hungry and didn't want to eat. I told him we were all going to eat together and that it was time to sit down. He walked into the kitchen complaining about wanting to play more. "And I'm not hungry!" he whined.

When he saw what was for dinner he started to whimper and whine more and said he didn't want chicken and vegetables. "That looks yucky!" He cried. He went to the refrigerator and pulled out a loaf of bread. I told him we weren't going to eat bread for dinner. We were all going to eat chicken and vegetables. But he brought the bread to the table, crying, and tried to undo the tie on the plastic wrap. I put my hand gently on his hand and said, "Sorry sweetie, we are not having bread tonight." He cried more and threw the loaf of bread to the floor. He pushed away his chicken and vegetables and told me to leave him alone. I told him I didn't want to leave him alone with these feelings. His sister got up from the table and put the bread in the refrigerator and he cried more.

I decided to take him to the other room so that the rest of the family could eat. He sat on my lap and cried more. I was hungry and wanted to eat, so when his crying slowed down, I gave in a little and offered him avocado instead of the mixed vegetables that were on his plate. He agreed to eat avocado and came back to the table with me.

When we got back to the table he ate half of the avocado and then tried some of the chicken on his plate that he had pushed away. A few minutes later he had devoured all of the chicken, another half of avocado, and two servings of the mixed vegetables—I couldn't believe how much dinner he ate! He was chatty and sweet at the table and lovely the rest of the evening.

HOW IT WORKED

Those of you with picky eaters are familiar with requests—or demands—for "something else" to eat. Rigidity around food is like rigidity around anything else: it signals a need for help. We often need to set a limit for a child who ventures off to replace our food selections with his own—in this case, bread. The child needs to shed his upset with someone who won't either give in to his rigidities or try to convince him that he should be content eating what's on his plate.

Lovingly, this mom continued to bring the limit of no bread by gently placing her hand on her son's. And when her son's feelings were disruptive to the rest of the family's dinner, rather than send him away alone, she removed him from the dinner table but stayed with him. Just because a child needs to feel doesn't mean that his feelings should hamper the functioning of the family. It's okay to say things like, "I don't want to leave you alone feeling badly, but we need to let your sister and Dad eat their dinner. I'm going to take you into the other room." If you don't set limits in this way, resentment can build between siblings and parents alike.

When this mom then Staylistened to her son's upset, she also took her own wellbeing into account. When she felt like her son had released a lot of what was upsetting him, she chose to be a bit flexible in her food limit so that she, herself, could eat. We parents are of no help to our children when we're running on empty, so let's not forget to feed ourselves! In the end, her offer of an avocado instead of mixed vegetables worked out great all the way around. It allowed her to get to the table to eat her dinner. And it was appealing enough to her son that he went back to the table, too. The combination of the child's release of upset and the mother's flexibility led the child to eat everything on his plate.

Cooperation: Sharing, Waiting, And Fairness

WHAT YOU NEED TO KNOW

When children feel connected to a loving adult and good inside, sharing comes naturally. Even a toddler will share his new toy with a friend. When children aren't able to share, it's usually for one of two reasons: they haven't felt connected in the past few hours, or something reminded them of times in the past when they felt afraid or alone.

Only when a child is tense must he have the blue shovel *now*. If a second child who wants the shovel is feeling connected, he'll find something else to do for a while. So problems with sharing arise primarily when both children are feeling rocky because they have lost their sense of connection.

We parents often want to fix sharing problems quickly. But fixing it— saying whose turn it is, and timing the turns so they're equal, for instance— makes us enforcers rather than connectors. Our children's deeper need to feel close to someone still throbs, and they'll continue to need help, incident after incident. And when adults establish turns, the child with the hard-won item may spend his energy being defensive, and lose the joy of playing. Or he may gloat that he has it, alienating his companions.

A policy that, over time, helps children play well together is this: *I'll be with you while you wait.*

The child with the item gets to keep it until he's done, and the adults in the situation listen to the children who want it. A child having feelings gets support; a child with a toy gets to explore it to his heart's content. You meet your child's (or his friend's) core need to get rid of deep feelings. You connect. When the storm is over, he'll know, "My Dad loves me no matter what, " and, "I wanted the first turn, but now it's all right."

When parents or caregivers adopt this policy, sooner or later every child gets the chance to be supported while he sheds his feelings of need. Shana gets the doll stroller for a long turn today while the teacher listens to Anita, who wants it. Tomorrow, Anita gets the stroller while Jordan is supported through a tantrum because he wants it. Shana had a good cry two days ago, so when she sees that Anita has it, she moves on to make a nest under the table instead. Each child gets an arm around them while they cry, and hears the reassuring words, "Anita will be through with it sometime. I'll stay with you while you wait." No one has to defend their toy. And if a child gives his toy to the friend who's crying, it's his own generous spirit that moves him. No adult said he must.

With this policy, you don't have to spend your energy trying to make things the same for each child in the short run. A child who wants to ride the only tricycle in the yard may get a whole twenty minutes while your child cries hard about wanting it. But your child gets your full attention, a far more significant prize than the tricycle.

When a child clings to a toy or other desired item for days at a time, you can set a limit. Let the child know that tomorrow will be different: "Soledad, tomorrow when Maggie comes to play, she's going to get to ride the bike first, and I'll help you wait." When Maggie gets there, Soledad will make a beeline for the bike! So you get there first, saying, "Solie, today Maggie gets the first turn. Let's move back a step so she can climb on." Soledad then gets to have the cry and the personal attention that will help her play more flexibly.

Over the years, thousands of parents and many daycare center directors have implemented this policy with excellent results. Here are some examples of how parents like you have used Hand in Hand tools to resolve struggles with sharing, waiting, and fairness.

This first anecdote shows how one parent used the "I'll be with you while you wait" policy to get out of a sticky sharing situation.

SHARING DURING PLAY DATES

TOOLS:  SETTING LIMITS    STAYLISTENING

We had a play date at our house with two other mothers and their three children. Before they came, I had been madly tidying up the house, and after they arrived I was preparing drinks and snacks.

I soon realized that my three-year-old son was having difficulty letting the other children touch his toys. He probably felt disconnected because I'd been so busy getting things ready. Every time his friends picked something up he would run over and snatch it away, saying, "I want to play with that!" He was starting to hold onto quite a collection.

I decided to help him, and I didn't have to wait long. The next time he tried to take a toy from one of his friends I moved in quickly, placed a hand on the toy and said, "Your friend is playing with this. You can play with something else or I can wait with you until your friend is finished playing with it."

With that limit and the offer of connection, my son began to storm and release tension. I sat with him while he raged and then cried, listening to him and acknowledging his feelings. Every now and then I spoke gently, "Yes, you wanted to play with that toy," "You'll have fun again soon," "I love you." I wanted him to know that I was here to help him when things got hard, and that I would stay with him and be ready to reconnect once he had worked through the emotions that were blocking his good judgment.

After five minutes or so my son wiped his eyes, looked at me and said he was ready to play. He was relaxed and easygoing for the rest of the play date, allowing the other children to use his toys and joining in with their play.

HOW IT WORKED

This parent noticed that her child was struggling with sharing. She recognized that setting a limit on his snatching toys was going to be her ticket to a successful gathering. She needed to help him wait for his turn, and she didn't waste time hoping that her son would stop. She realized that he must be feeling disconnected, so she expected the behavior to continue. Confident in her strategy, she was able to lovingly bring a limit by placing her hand gently on the desired toy the next time her son went for it. She offered him her kind presence and helped him wait, listening to his tears and protests as they flowed. After only five minutes, her son felt ready to rejoin the others and play generously.

"IT'S MINE!"

TOOL: 🎠 PLAYLISTENING

My youngest daughter Kendra, nineteen months, has been struggling with the concepts of what is hers, what is her sister's, what is shareable, and what is "special." We have suggested that our three-and-a-half-year-old tell Kendra that an item feels special right now if she does not want to share.

Two weeks ago, Kendra started labeling everything "special" and keeping it for herself. She began shoving and shouting, "Mine!" while she pushed us away and told us to move while she tried to hold onto what was hers.

A few days ago, she had her favorite stuffed gorilla on her lap during nursing. She told me that her gorilla wanted milkies. I moved Gorilla toward my breast to give her a turn. Kendra immediately shoved Gorilla away and said, "Mine!" I moved Gorilla back to my breast and said, "Special." She shoved Gorilla. I made Gorilla reply, "Mine," and she burst into uncontrollable laughter.

She has spent every nursing session over the last two days asking for this game. Most of the time was spent in laughter. This morning, she passed through the laughter and actually bit the gorilla on the nose. She then said "Sorry" and tried to comfort the gorilla.

We are not at the end of her healing through laughter, but I am amazed that she knew to initiate the game and she knew what she needed to do to take it to the next level to find her own healing. I am going to play along for as long as it feels right to her and trust that she is healing some hurt feelings and gaining power through this play.

HOW IT WORKED

Many times, children know exactly what they need in order to get back to their generous selves. Here, this very young toddler concocted a game of "Mine!" with her stuffed gorilla in order to get the giggles going. After several sessions of this game, she acted out her frustration on the gorilla, but then wanted to make amends. She was using her intelligence to work through her feelings around sharing, and with continued Playlistening and, perhaps some Setting Limits and Staylistening down the road, she'll be back to her cooperative self soon.

"YOU LOVE HER MORE!"

TOOL:  STAYLISTENING

My older daughter had been complaining about me giving more attention to her sister. She was so upset, and felt I really loved her sister more. She would cite examples and tell me I gave her breakfast first, or I asked her first how her day was at school. I didn't see the bias but had no intention of arguing with her. In the past I would have said, "Yes, but I did such and such with you yesterday, and don't you remember X, Y, and Z that we did last week?" Instead, I listened and told her I understood what she was saying. I said I could see how she would think that, and I was sorry if I made her feel slighted, but mostly I listened and let her cry while I told her I loved her and I was there to listen to her while she was upset. She came around full circle. She felt validated, became calm and relaxed, and was able to play easily with her sister and me. It was great.

HOW IT WORKED

If you have more than one child, it's likely that both of them have accused you of favoring the other. For many of us, this can trigger a wave of feelings inside. "Am I favoring one child over the other? Does this child sense that I am more challenged by his behavior and feel that I love him less?" And we might recognize that we're being triggered by feelings from our own childhood when we felt a sibling was favored.

In this situation, the parent seemed clear that her daughter's feelings were unfounded. She recognized that her past behavior of trying to convince her daughter that she loved her just as much as her sister had fallen on deaf ears. With feelings raging, her daughter was in no state to reason. Mom recognized her daughter's need to cry, and Staylistened with her. Once the tears were shed, her daughter regained her perspective and felt her mother's love.

GIFTS AND FAIRNESS

TOOL: STAYLISTENING

Somehow, my oldest child didn't think Santa was fair this year. She felt her sister's presents were bigger and better, and hers were smaller and worse. I felt badly for her because she truly felt wronged. I wanted to point out why hers were just as good and in some cases better, and I also had the urge to make her "shut up" and stop complaining about her presents. But I didn't. I listened to her while she complained and whined and explained to me how she didn't like Santa anymore and how Santa was a bad guy. I tried to tell her that Santa and I both loved her. I didn't take this personally, which I would have done in years past. I empathized and listened intently. She was sad for a while, but once I let her offload the hurt and gave her a chance to be heard, she started to let it go. She actually loved her gifts, and said so at the end of her upset. It was nice to see her come all the way through.

HOW IT WORKED

How many hours do we parents spend trying to make sure everything is fair? We measure ice cream scoops so they're the exact same size. We count shirts and pants to ensure that everyone gets an equal share of back-to-school clothes. We time our children's electronics usage so that one doesn't get a minute more than another. And if one child gets invited to a movie with a friend, we quickly think up a treat to offer the others, so they won't feel badly.

But, as my kids will tell you, "Life's not fair!" If one child has holes in his shoes and another's shoes are in good shape, only one child is in need of a new pair. If a ten-year-old functions well on ten hours sleep, but her younger brother needs twelve to make it through the day, it makes sense for her to have a later bedtime. In fact, trying to make life fair for our children works against them. We're essentially denying them the opportunity to learn to overcome upset.

Instead, let's give our children the attention they need to overcome disappointments and feelings of being slighted. This mother didn't run out to buy bigger and better Christmas presents. Instead, she Staylistened to her daughter. By offering her love and connection to heal from hurt, this mother gave her daughter the best gift there is—the ability to acknowledge her upset, feel her way through it, heal, and get back to enjoying life.

TACKLING OUR OWN FEELINGS AROUND FAIRNESS

TOOLS:  LISTENING PARTNERSHIP  STAYLISTENING

My daughter had started using the phrase, "It's not fair!" quite a lot at home. Each time she said it I felt triggered. I found myself either ranting at her or clamming up and ignoring her complaints.

I was the middle child in my family, and I remember the "It's not fair!" feeling well. I knew that I needed some listening time on this so I could work through my own feelings. I knew that this would help me be able to think and act more clearly to help my daughter.

I set up a Listening Partnership and began by talking about how hard it is for me when I hear my daughter say, "It's not fair!" As I spoke, my Listening Partner asked me what I had needed to hear when I was a child. I began to cry as heaviness came over me, and I said, "I just want to be heard. I just want someone to say, 'Yeah, it can feel unfair sometimes. I'm sorry you are feeling bad.'" My Listening Partner then said these words to me with such compassion and warmth that my tears kept falling. I felt decades worth of feelings dissolve as I soaked in those words I had been longing to hear.

The next time my daughter expressed her feelings about things being so unfair, I was able to listen to her with warmth and compassion, and she responded so well to me. I was able to think and act more freely, as my own "stuff" was now out of the way. I love the clarity and ability to remain present that my Listening Partnerships allow me.

HOW IT WORKED

Sometimes we are so triggered by our child's claim of injustice that we find it difficult to think straight. We're not sure how to respond, and mostly we're just upset. This mom recognized the feeling her daughter was experiencing from her own childhood and realized that she had some work of her own to do. She brought up these childhood feelings in her Listening Partnership, and with her listening partner's encouragement, she was able to cry the tears that she couldn't shed as a child. Hence, she was less triggered the next time her daughter cried, "Unfair!" Instead of blaming or shaming or ignoring her, she remained calm, thought clearly, and Staylistened with her daughter to heal the hurt.

WHEN EVERYTHING'S UNFAIR

TOOL:  STAYLISTENING

My daughter was having a really complain-y day. She was stuck in a rut. I decided to go with it and when she was complaining about something being unfair I sat down near her and asked, "What else is unfair?"

Holy cow, did she unleash! She went on and on for several minutes with a very long list from not being able to drive to not being able to cook her own dinner, to just wanting to know stuff. I just kept asking, "What else?" and saying things like, "That sounds so frustrating," and "I'm sorry you can't do that yet." She ended with some heavy sobbing and snuggling and actually said, "Thanks, Mom," when she was done.

She really seemed significantly less burdened for some time afterwards. We have revisited this interaction numerous times since then. I ask her what's unfair when I notice she's feeling particularly oppressed or small. She is super effective at voicing those feelings in this format.

HOW IT WORKED

Sometimes, if we can put all resistance aside, we come up with fabulous ideas! Here, this mom avoided a standoff. She recognized that her daughter's feelings were big, and not tied to any one thing. Instead of attempting to justify each little incident, she moved toward her daughter and encouraged her to share more of her feelings. By asking, "What else is unfair?" she sent her daughter the message, "I believe that you really feel this way, and I want to hear all about it." The result was that the girl was able let loose a litany of everything that felt unfair, and then she cried and let go of the upset that was driving her complaining. She felt lighter afterwards, and has continued to work with her mother in this way when dissatisfaction returns.

STICKING UP FOR YOUR CHILD

TOOL:  STAYLISTENING

It was sports day at my children's new school. My daughter, eight, was in the first of her races and she had her heart set on "getting a place," meaning she wanted to come in first, second, or third. She ran the first race and came in at the same time as another girl, in her mind at least, but she wasn't awarded a ribbon. She came to me deeply upset and angry.

"The man cheated! He was probably the dad of the child he gave a ribbon to," she told me angrily. She said she wasn't going to run in any of the other races because they'd cheated her. I struggled momentarily with what to do. Should I go and talk to the father who had awarded the ribbons? Would I seem like a pushy parent? It occurred to me that the best thing I could do for my daughter in that moment was to Staylisten. I gave her a warm hug, kept my arms around her, and said I was sorry this was so hard for her right now. She got angrier and repeated that she wasn't going to run in any more races and that she had been cheated. I kept my loving attention with her and acknowledged how she was feeling. Her anger broke into tears, and she cried and cried with my warm attention. I was so glad I was able to do this, and that no one interrupted us.

After she had cried hard, a friend from her team ran up to her, saying, "You're up! This is your next race!" To my surprise and delight, with no hesitation, she ran excitedly to the starting line, and won the race by a long way! Then, she jumped herself to victory in the sack race. She seemed to find a huge reserve of energy and confidence, and went on to have an engaged and happy sports day, competing and getting ribbons in a number of other races.

HOW IT WORKED

Sometimes it is necessary to step in and advocate for our children, whose intelligence is not always appreciated and whose rights are not often recognized. But oftentimes, the most empowering thing we can do is support our children to resolve the situation themselves. Had this mom opted to approach the father who awarded the ribbons, perhaps asking for an additional ribbon for her daughter, the feelings of injustice would likely have erupted at another event that day. Instead, by Staylistening and allowing her daughter to rid herself of the hurt of having felt slighted, she guided her daughter toward renewed confidence and joy in competing.

Cooperation: Homework

WHAT YOU NEED TO KNOW

It can be hard for children to sit down and concentrate after a long day at school, and it's hard for parents who are exhausted as well. A small investment of time connecting with your child through play or listening can lift his spirits and aid the learning process. Here's how the tools have worked for parents just like you.

WHINY RESISTANCE

TOOLS: SETTING LIMITS   STAYLISTENING

It was time for my six-year-old son to do his homework. Every time I suggested it, I was met with avoidance, tears and whining. I moved in close and set a gentle limit. "You know it's time to do your homework now," I said putting my arm around his waist. "No!" he said, and ran off. I followed him and set the limit gently again. This time, he started to cry, and through his tears, he said that he didn't know the words and that he was stupid.

He started to push hard against me, got angry and yelled. "You are making me do this! I am stupid! I am stupid! This is your fault!" He cried and showed anger for about fifteen minutes, and then was content to write up his words and do his reading effortlessly. He was also very proud when he had finished, and showed us how well he'd done his writing.

HOW IT WORKED

It can be challenging to read between the lines of our children's behavior. A whiny child resisting homework looks like, well, a whiny child resisting homework. With practice, you will begin to recognize, as this mother did, that her son's resistance to doing homework was a sign that he needed her support. And when she offered a firm but loving limit that allowed her son to push hard physically and to cry, she also learned what was at the root of his upset: he doubted his abilities. When Mom Staylistened, this boy was able to share his self-doubt, anger, and frustration. This release of emotion fostered healing. By not interrupting it, his mother was able to help him regain his confidence and his ability to think. He did his homework and felt proud of his accomplishment.

SETTING THE STAGE FOR HOMEWORK SUCCESS

TOOL: PLAYLISTENING

One day, my eight-year-old son came home from school, and was teasing and bugging his brothers, a sign that the afternoon would be difficult if I didn't step in. I knew that he had homework, and that it was going to be a challenge to get through it. I suddenly recalled that I had developed a strategy for plowing through my homework when I was growing up. I had pushed through my fears rather than work through them. I didn't want that for my son. I figured that vigorous play might be a great way for the two of us to reconnect after so many hours apart. I don't always have the patience to give my son the connection he needs, but this day I did! I said, "Hey baby, do you want to have a pillow fight?" "Yes!" he blurted out, excitedly.

We got out our pillow fight kit, complete with ten pillows that we had decorated together, and went at it. The spoken rules were that there's no hitting above the waist, and you have to stop when the other person says "Stop." The unspoken rule was that my son always wins. He pounded me, and I threw back, often missing him. He was getting into it. "Ha! You missed me!" he'd say, and he'd throw a pillow back at me. I used just the amount of strength and accuracy it took to bring more laughter. Eventually, the game turned into him wanting me to try to hit his legs with the pillows, while he attempted to jump out of the way. This was a real confidence builder. The longer we did it, the more he laughed, and the less disappointed he was when I did hit his legs. Instead of jumping straight into, "That didn't hit me!" which wasn't, in fact, true, he started to say, "Oh, that got me," without any overtones of, "I feel like a failure." We did this for ten minutes or so, until I said I needed to stop and get some other stuff done. He asked for one more round of pillows, and I agreed. We then cleaned up the pillows, and went our separate ways. He went right to the table to do his homework, unprompted, which had actually never happened before!

HOW IT WORKED

This parent interpreted her son teasing and bugging his brothers to mean, "Hey, Mom, I'm not feeling good. I need help, and you're the one I trust to help me out of this." She realized that he wasn't feeling good enough about himself to do his homework after being away all day. And she also realized she wanted her son's homework experience to be different than hers had been as a child.

The rough play helped her son feel seen and connected to her. It also led to loads of laughter, which is a release of light fear. After this mom's small investment of time, her son sailed through his homework.

WHEN HOMEWORK FEELS TOO HARD

TOOLS:  STAYLISTENING    LISTENING PARTNERSHIP

My son just started third grade. He loves school, but is very competitive and focused on getting things done best and first. The other day, I asked him to grab a new chapter book off his shelf and to go read on my bed while I put his little brothers to sleep. He has read many chapter books before, so I expected he'd just grab a new book and go read.

No such luck! Instead, he started crying about how the books were all too hard. I listened for a bit, and then reminded him that he had already read most of them. He continued to whine and cry about not wanting to read them and about them being too difficult. Then he grabbed one and said, "I'm just going to read this easy one then!" He stomped out of the room and plopped himself down on my bed. As I followed him, I felt my body tensing up. I asked him why he chose something that was so easy for him, and he immediately began crying about how all the books are too hard, and how even when he reads them he doesn't understand anything he's reading. He kept repeating that he never understands what he's reading.

As a mother with my own issues around education, I saw red lights flashing. "What if this is true? What if all this time he's been reading to finish the book, and hasn't understood a word!" My feelings were so strong that it took a minute to calm myself down enough to help him through this difficulty. At first I said, "Wow! If you're really not understanding, I think I will email your teacher about it." He screamed at me at this point, terrified that I was going to contact his teacher, and I realized that what I said felt to him like a punishment. I then changed my wording and tone of voice. "If you're not understanding what you're reading, I'll tell your teacher, so that she can help you with your reading comprehension. It's okay. That's her job. That's what she's there for."

He continued to scream, while I continued to alter my tone and words, trying to make it clear that my suggestion was an act of love, not punishment. He still screamed at me, begging me not to tell her. I made a mental note to bring my feelings to a Listening Partnership. I understood now that he was just offloading his feelings of fear about who knows what. This went on for about ten minutes.

Then, suddenly, he was quiet for a bit and took a new book off the shelf. He said, "We're learning about schema in class. I'm looking at the book cover and the title and the chapter names and the pictures. That gives me an idea of what the story is about." I said, "Great! Do you think you can read for a bit while I go put your brothers to sleep?" "Yes," he said. So I went and read books to my younger sons and put them to sleep. When I came back a half hour later, he was a few chapters into the book, and didn't even look up at me. I said, "Why don't you finish that chapter and then get in bed?" He asked if he could continue reading in bed, and I agreed. This was maybe five days ago now, and since then he has brought up the book several times, offering me summaries of various things that happened in the story. He's been excited to share.

HOW IT WORKED

Often, when a child gets upset about homework being too hard, it's a secret code that means, "I don't feel confident in my abilities. I'm scared I'm not going to be able to succeed at this." At first, this mom was triggered by the situation, worried that his reading comprehension was slipping. But when she reacted from that place of concern, her son's reaction reminded her that even if there was a learning issue, this was not the time to address it. He just needed her to listen. She quickly modified her words and tone of voice, so that her son could better tell that she was on his side, rather than out to punish or shame him. And she Stay-listened, while making it clear there was help for him if he needed it. Once this boy was able to cry and share his worries, he regained his reading confidence, chose a new, more challenging book, and even enjoyed it!

A BIG SCHOOL PROJECT

TOOLS: STAYLISTENING · LISTENING PARTNERSHIP

My daughter, Jamila, was given a month to learn the fifty US states and their capitals. I knew she would need some help with this. I offered to help her learn groups of about six states and capitals at a time, so that she could spread the memorization out and not get too overwhelmed.

After she memorized the first six, she felt she couldn't possibly learn all the capitals. She became upset, and had a huge cry. I stayed with her and listened to everything. I told her I thought she could do it, but mostly, I listened. A few days later, she memorized the second set of six states and capitals, but again at the end of it, she felt that all fifty would be too much for her. I listened while she had another long cry, but it was hard to keep listening. She was saying, 'I'll never learn this. I just can't do it!' over and over. She also got mad at me for trying to help, and cried hard about my "interference."

After that evening, I wondered if I actually had gotten too involved in this assignment. It's hard to help my children when they get mad at me for it! I'm a single mom, so there's no backup for her, no backup for me. I had a regular Listening Partnership session coming up, so I took my worries there. After working on how hard this was for me, I figured I needed to stay confident for her, and needed to keep listening. I hoped the process would work.

In a few days, I told her it was time to memorize some more capitals. Jamila felt hopeless again about learning them all, and had a third big cry. She felt she could never do the assignment, and she was angry with me, with the assignment, and with the world. I kept listening, now and then telling her I thought she was smart enough to do it. Again, I took my worry and frustration to my Listening Partnership, and kept wondering how this was all going to turn out.

After that third cry, everything changed! She learned the next sets of capitals quickly and easily. One day, she took on a set of eighteen states and capitals, and did them all at once. Three days before the test, she asked me to quiz her on them, and she knew them all. She was ecstatic, and I think amazed that she had done something she was sure she could never do. She was so proud of herself!

The day before the test, she was completely confident that she would get 100 percent, and she was actually looking forward to it. Jamila had always been anxious about tests, so I'd never seen her like this before. After the test, she told me she was sad that it was over. She wished she could do it again! She has referred to learning the capitals again and again as one of the major learning feats of her life, and she has thanked me repeatedly for my help. She's a more confident student now.

HOW IT WORKED

When we take the time to help our children through small struggles, we're often surprised to find that we've actually made a huge impact on their lives. This mom recognized that her daughter would need help, and broke the task down into smaller chunks. But even then, her child felt unable to accomplish the task. Her mom Staylistened. When Mom got worried about whether she was too over-bearing, and felt concerned about her daughter's anger, she went to a Listening Partner. There, she shared her thoughts and feelings until she was able to think clearly again about how to proceed. This back and forth between a Listening Partnership and helping a child is a great way to resolve parenting struggles over time.

After several big cries, her confidence was restored and learning became easy, even fun. She was actually looking forward to sharing her knowledge on the test. While this seemed like a one-time issue as it was unfolding, accomplishing this feat had a meaningful impact on her overall confidence as a learner.

Cooperation: Chores

REFUSAL TO CLEAN UP

TOOLS: STAYLISTENING  PLAYLISTENING

The day I decided we had to clean up the playroom, I was dreading it. The day before, we'd attempted to clean up my girls' room, a much smaller task, and I had turned into a yucky, bossy mom. Now we needed to clean up the mess that had a playroom underneath it. I told my six-year-old twins that we were going to clean up the playroom, and I think the neighbors could hear their groans.

I told them that we would start with one kind of thing at a time, say books, crayons, or My Little Pony figures. I picked up books that belonged in their room and put them in a pile. Sally immediately refused to take them to her room. I asked her to pick up crayons. No! Ponies? No! Katie watched from the side, waiting to see what would happen. I stared at the pile, feeling powerless and helpless. I was getting frustrated again.

Then an idea occurred to me. I picked up the pile of books and threw them on the floor. "Oops! I just made a mess," I said. Sally just watched me. So like any good kid, I lay on the floor, kicked my legs and flailed my arms and had a full-blown mock tantrum. "I don't wanna clean up! I don't wanna clean up!" And with that, the Playlistening began. Then, as I lay "helpless" on the floor, the kids put their ice-cold hands on my warm belly. First Sally, who started to laugh. Refusing to be left out, Katie added her icy mitts. Oh, the laughter as I whined and complained about how cold their hands were! I begged and pleaded for them to stop.

They didn't. Instead they got ice cubes and started chasing me around the house laughing hysterically. I screamed and whooped, trying to stay far enough ahead of them to make it a challenge, but remembering to trip and fall after a few rounds. The next thing I knew, I had ice in my shirt. I hollered, rolled around and did the ants in-my-pants dance. They laughed and laughed. I fought back just a bit, so each of them got the feel of ice on their skin, but they had the last laugh. I think we whooped it up for twenty minutes, a record Playlistening session for me.

After a little Staylistening with Sally, we returned to the playroom. Katie and I began to clean up, working collaboratively to pick up toys and sort through her bins. Sally joined us a little later, and cheerfully picked up toys. The three of us spent over three hours cleaning up, sorting bins and throwing out trash. And it was done in good spirits. I felt like a million bucks! Not only did my kids offload all the yuckiness they felt about cleaning up, but so did I. All the screaming, running, laughing, and ice play worked at least as well for me as it did for the kids. That was a thousand-watt realization. Playlistening: it's as good for you as it is for your kids!

HOW IT WORKED

What parent hasn't felt like he was going to explode with frustration from failed attempts to get a child to clean up? This mom was able to use Playlistening to loosen up both her own dread and her daughters' refusal to help clean up.

Without mocking her girls, she got their attention by pretending to have a meltdown about not wanting to clean up. At first the girls were hesitant, but then they made the game their own by shocking Mom with their cold hands and then upping the ante by stuffing ice cubes down Mom's shirt. Mom followed their cues, continuing to allow them to lead the play, but always moving toward whatever made them laugh. Her goal moved from getting the room picked up immediately to letting them get out their upset and build connection. In the end, everyone felt much more connected. They all cooperated in cleaning the play-room and enjoyed one another for the rest of the day.

CONNECTION DEFUSES A HATED CHORE

TOOL: PLAYLISTENING

My daughter is nine. She dislikes doing chores. One chore she absolutely will not do is clean up our dog's poop in the back yard, because she's extra sensitive to smells. I don't ask her to do this job as it's a lost cause.

One Saturday, my usual poop-scooping day, she was really energetic, and I was feeling good, so I engaged her in a good wrestle. I outweigh her by a lot, but she's strong and fast, so we had a long, sweaty, full-of-laughter tussle on the carpet in the living room. She was having a great time lording it over me, pinning me down, and managing to "get" me again and again, no matter how many smart moves and escapes I came up with. We really had fun. I think it was one of the longer wrestling playtimes we've had. When I finally was too tired to play more, we got up and dusted ourselves off. I told her I was going to go out in the back yard and scoop poop, and she said, "OK, Mom. I'll help you." I thought I would fall over! She went right to work and we had the job done in just a few minutes, while chatting happily together. Connection makes such a difference!

HOW IT WORKED

It's such a treat when cooperation comes unexpectedly. Here, this mom was simply feeling good and seized an opportunity to roughhouse. She put up a good fight, but was always sure to let her daughter "win." As your children grow, you'll find you need to adjust the amount of resistance you offer in your Playlistening with them. This mom made sure not to overpower her daughter with her strength, nor to play so weakly that her daughter felt like Mom was letting her win. It's a balancing act that you will get better at the more you practice.

———◆———

SHIFTING CLEANUP RESPONSIBILITY TO YOUR CHILD

TOOLS: SETTING LIMITS   STAYLISTENING

Cleanup is not the most popular time in our house. I haven't wanted to be harsh with my daughter, so have often just done it myself. My husband and I recently decided to make a change.

After a fun playtime, we asked our daughter to help with the cleanup. She proclaimed herself to be too tired to clean up. We sat down next to her and said that we knew she felt tired, but that she could still clean up some of her toys. She started to cry. We offered to help and stay close, but insisted that she could do it. She refused and her cries got louder. She started to storm, insisting that she couldn't do it. We stayed close as she protested loudly, crying, sweating, and storming about in our arms. We provided resistance so that she could struggle more fully. We listened and continued to hold the limit around cleanup for about twenty minutes. That can feel like an eternity when you are up close and listening to your five-year-old show deep feelings. Your child is clearly counting on you to stay and listen, while you are getting tired and are ready to call someone to listen to you! We hung in there.

Then, the storm was over. She started to actually clean things up. We did it cooperatively. We all put toys away, relaxed, and connected so that it felt like a good time together. What a discovery! My husband and I looked at each other, pleased that we had taken on this project that had seemed daunting because of our own feelings! Then, the three of us moved toward bedtime, relaxed, and giggled our way under the covers.

HOW IT WORKED

Understandably, many of us give up on gaining our children's cooperation. Like these parents, we don't want to be harsh with our children, but we don't know what else to do. Or, we may act harshly over a period of time, but it doesn't

work, so we give up. Sometimes we just don't have the time to devote to the issue. It's faster to just do the job oneself. For many of us, listening to our child's upset about having to do chores is upsetting.

These parents got to a point where they were ready to change both their behavior and their daughter's. They set a loving limit that she would and could help them clean up, and then Staylistened to her as she emptied her emotional backpack. As hard as it was, they didn't interrupt her crying or try to stop it. The reward was a cooperative girl, willing and able to join in the cleanup. And a relaxed evening to boot!

Cooperation: Screens And Devices

IT'S TIME TO TURN IT OFF

TOOLS: SETTING LIMITS   STAYLISTENING

At times during our three-year-old's early childhood, she insisted upon watching the videos I'd recorded of her on my cell phone. One evening at dinnertime, she didn't want to put the phone down. Though it wasn't exactly off-track behavior, it was clearly compulsive, and we decided to set a limit and insist she stop the videos. She had a hard, but fairly brief cry, and I listened. Then she jumped around the living room shouting, "I'm so happy because I'm jumping!" Perhaps it came out backward, but we got the point, "I'm jumping because I'm so happy!" It was obvious that it felt so good to get free of the feelings that fueled the compulsive behavior; she was bursting with wellbeing! It was good reinforcement for us to see the benefits of a gentle but clear limit coupled with warm listening.

HOW IT WORKED

Screens are addictive. At times, we may decide that it's fine for our children to watch a little longer—or a lot longer. But other times it makes sense to set a limit. There is no formula. Each family gets to create rules that work for them.

In this case, these parents felt their daughter needed help to put down the phone she was watching. They set their limit, unleashing tears. Then they Stay-listened until her upset had passed. They didn't negotiate, which probably would just have postponed the upset. They didn't promise her the phone after dinner. They simply accepted her upset and helped her move through it by offering connection. When her tears had passed, their daughter was feeling much better!

————◇————

FINDING A ROLE FOR ELECTRONICS

TOOL: SPECIAL TIME

I, like so many other parents, have a difficult time with electronics. In our house we watch very little TV, and we limit the use of iPads and iPods to special occasions and trips.

This, however, does not keep my school-age girls from asking to use their devices either on their own or during Special Time. When I first began using Hand in Hand Parenting, I was dead set against allowing the girls to use this sacred time to "dumbly" sit in front of a computer or their iPad. As the begging continued, I decided to occasionally allow use of their electronics. When I told them they could use iPads for Special Time it was like they'd won the lottery!

I sat with each of them and studied their games, pouring all of my undivided attention into these silly devices. I found that it wasn't so bad! They loved their games of painting nails and washing dogs. It was cute how engaged they were, and how naturally intuitive they are with their electronics. I became more at ease with allowing them to have some additional screen time.

My girls were thrilled, and I seemed to have gained all kinds of "cool mom" points. It was definitely a win. They continued to ask for Electronic Special Time, as they like to call it, and I indulge them occasionally. But what I did next made the biggest difference in relieving some tension around Special Time and the use of screens.

Special Time isn't always easy to do with two kids and one adult in the house. So sometimes I allow one girl to use her iPad while I play with the other for twenty minutes, and then we switch. Everyone gets time with Mommy and time on their beloved device. They love it, and it allows me to be actively engaged with one daughter while the other one is occupied.

These strategies have helped me feel lighter and less worried about electronic use, and I've garnered a little street cred with the kids!

HOW IT WORKED

Because we parents haven't yet figured out how to incorporate electronics into our own lives in a balanced way, and because they are addictive, we're often full of concern about our children's use of them. Getting annoyed with our children and their technology obsessions only makes the situation worse. When you can find a way to partake in your child's technology interests, you can actually loosen up your child's desperation to use the device. It adds your warmth and admiration to what's usually a solitary pursuit. Special Time with technology allowed also gives us a few safe (and short!) moments when we can let go of our worries and find some joy in our children's plugged-in worlds.

This mom recognized that her rigidity around not using electronics during Special Time was creating distance between her and her girls, so she let them know that some electronic Special Time was OK. It offered her a path into their hearts and minds, and released some of the tension in their home around electronic use. She maintained flexible limits, allowing electronics sometimes, but not always, and learned to use the devices to get uninterrupted Special Time with one child or the other.

WHEN ELECTRONICS BECOME AN ESCAPE

TOOLS:  LISTENING PARTNERSHIP  SETTING LIMITS  STAYLISTENING

I came home from work on Wednesday, and my six-year-old daughter seemed to be in a brittle mood. It was her first day back in school after being home sick for two days. She started to ask for Cheerios, which she knew I would refuse to give her before dinner. Then quickly, she started to ask for her Grandma's iPad, which she only got to play with during my parents' visits. Seeing that my daughter was tense, and having had my listening time earlier that day, I had the clear head to set a limit.

I said firmly and gently, "No, sweetie, I see that you are upset right now, so we're going to wait on the iPad for now." Sure enough, the limit was all that she needed to let me know how she was really feeling. She told me that it wasn't fair that she couldn't play with the iPad, that her brother had had a turn, and that she wanted it now! She cried big tears, screamed at me, and pushed up against me with all her might. I was feeling well resourced that evening: my Mom had kindly made dinner so that I didn't have to choose between listening and cooking, I'd had my listening time, and I had the patience and compassion to see that my daughter needed my support and openness, even though she was directing her upset at me.

After fifteen or twenty minutes of working through her feelings, my daughter settled down and was ready to go in for dinner. Grandma's iPad was forgotten for the rest of the evening, and the following day when she asked for it again, it was a lighthearted, take it or leave it request.

HOW IT WORKED

Electronics, like all things children love, sometimes become a pretext for working through their upsets. After Mom refused to let her bury her upset in a bowl of Cheerios, she tried for the iPad. Fortunately, this mother benefited from a Listening Partnership earlier that day—she was feeling good and thinking clearly. She recognized her daughter's desperation as a call for help, and moved in quickly with a loving limit. One soft "No" was all this girl needed to release pent up feelings through tears, strong words, and physical might. Then, feeling reconnected to her mom, the iPad (and the Cheerios) returned to the status of "things I like, but know I can't have right now." The charge was gone, even the next day.

TEENS AND ELECTRONICS

TOOLS:  SETTING LIMITS  STAYLISTENING

One night my fourteen-year-old daughter had a headache. She had been using her laptop and her cellphone a lot during the day. She also hadn't been sleeping well, and I don't think she'd been eating well either. My husband and I decided to set a limit on how much she could use the computer and cellphone at night. We decided to remove them at nine o'clock, to help her get a good night's sleep.

The first night my husband told her that the laptop and the cellphone needed to be out of her room by nine. She asked, "Why?" and then said, "I need them for my homework." My husband answered with a soft tone of voice, "You can finish your homework before nine o'clock." Our daughter got angry and ran up the stairs and into her room. I went up to her room and said to her, "I'm sorry that sometimes you can't get what you want, but I think this is for your own good." She responded to me with, "No, this is not fair. I have good grades in all my classes. Now I'm not going to have good grades anymore because I won't be able to do my homework, and it's going to be your fault. And I'm not going to have any more friends because you're taking away my cellphone. Get out of my room!"

I told her I would leave once she gave me the cellphone and laptop. She didn't want to give them to me. I told her she would get them back in the morning. I took the laptop, but she still didn't want to hand over her cellphone. "I'm still waiting for the cellphone," I said to her in a low and calm voice. She yelled at me and repeated, "I'm not giving it to you. I don't know why you are doing this. I have good grades and now I'm not going to get good grades because I won't be able to do my homework. And it's going to be your fault." I think she was trying to make me feel guilty, but I still felt good about trying to help her get a good night's sleep.

Finally she threw the cellphone on the bed and pulled the blankets over her face. I removed the blanket from her face very slowly and told her I loved her. I stayed with her for some minutes, and then she said, "Mom, can you go to your room?" She sounded mad and wanted to read a book. I asked if I could stay for five more minutes and she said OK. I stayed with her, looking at her, touching her feet gently while she was reading. After five minutes, I kissed her and said, "Goodnight, I love you." She said, "I love you, too."

I want to be consistent with this limit because I can see how my daughter is getting better. She says she's not getting headaches, and she's also sleeping better. Now it's not a struggle to have her hand over her electronics to us when we ask. I also feel that now we are more connected and are having more fun together.

HOW IT WORKED

One of the keys to Setting Limits successfully is being clear with ourselves that the limit we're setting makes sense. If we're not sure, it can get confusing when our teenager starts giving us justifications for why she needs her phone. These parents noticed several negative repercussions of their daughter spending too much late-night time on electronics, and made a firm decision. They worked together, keeping their tone of voice warm, and stood by their limit. They didn't negotiate with their daughter or try to control how she felt about their limit. They also continued to show their love throughout her upset. They simply repeated their limit and Staylistened. The result was that their daughter began to feel better, realized the bad effects her habit had inflicted, and began to voluntarily hand over her electronics at nine o'clock.

10
Toward Sweeter Separations

WHAT YOU NEED TO KNOW

I have yet to meet a parent who doesn't struggle with supporting their child through separation issues. Do any of these scenarios ring a bell?

- You have got a nine o'clock meeting at work. It's eight-thirty at preschool drop off, but instead of a pleasant wave goodbye, your three-year-old clings to your leg and screams like you've thrown him to the lions.

- It's been an exhausting day at work, followed by sports practices and dinner preperation, and your eldest needs homework help. You take your four-year-old to bed for a quick read and a kiss. You emerge over an hour later, too tired to help your older one.

- Finally, you've found a babysitter your kids really like, so you and your partner are headed out to dinner and a movie. The sitter arrives and everyone's happy. But when you kiss your two-year-old goodbye, big tears begin to flow and he begs to come along.

Separation is a core challenge for almost every child at some time. We parents do the best we can to make it through these painful partings. We bribe our kids with promises of special treats. We lie down with them while they take hours to fall asleep, and then slide out of the bed, exhausted. We cancel date nights at the expense of our relationships because we can't bear to see our little one's heart break. Yet these strategies don't help our children overcome their fears. The next bedtime, goodbye, or date night sparks the same old struggle.

Separation anxiety is understandable because our young children are wholly dependent upon us. We are their safe haven. Their lack of experience means that even though we're close by, simply walking into the bathroom and shutting the door can trigger feelings of fear. We know we'll return shortly, but early in their lives, they can't make that leap two minutes into the future.

Many parents try to shield their children from separation hurt, but it's as common as a skinned knee. Mommies and daddies talk on the phone. They run errands. They have to go off to work. Sometimes parents can't be present due to illness or the effects of stress. The entry into daycare or preschool can be a jolt. Many children must adjust to divorce, changing schools, or moving to a new community. Others face the death of a loved one. Despite our best efforts, every child's sense of safety is rattled, sooner or later, by the hurt of separation.

Complications occur when a child doesn't have the support he needs to grieve until the hurt from separation is healed. Any leftover fears he carries are stored away, and they cause trouble down the line. Even an insignificant separation, like putting your child down for a nap, can bring up outsized emotion from the past. For instance, a few weeks after his grandfather dies, you might be shocked to find that your son has escaped his babysitter and is chasing your car down the street, afraid you'll die while you're at the grocery store.

When your child is deeply frightened by separation, it may be that a very early hurt is at the root of things. Take the birth experience, for example. Your child came to you ready to be welcomed, cradled, and protected by his loved ones at birth. Anything short of that can be a shocking experience. When a newborn goes through a difficult birth, his system responds with alarm. And if he must be whisked away from his mother for any reason, his nervous system is fully aware that he's in big trouble, far from all he has known. Even one unwanted separation, large or small, can leave behind feelings that set your child up to be fearful months or years later when you leave. But rest assured that, however intense your child's separation fears might be, you can help him recover.

Over the years, a child will keep encountering new situations that trigger those earlier unhealed feelings. He might have a string of intense outbursts the week before he starts first grade, and again three years later when he's scheduled to take a trip to see his grandparents. Deep feelings recur, but when you use Listening Tools your child can make progress with each round of upset. Separation upsets are opportunities in disguise! As you Staylisten, painful feelings will pour out and your confidence will flow in. Your child's load of fear will lighten, and he'll enjoy his increased confidence. So will you.

TACKLING SEPARATION FEARS USING LISTENING TOOLS

The first step in moving toward confident separations is to plan for emotional ones. You're ready to be an agent of change when you've anticipated the upset that is surely coming.

Second, understand that your child's upsets reflect underlying fear, not a deliberate desire to ruin your plans. Think about where your child's fears might come from. If your son clings tightly to you at bedtime, consider what earlier separations he might be recalling. Has the daughter who won't participate in that gymnastics class she wanted so badly had difficulties in groups of children before? You may be able to identify a few of the hard times that could be contributing to your child's separation fears. But don't worry if you can't think of anything. He can shed his fears without either of you knowing their origin.

The third step in helping your child through separation struggles is to address your own fears and worries. As your child shows you how threatened he feels, your own feelings can be triggered so that you become unsure of his safety, too! Your worries will be transmitted to him without a word.

Things will go better when you get the support you need to release these feelings. Remember how you felt leaving your crying child to get to work on time? Or how it felt moving your child from a crib to a "big kid" bed? Do you remember longing for your own mom? Your dad? Listening Partnerships work well for identifying and venting feelings from memories like these.

In the throes of a difficult separation, Setting Limits and Staylistening are your go-to tools. You'll want to let your child know ahead of time that a separation is coming up. He needs to know where you are going, when you are coming back, and who will stay with him. If he begins crying at this news, Staylisten. He's using the healing process already.

When your child's fears run deep, start saying goodbye to him a whole hour before you must part. This allows you to be your child's anchor through his feelings of grief. Simply propose to leave, then Staylisten. When his tears subside, say again, "Sweetheart, I'm going to go. I'll come back. I'll always come back." He will re-intensify his shedding of grief and fear with you right there. At some point, after he's done the crying he needs to do, he will be able to say goodbye, and enjoy his time with the safe adult you've chosen to be with him.

You are using Setting Limits and Staylistening, but drawing out the process, so that when you set the limit, there's no action on your part except Staylistening. This gives his system plenty of time to unload its burdens. He can focus on his feelings, rather than trying to comprehend a rapidly changing situation. The key healing factor is your confidence that he's OK as he cries. You'll need to keep remembering that he is not a heartbroken waif. He is a strong, fortunate child who is releasing stored feelings in the safest possible setting—with you by his side!

Here's what one mom was able to accomplish after getting some good Listening Time for herself:

———◇———

My son is five years old. One of his biggest emotional projects is separation anxiety. I recently signed him up for a martial arts class after school on Mondays. This has turned out to be a prime time for working on separation. The first several classes did not go well. He participated some, but spent most of the time flopped over in my lap. I spent most of the time worrying about what others were thinking about us. I realized that I had to get some extra listening time, so I did. And it helped.

The next Monday at class, I told him that while he was in the opening circle, I needed to leave the room for three minutes to go across the hall to ask a question in the office. We'd spent some nice time connecting after school, but my words elicited tears. "No, Mama. I don't want you to go. Let me come with you," he begged, clinging to me. After he calmed down, I mentioned again that I needed to go to the office, that he was safe, and that I would be right back. Again, he cried. Occasionally, I nudged him off my lap, so that he could feel the separation a little more. Each time he calmed down, I again set the limit that I had to go, that he couldn't come with me, and that he had to stay in the room. We did this for most of the hour. Halfway through, I was wondering if this was doing any good. But since I was still feeling OK, I decided that we could keep going.

The first major change I noticed was at bedtime. He mentioned that he was hungry, and that he wanted one raisin. Anytime he says this, I've figured out that he's missing me, and the closeness we used to have while breastfeeding at bedtime. I said, "You had a good dinner, and you can wait until morning to eat." He completely surprised me when he said, "OK. I'll have some water and it can fill the spot until breakfast." Wow! The surprises continued the next morning at school drop-off. I mentioned that I couldn't stay for second breakfast with the class. For the first time ever, he said, "Yay!" And when I said goodbye to him at the classroom, he forgot to give me a hug. I had to remind him! Usually the magic hug is a really big deal, but today he was confident and ready.

Setting limits at martial arts class, and the Staylistening that followed, made a big difference for him. I'm grateful that I've gotten myself the support I need to be able to support him. I'm even looking forward to next week's martial arts class, even if he doesn't participate.

———◇———

Here's the story of a mom who took a broad perspective on her son's separation issues, chose to set a limit and Staylisten, and watched big new doors open for him.

———◇———

When my son was in sixth grade, he was still too frightened to go on sleepovers. I didn't want to push him to do something he wasn't ready for, but all his friends were sleeping at each other's houses, and I sensed that my son really wanted to as well. I felt that his fears were holding him back. After sharing my feelings about this issue several times with a Listening Partner, I decided that I was ready to help my son.

I had gone to overnight camp myself when I was young, and I wanted my son to begin going to the same camp. I knew he'd love it, and I'd heard that one of his close friends was also going. I knew that if I set a limit here, I'd need to Staylisten, and this would move him into a more rational and relaxed space.

One day, the two of us were home alone and I said to my son, "I've decided I'd like you to go to sleepaway camp this summer. The session that fits with our schedule is full, but I put you on the waitlist." I knew that he would be upset by this proposition, but I didn't realize just how scared he would be! He began trembling. He begged me not to send him. He told me that he couldn't be away from me for that long—that he would die! At first I was taken aback by the rush of emotion and the intensity of my son's words. But I quickly realized that this limit was important.

His upset and trembling continued for a good hour. I listened. Then he calmed down and asked, "Do you think I'll like it?" He was still hesitant, but he had shed enough fear that he could see the possibility that my decision to send him to camp was a good one. We talked for a while, and then moved on to other things.

The next day I heard my son say to his brother, "I'm going to sleepaway camp this summer! Well, if there's space. I'm on the waitlist." He was proud. And then he turned to me and asked if he could spend the night at a friend's house that same night. While I remained calm, inside I was bursting with excitement at my son's newfound freedom. "Absolutely! Why don't you give him a call and see if tonight works." Since that day, my son has been sleeping at friends' houses regularly. And that summer he had the time of his life at camp. His first words off the bus when he got home? "Can I go to Session Three next summer? It's longer!"

———◇———

Setting Limits and Staylistening will work wonders to help a confident child with a sudden bout of fear. But if your child expresses upset every time you drop him off for a play date, or every night as you settle him down to sleep, you'll want to balance the deeper work he needs to do with play and the opportunity for your child to take charge. Playlistening and Special Time need to be part of your toolbox to address his emotional project.

A simple game of peek-a-boo that gets your little one laughing is a wonderful way to help your young child offload light fears about separation. You hide your face for only a short moment, but your child senses the disconnection and is relieved when you "suddenly" reappear with a smile. He laughs. He heals. His trust in you builds, as does his belief that you will return.

As your child grows, peek-a-boo will no longer bring the laughter, and you will need to up the ante. Hide and seek might be a good next step. Or, try a good chase in which he gets to be more coordinated and powerful than you. You almost catch him—but then he's able to tug his shirttail away from your grasp. With each game there is laughter. The more laughter, the more quickly the layers of fear will fall away.

These parents showered their son with affection in a game of "I want him!" to ease his separation fears:

———◇———

My son had been going through a l-o-n-g mommy-focused time. We had mostly bent to his wishes, as he would otherwise scream and cry. With my new knowledge of the Hand in Hand tools, we started setting some limits around his preferences when he was around two years old. I had a helpful Listening Partnership and was feeling more tolerant of his strong feelings. Also, we'd done some Staylistening with the warm but firm limit of, "It's time for you to be with your dad now." All of these approaches had yielded some success.

But one particular night, after deciding that it was Dad's turn to offer books, snuggles, and tuck-ins, we tried a different approach. When I gave my son a hug and tried to pass him to Dad in the rocking chair, he clung to me and started to fuss. I dramatically pulled him back from my husband's arms and said loudly,

"No, no, you *can't* have my baby! He's mine, *mine*!!"

My husband retorted with, "Please let me have him! I want him so!"

I swung my son in my arms as he giggled and I counted, "One, two, three—as if to toss him to his dad. Then I said, "Oh—no, no, no, you can't have him!"

We went back and forth, play-arguing over who would have him. I would almost drop him in his father's lap, but then run back across the room with him in my arms, saying, "No, no, no!"

After about ten minutes of play and prolific giggles, I finally plopped him in his dad's lap, and he snuggled right in and waved goodbye to me. I left, Dad completed the bedtime routine, and our son slept soundly through the night (not an everyday occurrence).

———◇———

Regular Special Time with a frightened child, even if you've only got five minutes at a time, will help greatly with separation challenges, as it builds the connection between you and your child. It offers him the opportunity to be in control of his world, a stark contrast to how he feels when you need to leave him. He might lead you in games that help you connect the dots and discover the origins of his fears. Pouring in your love and attention while following his lead will boost his confidence. And when the timer signals the end of Special Time, your child may be overcome by feelings and cry or scream, giving you another chance to help him heal his hurt at its core.

The following sections delve into the most common separation issues faced by parents. Even if you don't find your particular struggle addressed, these nitty-gritty parent stories will spark your imagination and suggest varied ways to heal the hurt of past separations, setting your family up for more peaceful, confident separations moving forward.

———————————— ◆◆◆ ————————————

Separations: Goodbyes

ENDING A PLAY DATE

TOOL: PLAYLISTENING

When my six-year-old daughter had play dates in preschool, as well as this past year in kindergarten, there was often a lot of angst at the end when the kids had to separate. There were bad scenes—tantrums, crying, the kids trying to run away and hide. One parent even bribed the kids with candy, only to have them run away again right after getting it!

So I was struck by the brilliant Hand in Hand idea to end a play date with connection. Recently, when we had another girl over at our house and the play date was ending, I went into the closet where the two girls were playing with a toy fairy castle and warmly observed, interacting with them for a few minutes. I told them it would be time to go soon and asked if there was one more fun thing they would like to do before the play date was over.

My daughter's friend suggested an obstacle course, and I responded enthusiastically. So we created an obstacle course together. It involved
jumping over stuffed animals, pillows, and through Hula-hoops, which I
purposely arranged to lead from my daughter's room, out our front door,
and right up to the fence of our front yard. I put our guests' shoes at the end
of the obstacle course so that putting them on would be the final hurdle,
and enlisted my husband to time the proceedings with a stopwatch while I
narrated the proceedings like a sports announcer.

We all laughed a lot as the kids made their way through the course.
It went great! Sure beats the standard five-minute warning, chorus of
"Nooooo," and all that resistance.

HOW IT WORKED

*There are neurological reasons why connection helps children cooperate, but
when you're used to constant struggles, the results of connecting with your children can feel like magic!*

*This mom enlisted the girls' thinking to come up with a playful idea for
ending their time together. They hatched a creative plan, and the parents worked
with the girls to make it happen. Fun and laughter ensued, with the visit ending
on a happy note.*

*This might sound like a huge outlay of energy to you, but once you get the
hang of Playlistening, the benefits are richly rewarding. Who wouldn't rather play
a game than have an argument?*

———◇———

PARTING AFTER A VISIT

TOOLS: 🚦 SETTING LIMITS   💞 STAYLISTENING

Our week had been really busy, with visiting family that included my
two-year-old nephew. My two children had played really well with their cousin. However, there always comes a point during family visits or holidays
when my son's feelings overwhelm him. Even excitement, often viewed as
a positive emotion, can be hard for him to handle.

So on the last morning of the family visit, my son was predictably upset about saying goodbye, and went off track, not playing well with the others anymore, and doing little forbidden things. I've learned that this signal means he needs connection. But I was also busy getting things together so my extended family could go to town and catch their train to the airport. I needed to move a car seat to another vehicle and casually mentioned that I was off to do this. My son followed me, really agitated that I was going to take his seat out of the car and put it in his grandma's car for his little cousin.

I tried to explain they weren't keeping it, and that it was coming back soon, but he felt so disconnected that he couldn't think and listen to my reasoning. I decided it would be best to listen to this upset, and see where it would lead. Perhaps I could help him release tension.

I calmly explained that I would be taking the seat out of the car. He immediately jumped up and sat in it, yelling and telling me "No! You can't do that!" I kept letting him know that yes, I was going to take it out, but I didn't actually make any move to do so. All the while I kept my voice warm and kind. He started pushing really hard against the edge of the seat, yelling and crying for me not to move it, even though I wasn't doing so. I thought to myself that this was a positive step for him, and I was happy to help him. Also, we were not near the others, so I knew we wouldn't be distracted at all.

As his sobs eased off, I made a move to unclip the seat, and he started yelling and pushing me away, and pushing the car seat down to keep it in place. I listened in this way for about five minutes, offering connection and love until he stopped crying and looked up at me, asking if I still needed the seat. I told him that his cousin needed it, and asked if I could take it now, please. He agreed and hopped out of the car while I unclipped it. He watched me put it in the other car, now quite happy with what was going on!

At this point my son was visibly more relaxed, and ran over to his grandmother and told her that we had put the seat in her car for his cousin! Then, he went and joined in the game the other children were playing with their fathers. He was happily sharing, inclusive, and also able to express his sadness verbally about saying goodbye to his cousin, aunt, and uncle.

I knew that my morning at home with him would now go a little more smoothly, too, and it did. I was thankful I had the time to listen to my son's upset about his car seat, and that I had the knowledge of how to listen.

HOW IT WORKED

Whether it's a family visit, or a visit from a friend, goodbyes can be hard for children. Where we might give a hug, shed a tear, or express our appreciation for the visit, young children often express their upset and disappointment through off-track behaviors.

This mother recognized her son's unacceptable behavior as a cry for help. By setting a limit with a loving tone of voice and listening to her son's resulting upset, she allowed her boy to express his feelings openly, dump his emotional load, and regain the ability to connect and cooperate. She offered her son a limit to push against, so that his upset could be directed at something specific, rather than spilling out all over his cousins, aunt, and uncle. Then, he was able to do the work of healing, and the goodbye was sweet.

———◇———

LISTENING TO A FRIEND'S CHILD

TOOL:  STAYLISTENING

A three-year-old boy and his older brother were going to stay with me and my daughters while their mom, who is my dear friend, went to a work meeting. We are very close, but hadn't seen each other all summer. On their way to our house, Sam fell asleep, so his mom had to wake him up right before saying goodbye.

When she started to leave, he got very upset and started to cry, not wanting to let go of her. She didn't want to be late, so I had to hold Sam while she left. I sat on the floor and held him gently in my lap, ready to Staylisten. My daughter, also three, sat next to me. Sam saw his mom leave through the window and screamed, "Mommy, don't go!"

With a very calm tone, I said, "Your mom will come back. I love you very much, and I will take good care of you." His crying escalated, and he started trying to kick the door. His brother tried again and again to distract him, but Sam was working really hard on expelling his feelings and kept on crying.

Listening to him wasn't as difficult for me as Staylistening with my girls can be, but it wasn't easy for his brother or my youngest daughter, for whom the issue of separation is a tender one. The challenge I faced, besides anchoring Sam while he cried passionately, was to reassure his brother and my daughter that everything was going to be OK. Gentle eye contact and statements like, "It's fine if he needs to cry," made with a neutral tone, were needed to convey a sense of safety for all.

After a few minutes of reassuring Sam that he was safe, he finally looked at me, sighed, and slowly stopped crying. He then got up, went to see what his brother was doing, and accepted the snack he had rejected before. For the rest of the afternoon, he was really easygoing: he made relaxed eye contact, was able to express his needs with clarity, and played beautifully with his brother and my girls.

When my friend came back, he ran to her arms with a big smile on his face. My daughters later commented on how happy Sam had been after having cried so hard. Seeing him go through this deep process made a big impact on them. We were all wondering how things would go the next time he had to stay with us.

A few weeks later, when his mom had another meeting, we found out. He walked into our house, waved bye-bye to his mom, and ran off happily to play. Just like that!

HOW IT WORKED

This mom, familiar with Hand in Hand, was able to give her friend's child a great gift. She did a beautiful job caring for the upset child. She assured him that she loved him, that he was safe, and that his mom would return. And then she Staylistened with him until he was able to join the other kids and play happily.

She also made sure to reassure the other children, letting them know that Sam was OK and just needed to cry. And while they weren't so sure that she was right at first, by the end of their time together, they realized how happy Sam had been after letting go of all that emotional hurt.

———————————— ◆◆◆ ————————————

Separations: Bedtime

WHAT YOU NEED TO KNOW

Hand in Hand Parenting doesn't advocate a particular sleeping recipe. Our children sleep with us, sleep in their own separate rooms, and have led us to experiment with just about every setup in between. We have seen that when parents are attentive and use Listening Tools during waking hours, the parent-child bond stays strong into adulthood, whether children have slept quite close to their parents in childhood or not. We support your thinking, and trust that you will figure out what makes best sense for your family!

Whatever your sleeping arrangement, offer your child loving attention and listen to him as his feelings bubble up around sleep. In time, often quite quickly, he will learn to go to sleep and stay asleep, unafraid and without you when necessary. Help him face his fears when they compromise a good night's sleep for you, because he needs a parent who can function well during waking hours. Sometimes this requires pairing Special Time with setting limits lovingly, and then Staylistening. Other times, lots of Playlistening and vigorous snuggles will help dissolve your child's fears. We don't recommend letting your child "cry it out." Leaving your child alone, scared, and crying for connection reinforces his fears and sets in a sense of helplessness. Because deep-seated fears often rise to the surface at night, helping your child with sleep issues can take some time. Be sure to shore up your Listening Partnership time as you proceed.

EVENING MELTDOWNS

TOOL: PLAYLISTENING

My son is almost three. The evenings have been a prime time for his meltdowns. At the end of a long day my wife and I are exhausted. I frantically try to get dinner ready and worry whether my son will eat it. Needless to say, I run low on patience! I feel rushed, tired, and all I want to do is sit at the table and eat in peace!

But in the last couple of weeks, I've done Playlistening with him after dinner. What a difference! Lately, my son has been eating his dinner. When he's done, he can't wait to grab my hand to go into the living room for some goofing around! And I am surprised to find how much I love Playlistening, and how much fun it has brought into our home.

When we get to the living room, the house transforms. He'll climb on my back and ask me to be an elephant or a gorilla or an airplane flying around the house. Then we'll play hide and seek, and I call out, "Peep-squawk" to give away my hiding spot. I really love it because there is so much laughter between us, right when it's really needed to bring connection back. It's amazing how much lighter things feel after a good play and laugh!

The rest of the evening routine has become a lot easier as well. If he's on my back and I am pretending to be an airplane, I can fly into the bathroom, and the task of bathing him and brushing his teeth becomes part of our play. We now also get less resistance from him at bedtime. Our evenings have never felt easier.

HOW IT WORKED

Never underestimate the power of play to shift moods and help you connect with your child! By introducing Playlistening into his evening routine, this dad has transformed dreaded dinners and frustrating bedtime routines into fun times of connection and cooperation.

———◇———

TROUBLE GOING TO SLEEP

TOOLS:  SETTING LIMITS  STAYLISTENING

One of the children who had graduated from the infant-toddler center I directed couldn't go to sleep by herself. She needed either her mom or her dad to lie down with her, and it often took her a long time to finally fall asleep. The lack of sleep and long bedtime routine was affecting the parents' relationship with one another, so they decided to help her face her fears. They asked my advice about how to help wean her from their presence after some snuggles at bedtime. I suggested that they tell their daughter they'd help her until she felt safe in her bed alone, and then initiate small steps of separation to let her feel fears while they listened and supported her.

They talked with their three-year-old about this project, expecting it to take many nights. And Rebecca began to cry that night, worried about how she would feel when her mommy and daddy left the room. They listened to her, reassured her that they would be nearby, and told her she would be safe in her bed. They snuggled with her for about ten minutes, and then made the move to sit up. She began to cry, so they sat on the bed, listening to her cry and letting her reach for them. She would reach and cry, hold on and cry, and when her crying subsided, they would peel her clutching arms away slightly to help her feel the prospect of separation again. Slowly, over a period of two hours in her room, they moved inch by inch away from her. She cried, sweated, and trembled, but they kept reassuring Rebecca that all was well. They said that they would watch over her from a distance, keeping her safe. By the time she fell asleep, they were listening to her from across the room, near her doorjamb, but they had not left the room. They'd kept eye contact with her the whole time.

They were both relieved and worried when she finally slept. She had cried so long! Would she be less trusting of them in the morning? What if they had made a terrible mistake?

But Rebecca awoke feeling energetic, warmly connected, and eager to go to preschool. Her parents didn't see the sad, distant child that they had imagined the night before. Rebecca said goodbye easily at preschool, and seemed happy to be there. At the end of the day, her teacher told her mom, "She's been shy since she arrived here, always hovering around the edge of play. But today, she jumped right in, laughed, entered games that included several children, and had a great time. We've never seen her like this before!"

Her parents were amazed and relieved. The work Rebecca had done the night before had not only made a huge difference in her day, but that night, she went to sleep contentedly after a snuggle and a story.

HOW IT WORKED

Many parents feel trapped at bedtime, caught between a healthy desire to help their child settle into sleep peacefully and a genuine need for some alone time to refuel. Choose the former, and your evening is gone. Choose the latter, and your heart breaks as you try to ignore your child's sobs and pleas for comfort. There is another way.

In one night, these parents enabled their daughter to go to sleep peacefully on her own. And they did it while staying with her and pouring in their love. Instead of leaving in one big break—and break of trust—these parents moved away gently, and only as much as they needed to in order to allow their daughter to release her feelings of fear about their departure. Taking very small steps toward the door created the perfect balance of, "You're safe," "We love you," and "You can do this." Their daughter felt scared, but her parents' continued presence served as a constant reminder that she was safe. In this situation, the tears that flowed were tears of healing. This child offloaded fear that was not serving her well.

WHEN YOUR CHILD IS AFRAID TO SLEEP ALONE

TOOL: STAYLISTENING

My daughter, who is seven, always wanted to sleep in my bed. She went through a period of crying every night about sleeping alone. I listened to her cry each time, hoping it was doing some good, but I saw little relief or change.

One night, however, she became very mad and started trying to punch and kick me. I had just watched a Hand in Hand video on working with aggression, so I felt clearer about what to do. I met her aggression with warmth, kissing her hands when she punched, deflecting her kicks, and letting her know that I saw how upset she was.

After a long, vigorous protest, she relaxed, lay on the bed, and told me about something that happened at gym that day. They had played a game with a big parachute silk, which she had never done before. It was familiar to all the other children at her new school, but she was confused about what to do, and felt scared when she found herself covered by the parachute. She said everyone loved the game, but she hated it.

She seemed to want to kick some more, so I held up a pillow and encouraged her to pretend it was the parachute, and to kick it. She did, and she loved kicking it! She then got up to punch it down with a karate chop again and again. Then, she threw it back over her head and down the hall repeatedly, calling it a "Stupid, f___ pillow." "F___" is a word she has been fascinated with—it holds a lot of power for her. I felt like this aggression would go on forever, but I let her keep going because she seemed to be getting so much out of it.

After a while longer, I realized that it was late for a school-night bedtime, and I suggested she could continue another time. She seemed satisfied with that, and went to bed without crying. Sleeping alone still holds some fear for her, but since that night, she hasn't cried once at bedtime. The difference in her after that night is remarkable! I was surprised and happy that one Staylistening time had such a big impact.

HOW IT WORKED

Sometimes our children beg to sleep with us, but we choose not to let them. Perhaps we don't get a good night's sleep when they're in our bed, or we recognize our own need for some time apart from our children to refuel. Maybe we've recognized that their fears around sleeping by themselves might be holding them back in other areas of their life, and we want to help them. We heed their call for connection, but acknowledge our own needs as well.

This mom set a limit: her daughter needed to sleep in her own bed. Rather than reacting to her daughter's aggression with anger, she recognized her fear, and moved to connect with her. By responding to her daughter's kicks with love and compassion, she sent the message, "I love you no matter what!" That was just what her girl needed, and she felt safe enough to say what was really bothering her.

The mother then used that incident as an inroad, and helped her child work on releasing the hurt. Her daughter kicked and punched and swore at a pillow. This "freedom of the mouth," as we like to call it, is something we recommend parents adopt during Staylistening sessions. Contrary to what you might think, we have not seen foul language slip into these children's daily lexicons. This mom was creative in directing her daughter's anger and protest, giving her a way to feel powerful instead of frightened, and a way to offload enough upset that she could relax that evening and for many nights to come. However, a parent who can't abide their child's chosen words could encourage their child to throw their intensity into some other word, like "rutabaga!" or "fruitloop!" The permission to be angry is the healing factor; the exact words used are less important.

Separations: School And Childcare

CLINGY DROP-OFFS

TOOL: ⧗ SPECIAL TIME

I was dropping off my son at his new preschool the other morning and when we arrived, his class had already moved outdoors for playtime. One of the teachers was still in the classroom and she greeted him and offered to take him out to play. He started clinging to me and was not very pleased that he was the only one in the room. I asked for a few minutes with him and said that I would walk him down to the play area when we were ready.

Then I took my cell phone out and showed my son the timer. I said, "How about I give you five minutes of Special Time?" He agreed. He began to settle down and grabbed my hand to walk me around his new classroom. He showed me all the toys and different things that he liked to do. It was like a mini-tour.

My timer went off. "Special Time is finished," I said. I asked if he'd like to show me where he goes out to play. He grabbed my hand, and we walked outside toward the play area. When we got down there, his teacher greeted him. After I gave him a hug and a kiss goodbye, he went off to play. He felt much happier and connected, and I felt better, too. I was a bit anxious when I picked him up, not knowing if he had an OK day or not. But everything was fine and I was told that his day was great!

HOW IT WORKED

Transitions can often be difficult for children, and the fact that we parents are often rushing doesn't help. When we can take our time, like this parent did, there's often a Hand in Hand tool that can help our child transition smoothly. Special Time offered this boy an opportunity to stay connected to his dad as he explored his classroom, processing his transition from home to school. By the time the five-minute timer went off, he was ready to cheerfully wave his dad goodbye.

SHYNESS AT DROP-OFF

TOOL:  PLAYLISTENING

When Maria was younger, about five, she became shy every day as we approached her school. She knew everyone there very well, and they were patient and warm with her. She always opened up soon after arriving, but she started each day not looking at or speaking to those who greeted her at the door.

I tried an approach my Hand in Hand consultant suggested: I acted as if I were the shy one. Each day, I would pretend that I didn't want to go in. I would go up the walkway, holding Maria's hand, and then turn around and run. I would let out a little screech if I thought anyone saw me through the windows as we walked up. I'd keep trying to pull Maria back to the car, saying I didn't want to go in. Maria loved this game. She would patiently and warmly hold my hand and encourage me to keep walking toward the classroom. She laughed and smiled while we played, and after a while, she stopped being withdrawn at the start of the day.

HOW IT WORKED

Kids aren't naturally shy. They feel shy at times because of other feelings, like fear, that get in the way of them living a big life. This mom recognized that her daughter's fears were holding her back and used Playlistening to help her laugh away her shyness and step more confidently into the classroom at the beginning of the day.

DROP-OFF AT A LESSON

TOOLS:  SETTING LIMITS STAYLISTENING

My five-year-old daughter had recently begun primary school. Although she'd settled in nicely after a rocky first week at school, the separation anxiety was still present in other areas, like swim class.

She'd taken swimming lessons since age four and never had any issues, happily following instructions in the pool. However, after school started this year, she began crying when she had to get into the pool. Using the Hand in Hand tools, I went to her, knelt down, and simply listened. She wasn't worried about the swimming class itself, but about me leaving the pool area while she was in the water. This fear was immobilizing her.

I acknowledged her fears and stayed with her while she cried, resisting the urge to do what I might have done previously—to reason with her ("I'm just up there in the viewing area"), or bribe her ("If you go swimming, I'll give you a candy"), or even scold her ("If you don't get into the pool, I am going to get very angry"). I did reassure her every now and then that I wasn't going to go. She eventually got in the pool. She continued crying, staying close to where I was on the edge until the lesson was over. The next week the same thing happened, but by the end of the lesson she was participating in the class with me still at the edge of the pool.

When the subject came up at home, I reassured her that I would be there and not leave, and I continued to listen to her fears and deep sadness. I told her that I would come down to the poolside if she needed me in the beginning, but that I really thought that she would be OK.

The next week, she was a bit nervous and said she didn't want to go, but I gently said she did need to go swimming, and that I would be there for her. We got there, she began walking to the pool, and then she stopped and said, "Actually, you can wait here." I agreed and waited on the steps. Then she turned to me again and said, "Actually, you can just go there," and she pointed to the viewing area where I normally sat during her lessons. I asked if she was sure. She nodded happily and went down to join her class.

She was so happy during that lesson. She was back to her confident, bubbly self, and giggled and laughed more in that lesson than ever before! I couldn't believe the power of Staylistening. It was one of my first few experiences with Staylistening, and I myself was trembling with the after-effects!

HOW IT WORKED

When your child who's doing swimmingly suddenly becomes clingy, it's a good sign that some hurt has bubbled up and is ready to be shed. Staylistening is often your go-to tool for helping your child get back to her spirited self.

This mother recognized her daughter's shift in behavior and realized that the change occurred alongside the start of school. She decided to set limits around going to swim lessons, something that she knew her daughter really enjoyed. She expected major feelings to follow, so she wasn't surprised at her daughter's crying or her pleas to stay out of the water. Following several weeks of setting limits and Staylistening at the swim lessons, her daughter regained confidence and joined the class with pleasure. By setting a limit and allowing her daughter to work through her fears, she counted on her daughter's ability to heal from hurt and regain confidence. She taught her that fear can be overcome with loving support.

LONG, EMOTIONAL DROP-OFFS

TOOLS:  LISTENING PARTNERSHIP  SETTING LIMITS STAYLISTENING

We had just come off a two-week break from preschool, during which my four-year-old son had been very ill. I had been by his side constantly, taking care of him. I gave him a heads-up about school starting, and he was not excited about this at all. He would say, "I don't like school. I don't want to go!" I listened.

I knew this transition had the potential to be hard. I got some listening time around this before he started back to help loosen my anxiety around this sensitive spot.

The first day back I stayed extra long in the morning, and was able to leave pretty smoothly. On the second day I stayed again, but this time I wanted to do a long goodbye so that he could release some of the fear I sensed he was holding. The teacher was available to help, so we worked together. She held him close, and I slowly moved away. As soon as I couldn't quite touch his outreached finger, he began to cry. I stayed with it, going back and forth to help his feelings pour out. We did this for a good ten minutes and then he wanted me to push him on the swing before I left. I did, and then the teacher suggested that he push me out the door. He liked that, and off I went.

When I picked him up at school he was happily playing with another boy. I asked him how his day was, and he said, "Good." I checked in with the teachers and they told me his day had gone well. Now, I was happy, too!

HOW IT WORKED

Rather than put a patch on her child's upset, this mom beefed up her stamina in her Listening Partnership, and then enlisted the support of her child's teacher to help her child heal from separation fears by setting a limit. Because she stayed close but proposed to leave, her son felt safe enough to cry. After a while, he relaxed and came up with another way to connect with his mom: having her push him on the swing. One last infusion of love, and then he was ready to send his mom off with a smile.

WHEN IT'S HARD FOR US TO SAY GOODBYE

TOOL: LISTENING PARTNERSHIP

My daughter was starting nursery school, and although I trusted that she could handle it, I had various concerns. School wasn't my first choice; I would rather have kept her at home. It felt unfair, as her older brother hadn't gone, and I was scared she might lose some of her wildness and exuberance and become obedient!

I took this to my Listening Partnerships. The first time, I expressed my concerns and my listening partner said, with a twinkle, "It's not as if you are sending her to boarding school!" I laughed! She had helped me to remember that I'd carefully selected a safe, cozy environment.

In another session with a different listening partner, I cried about feeling that she was too little, and that I didn't want to send my baby away. My listening partner asked me what was the worst thing that could happen, which allowed me to release some fears. I didn't know if she would be OK without me, and it was daunting to think that I would have no control over part of her life, no ability to protect her while she was there. One thing I love about my daughter is that she is so clear about what she needs and is good at asking for it, and I was scared she could lose this strong voice. My listening partner affirmed that it was possible she might thrive there. This led me to remember my own experience of being at preschool, and some other scary memories. After offloading these, I felt I could approach my daughter's start at school from a much more positive and balanced place.

During the actual week nursery school started, my husband or I stayed with our daughter each morning. On the day I went, I had to send out a plea for emergency listening time! One of my listening partners responded and gave me her attention as I described my disappointment about my daughter's new teacher. I swore a lot, pretended my partner was the teacher, and said all the things I'd wanted to say to her, but obviously wouldn't in real life. I cried that I wasn't keeping my daughter at home with me.

My husband and I had been on the brink of renouncing the whole idea of preschool, but after releasing so much of my upset, I was able to think more clearly. I realized that our worries might be unfounded. We knew our daughter was bold, resourceful, and robust, and we wanted her to gain confidence from seeing the process through.

The next day, my husband went with her but felt really unwell. He gave her the option to go home with him or stay and be picked up later. She chose to stay! When I went to collect her, I watched her for a while before she noticed me. She was her usual happy self and had lost none of her exuberance. I learned that my daughter has had a very different foundation from the one I'd had, and she experiences the world very differently! I saw the value in allowing a child to stretch their comfort zone and gain self-confidence from doing so. She transitioned seamlessly. While other children, even those who have been there for some time, cry and cling to their parents as they leave, our daughter happily involves herself in play. She has had the flexibility to adapt to the various rules that she had not been used to at home. All those worries, it seems, were ours, not hers!

HOW IT WORKS

Sometimes it turns out that our children are just fine with a separation, and it's our own worries that stand in our children's way. Here, this mother uses her Listening Partnerships to dig deeply and release lots of fear and worry about leaving her little girl. As a result, her thinking clears and she's able to separate her own feelings from those of her daughter, and to acknowledge that her daughter is her own person. It is she who feels her daughter is too little to go. Her daughter is ready to put on her shoes and head out the door! Had this mother given in to her worries, this little girl wouldn't have experienced all the fun and growth that takes place in a nurturing childcare environment, something she was fearless to try.

Separations: When Your Child Rejects A Parent

WHEN YOUR BABY ONLY WANTS YOU

TOOLS: 🚦 SETTING LIMITS   ⟳ STAYLISTENING

When my daughter was about six months old, she didn't want to be held by her dad when he came home from work in the evenings. So we decided to Staylisten with her about her fears of separating from me.

One Saturday morning, my husband held our daughter. She cried and reached out to me to hold her. My husband was sitting on the couch, holding her, and I sat beside them. My daughter could see me, and kept reaching and crying. I said to her in a whisper, "Daddy is holding you now. You are safe with Daddy. We love you very much!" She cried loudly and stretched her arms out to me. My husband held her while she struggled. He said, "I love you very much, sweetheart. I love to be with you." When he said this, she cried even louder, screamed, and held her body rigidly. Occasionally, she looked at my husband, then turned her head away and cried again.

She cried like that for about fifty minutes, and her body was very sweaty. She was very strong as she twisted and struggled in my husband's arms, making him sweaty, too. At one point, he felt like he wanted to give her to me, but I encouraged him to continue, as he is kind and thoughtful, and a good person for her to be with. When she was done, she was tired, and she took a long nap.

While she slept, my husband and I had a good talk about the feelings we have when we listen to our daughter cry. I knew it was a big challenge for him to listen to her for so long. I told him that he did a great job. He is a wonderful dad.

Since this listening time, our daughter is happy to have him hold her when he comes home. They play a lot every night and have lots of fun together.

HOW IT WORKED

This mom knew that her daughter's rejection of her daddy must be based in some feelings of upset, because he is an attentive, loving dad. Children often store their feelings of upset from their parent's daily departures, and these feelings prevent the child from feeling totally safe with the parent who departed. This mother simply set a limit. Daddy is a loving person, so you are in no danger in his arms, she explained. I'll stay right next to you. Together, we'll listen to you if hurt feelings arise. Hurt feelings did come up, and one good listening time restored this baby's sense of safety with her daddy. And the parents talked through their feelings after this big listening interlude, so they could better understand the issues that surfaced for each of them during their baby's long cry.

WHEN YOUR CHILD WANTS THE OTHER PARENT

TOOLS:  LISTENING PARTNERSHIP   STAYLISTENING

Our son is nearly three years old. He still goes through some separation anxiety when he's without his mom. We usually put him to bed together, but the other night, my wife needed a break. So our routine began. I read him a book, tucked him in, and said goodnight. The minute the lights went out, he got anxious and climbed out of bed, wanting to go find Mommy. He walked toward the door and screamed for me to open it. I gave in and opened it. He looked, but couldn't find her. He began stomping his feet and screamed out, "Call Mommy!"

I moved in and held him. He was frantic and kept crying, "I want Mommy!" As I held him I said, "I hear how scary it is for you! I am here for you." I carried him back into his bedroom and sat us both down on the floor. He was in my lap, and he cried hard into my shoulder. I kept holding him, acknowledging his feelings. "I am here for you and I will support you through this." Although he kept screaming for Mommy, after awhile I noticed a change. His cries deepened, and there was a sense of sadness. I stayed with him, telling him, "I will not leave you alone. I am going to be right here for you!"

He got tired and said he wanted to lie down. I carried him to bed, and he continued crying with me by his side. After a good while, he settled down. He said, "Mommy needs space," and I responded, "Yes, she needs a break. Mommy loves you very much." He then slowly drifted off to sleep.

Staylistening with my son felt different for me this time. Hearing his cries can be quite triggering for me when they are filled with fear and panic. This time around, I noticed that they reminded me of my crying as a little boy, but I wasn't triggered by it. All that work I had done in Listening Partnerships had paid off. I am so glad that I was able to stay present, and help him through his fears. The next morning he woke up happy. He was full of himself!

HOW IT WORKED

There's nothing that pushes a parent's buttons quite like a child "needing" the other parent. We often feel hurt, or like something's wrong with us. But a child who's feeling discontent with one parent or the other is just lost in feelings, unable to remember how special each parent is to him. It's not about you!

This dad had worked hard in his Listening Partnerships on his own struggles and triggers, and so was able to stay fully present when his son needed him. Dad didn't take his son's words personally. Instead, he kept him close and listened to his upset, including his pleas for Mom. The boy was able to cry and cry, and eventually share his newfound understanding of why Mom couldn't be there. He was then able to relax, get a good sleep, and wake up feeling fine.

———◇———

WHEN A PARENT WORKS LONG HOURS

TOOLS: ⧗ SPECIAL TIME   ◉ STAYLISTENING

Soon after her sister was born, my two-year-old started longing for her dad. She would begin whining the moment he left for work in the morning, and ask for him throughout the day. She would get upset with me and say she didn't want me, she wanted daddy. But when he came home she would run from him, saying, " I don't like you, Daddy. I want Mommy." This was followed by a big cry and lots of Staylistening. It made our evening routine pretty stressful.

We started making sure she got ten or fifteen minutes of Special Time with her dad when he got home. He also makes sure to give her five minutes in the morning before going to work.

When we first started her morning Special Time, it would often end in tears. She didn't want him to go to work. After a few weeks there were no more tears at the end of Special Time in the morning, and she was able to say goodbye to him. She was also excited at the promise of more Special Time in the evening. The work she did completely changed things for my daughter. She now jumps out of bed in the mornings for her time with Daddy. Our mornings run a lot more smoothly as well, as her cup has been filled at the start of the day. Our evenings are filled more with laughter than with tears now, and our evening routine is less stressful.

HOW IT WORKED

This girl was missing her daddy, who would disappear daily for hours on end. Perhaps the birth of her sister had heightened her sensitivity. In any case, her feelings manifested in lots of upsets directed at Mom, then Dad, and lots of tears. Her parents used Special Time, one of the absolute best ways to build or rebuild connection between a child and a parent. Short Special Times with Dad each evening reassured their daughter of her Dad's love. The morning Special Times also helped, and when Dad went off to work, she had a daily opportunity to be listened to as she mourned his departure. Eventually, her reservoir of upset emptied. The father/daughter relationship grew stronger, and this child's newfound confidence has transformed her mornings and evenings.

———◇———

CHANGING THE BEDTIME ROUTINE

TOOL: PLAYLISTENING

My youngest daughter was struggling with separations. Daycare and nighttime separations were particularly hard. One day, she had struggled with the separation from me at daycare. So I thought that some Playlistening at night would help her release some of her fears around sleep time. I planned to play, and then ask Daddy to put her to sleep that night, thinking that would trigger a big release from the day's tensions.

We played many different games that made her laugh and gave her a sense of power. For example, she rode on me like a "bucking bronco," as I tried to shake her off. She thought it was so funny and jumped back on many times. Another game was flying on my feet, but instead of flying on both my feet she wanted to just fly on just one. This resulted in lots of laughter as she flipped upside down and on her head, making it very hard for me, thus giving her power and control. She even made up a game where we ran through the house with pillows, trying to hit each other. She was in hysterics. It was great because she made the game up and laughed all over the house. Another game consisted of me saying that Daddy would put her to sleep. It became play as she moved my cheeks and face in a funny way so that my voice was distorted and I had ridiculous expressions on my face. She was laughing hard and kept moving my cheeks so that I would continue to do this. This last one was particularly powerful when she laughed, as it was dealing with a sensitive topic—separation from me.

Following this play I was expecting a big cry when I told her that Daddy would put her to sleep, as building safety through Playlistening can often result in hurts bubbling up to the surface. Instead she was completely fine with it! Unbelievable! I could not believe it, as previously she had protested and been very upset when I suggested that Daddy would put her to sleep! I knew that Playlistening was the reason for this. It managed to bring about connection and nurturing while releasing the stored tension and separation fears through laughter. Furthermore, it was fun and exciting, as I never knew what was going to come next. This Playlistening session clearly seemed to loosen up her fears, enabling her to drift off into a beautiful sound sleep.

HOW IT WORKS

Playlistening is incredibly empowering for children. It allows them to laugh their fears away, be creative in their silliness, and exercise their power over the adults who spend much time telling them what to do. Here, this mom planned a Playlistening session specifically to work on her daughter's separation issues. She knew it would build connection between them, and that it would likely create the safety necessary for her daughter to have a big healing cry when she handed her over to Dad at bedtime. As it turned out, her daughter laughed a ton and orchestrated a Playlistening game specific to her feelings about her dad putting her to sleep. When bedtime rolled around, she was feeling so good that she was absolutely content to go off with her dad.

Separations: Handling Rocky Reunions

REUNITING AFTER A FEW DAYS APART

TOOL: PLAYLISTENING

My husband took our children, six and three, off on a four-day trip. After I picked them up from the train station, we all went swimming. The children signaled very plainly that they still felt disconnected by saying things like, "I hate Mommy." They didn't want me to touch them or to be the one who changed their clothes. So when we all got in the pool together, I instigated a game of "That's my child." My husband would try to take a child from me, and I would vie to get one back from him.

For a long time the children would cling to him, kicking me if I went too close and calling me a "stupid idiot." I didn't take it personally. I just kept trying over and over again to get them back, and I made sure I "failed" often. When they tried to kick me I just held the offending foot, or moved out of the way and said, "Oops! Can't do that!" When I was after him, my son would trick me by saying he would help me get his sister. I would let go of him, and he would escape. I hammed up my helplessness, and played that I was sad to have no children.

Over the course of half an hour, I could see them very gradually warm to me. They would stay with me a little longer each time, and eventually they would reach out to me. By the end of the swim they were feeling happy and connected to me again. My daughter was jumping into my arms, and my son was diving for the weight I was throwing. We were together again.

HOW IT WORKED

This mom recognized her children's mean words and aggressive behaviors as calls for help. She knew that Playlistening would bridge the distance between where she was standing and the sweet connection they all wanted. By launching into a game that sends the message "I love you," she created an opportunity for her kids to fight back, showing their upset and anger about having been separated from her for the last few days. She was careful to always play the less powerful role in the game, a sure way to help a child laugh. Slowly, slowly, her children released their upset and regained their ability to be close to her.

RECONNECTING AFTER A LONG DAY AWAY

TOOL:  SPECIAL TIME

All day long, I'd had to figure things out on the fly. By the time my ten-year-old son left school, my schedule had changed half a dozen times. I had arranged for some friends to take my son to a nearby park for a birthday party, where my daughter and I would meet them after an impromptu doctor's appointment.

After all that chaos, it was a relief to arrive at the park. It was our first day of beautiful spring weather, and lots of school families were at the park flying kites together. The change of pace from my busy day felt great. I relaxed and started talking with friends, checking in just once with my son, who also had several friends his age at the party.

After about an hour, my son came over to me as I was chatting and asked, "Mom, can we do Special Time?" I was taken aback at first. "But we are at a party," I thought. "Why on earth would we do it now?" But I said, "Um. I guess. But give me ten minutes." "Okay," he said.

I talked some more with my friend. After a bit, my son came back and asked again. I could tell this was important to him, so I said, "Sure."

He and I played football together for fifteen minutes, just the two of us in the midst of all of the other families. I really enjoy Special Time with my kids, and I was completely delighted by him and attentive to him. We had lots of fun chasing each other. When our fifteen minutes ended, we prepared to leave. My son was relaxed and happy.

It wasn't until the next day that I realized that he asked for Special Time during the birthday party because he was feeling alone. He and I usually have a nice connection time after school and it didn't happen at all that day. I was so distracted with my own busy day that I didn't notice; I just assumed that all was well with him, since the weather was beautiful, we were at a birthday party, and everyone was playing.

I was so proud of him for having realized he wasn't feeling well inside, and for knowing that he could come to me and ask for what he needed. He knew he could get a boost from Special Time to feel well and connected again.

HOW IT WORKED

So often we say hello again to our children after school or work in a whirlwind of dinner preperation, homework, or some other distraction. In this case, it was a party. Everyone loves a party, but it can be really hard for a child to enjoy himself when he doesn't feel connected.

Here, the child took the lead in reconnecting with his mother. He was used to having time each day where he soaked up her love, and he recognized that he needed it, even before his behavior went off track! This is the blessing of naming Special Time. As your child grows, he learns how it makes him feel, and he can ask for Special Time when he needs to feel seen and accepted for who he is. All you have to do is answer the call.

VISITING WITH A PARENT WHO LIVES SEPARATELY

TOOLS: SPECIAL TIME   STAYLISTENING   PLAYLISTENING

My daughter lives with me and sees her dad twice weekly in my home. When she was around two years old, and prior to that as well, their time together was not always consistent. This caused some insecurity and fear for her in their relationship. When my daughter was able to see her father consistently, they generally had a close and comfortable time together. But when they reconnected after a more prolonged separation, my daughter didn't want to spend time alone with her father; when we were both present, she would not want me to leave the room.

To help with this challenge, I started doing Special Time just before my daughter's dad's visits. I noticed that this helped loosen up feelings. I found that during her dad's visits she started having more and more outright upsets. Something would trigger her, she would get upset and come to me, refusing to talk or play with her dad.

I would move in close and listen, not trying to fix anything but just sitting with her. She would cry and rage about whatever upset had happened and would not want to see or even look at him, saying she didn't want him, or that she never wanted to see him again and he must go away. Often, she would be crying on the floor with me, in a room away from her father. Once she had finished her big cry, as quickly as the upset had flooded in, she would jump up and bounce back into connection with her dad. It was remarkable how easily she was able to move back toward him, reconnecting with joy and openness.

I told her as she cried, "Your dad is a good man," and "Your dad loves you so much, sweetheart." I think it was important for her to hear me saying these words. I am sure that the tension between him and me in the past had left her confused.

There were also a few occasions where she had long cries as I was about to leave her with her father. This was a bit trickier, as he then wanted me to leave quickly rather than "prolong the agony." In our parenting meetings with each other, we talked about the Listening Tools and how they work. Although he understood and appreciated their value, without the support of listening time for himself, he often couldn't bear to listen as his daughter totally rejected him. But I remained clear about my goal. I talked about the approach in meetings with him, rather than in the middle of a difficult incident during his visits, and he came to see that listening to her feelings really improved their relationship. Over time, these occasions became easier.

My daughter would also initiate Playlistening and ask for Special Time during her dad's visits. He would help her do rough and tumble play or airplane jumps off the couch, and she would ask him to help her "fly."

Once, after a period of several big Staylistening sessions, her father and I were having a parenting meeting and he opened up about the changes he had noticed. He talked about his own difficulties with staying present when she cries or stomps away, and yet he recognized how it helped her to release these big feelings. He remarked on how much their physical play helped them to reconnect, especially after longer periods of separation. He expressed deep gratitude at how close he feels to our daughter as a result. This was a remarkable development, given that his upbringing was very different from the Hand in Hand approach.

HOW IT WORKED

If you are divorced or separated, you likely often feel challenged by passionate feelings your children have when moving back and forth between you and your ex. This anecdote suggests that the situation can improve.

This mother used Special Time to warm her relationship with her daughter, building a connection that enabled the girl to share painful feelings when they arose. Mom was there to listen. This mother also never lost sight of the goodness of her child's father, the importance of his connection to their daughter, and their shared desire for their child to have a good life. Despite the tensions between them, she was able to let their daughter know that her father was a good man and that he loved her. And the father was, despite his discomfort, able to tolerate his daughter's negative feelings, and managed to keep an open mind throughout a challenging situation.

Lastly, because this mother used Playlistening and Special Time with her daughter regularly, her daughter knew how great she felt during play. Knowing what she wanted, she could initiate the play she loved in her visits with Dad. This helped to build closeness and strengthen their connection, too.

11
Lifting Fear

WHAT YOU NEED TO KNOW

Children find lots of creative ways to show us when they feel scared or worried. Some young ones erupt with crying, screaming, swearing, or acting aggressively. Other children clam up and turn inward when they're frightened, so their signals are less overt and harder to decipher. Kids will suck their thumbs, bite their nails, chew on their shirts, twirl their hair, read obsessively, or skip quickly from one activity to another, all in an attempt to quiet the rumblings of fear. Though these habits aren't flashy, they are reliable signs that a child is scared.

Fear underlies many of our children's persistent struggles. It makes it hard for them to say a calm goodbye as we head off to work. Fear drives physical outbursts of aggression, and the impulse to grab rather than wait for a turn. The child who shies away from participating in an activity he loves is probably scared. So is the child who never raises his hand in class, and the one who constantly disrupts. Fear keeps our kids from living the secure, relaxed life we want them to have.

WHERE DO CHILDREN'S FEARS COME FROM?

You may be able to put your finger on a few incidents that might have frightened your child, such as a difficult birth, an accident, an illness, or sudden changes at home. But experiences that seem harmless and mat-ter-of-fact to you can also cause trouble. A few claps of thunder, your car running out of gas on the highway, one shouting match with your part-ner—any of these events could frighten your child, and make relaxation difficult for him without your help. In fact, fear is often the reason your child goes off track the moment your day becomes difficult. He takes his cues about the safety of his surroundings from you and the other adults around him. When you're tense or unsure, your child can sense it, and your fear becomes his.

Fortunately, he is built to heal from his fears, and you can help him!

HOW CHILDREN RECOVER FROM FEAR

A scared child—like scared people of all ages—is suddenly flooded with emotion. He feels unsafe, whether there's real danger or not. As he reacts, he will fight, flee, or freeze. He needs your presence, but as you've probably discovered, your presence alone doesn't make him *feel* better.

A fearful child feels profoundly alone. In defensive mode, he may argue, lash out, or grab for something he knows is off limits. If he's in flight mode, he'll back away from a situation, refuse to engage, or actually run. And if the situation is truly overwhelming, so much of his mind shuts down that his protective instincts drain right out of him. His system decides that he's safer playing possum. Terrified inside, he acts as if things are normal until the danger passes. When a child becomes that frightened, he may not be able to talk about what happened to anyone. Only his off-track behavior will indicate that something troubling has occurred.

Whether he fights, flees, or freezes, your child can't think when he's scared. And without help from a caring person, he can't get his mind back in gear. So reactive behavior may crop up often. Sadly, when an off-track child triggers unhappy reactions in those around him, it's like lighting a match near an oil spill—their disapproval makes a bad situation worse.

It's not easy to reach out to a frightened child and handle the behaviors that have evolved to protect him from harm. But a frightened child needs someone to invite him to connect. As soon as he feels safe enough, he'll burst with emotion. Listening to him as he finally shows how frightened he is will then open the door to his recovery.

Children shed fear through laughter, which relieves some of their lighter fears. The deeper layers of fear are released in crying, trembling, perspiring, and sometimes struggling, while the child is safely listened to by a loving adult. Most of us have been taught to quiet those big tears, screams, and shaky breaths. But they are the body's remarkable means for becoming un-scared. Listening to a child all the way through a flailing cry after something scary has happened will restore his sense of safety and connection. After all that fear has been expressed, a bad experience becomes one that was mildly interesting. It's almost as simple as that.

But there is one wrinkle! If no one listens to the intense feelings that come up the moment a child gets scared, those feelings are stored away, raw and powerful still, in the child's emotional memory. There they sit uneasily, tangled with information about the sights, sounds, smells, tastes, and textures of the experience. So a day, a week, or even years later, your child may experience a flashback, and once again be gripped by that stored fear in the course of his daily life. For example, if your child was frightened by a dog when he was two, and months later sees a dozing rabbit in a cage, he may feel as terrified of the rabbit as he was of the dog. The rabbit has fur and ears. Those harmless cues trigger your child's fears, though their source may be months behind and miles away.

One mother shares how powerful these delayed fear reactions can be—and how a child can heal with the support of a loving parent:

———◇———

My four-year-old daughter had requested Special Time, and we were in the middle of it. She had directed me to try to wrestle a balloon from her grasp. I was moving in close, with affection, and she was giggling with glee. After just a few moments, unexpectedly, she became intensely emotional. She flipped into disorganized physicality, throwing her body in all directions, as only she can. There was lots of energetic movement, lots of pushing and bouncing off the furniture. She even gathered up the rug on the floor and lugged it into the hallway, as she commanded me, rejected me, yelled, and screamed!

I Staylistened. Such massive feelings were coming out of such a small being! Fortunately, I remained mostly calm. I let her know, "I am here." I also occasionally whispered, "You are safe." Mostly I said nothing. I stayed with her, looking out for her physical safety and hoping that eye contact and my presence were enough.

She went in and out of this intensity for an hour. I continued to Staylisten. Each time I moved in a bit closer there would be another surge of expression, of emotional release. It was clear she was done when, just as quickly as the outpouring had started, she flipped into smiles, lots of hugs, and affection. The afternoon progressed smoothly, with much cooperation.

The next day, I discovered there had been a situation at school. A child in her classroom had become unsettled to the extent that two teachers were needed to carry him from the classroom, kicking and screaming. I could imagine that this scenario would have been incredibly emotive for her, possibly bringing up deep, unresolved hurts and fears. You see, my daughter is adopted. She was removed from foster care at a time when she had no words to express how she felt. She was removed in a manner that mirrored the removal of the child from her classroom. It was as if she knew she needed to get some feelings out as she asked for Special Time. Then, with Staylistening, she released the hurts of her day, and possibly tapped into those very early hurts and fears and gave them some release, too. I like to think so.

———◇———

When your child shows you he's scared by lashing out or by shrinking into himself, he is asking for your help. He reacts instinctively, guided by his body's urge to stay safe. The behavior he uses as his flare isn't his choice. It's a distress signal. It leaps out without a thought. His behavior says, "I'm in trouble here!"

Of course, seeing your child's fear-driven behavior is bound to be upsetting. "What in the world is the matter with you?" is a mild way to state the reactions we're likely to have. But with this new perspective, it may be possible to see your child's reactive moments as a gift. He's telling you as clearly as he can that he's scared, and that he needs your listening to heal.

Not all children are fiery when they're scared. Some children lead their lives cautiously, quietly. They seek to control their environment and they may not interact with others easily. If your child is like this, he will benefit from an extended lead-in with Special Time, Playlistening, and other connective times with you. As these tools reassure him more fully, he will show you the feelings that lie beneath the surface. You'll get freshly minted chances to set limits and Staylisten.

This parent traveled such a route:

———◇———

My four-year-old son had always been a little reserved, socially awkward, and prone to run away from confrontation. We saw him as easy going, introverted, and compliant, with very few needs. Last year, though, we got signals from one of his teachers and a doctor that he might have some developmental challenges, and we began to wonder whether we'd been reading his behavior right.

We began to focus more on his needs, asked for his opinions, and encouraged him to express his feelings. I started doing a lot more roughhousing play with him, giving him space to choose how we played, to boss me around, and be more physical in play. I made time in our schedule so that he and I could be together, away from his verbal and extroverted sister, who tends to dominate the play at home.

Our investment in play was like putting spare coins in a piggy bank. There were no overnight changes or dramatic emotional releases. It took a few months of this additional attention, as well as a change in schools and help from an occupational therapist, to begin to see real change in my son's confidence, assertiveness, verbal skills, and engagement with other children.

My son finally started to get whiny and clingy, so unlike that easy and seemingly independent little boy. Then, we spent a two-week holiday vacation at home. We spent a lot of time together, and he connected really well with his sister, because his play skills had improved.

On the last Sunday of our vacation, a barrier finally broke. We had talked about how he would go back to school and I would return to work the following day. My son started to cry, and cry, and cry. He also tensed his body, sweating and struggling through his feelings. He was working on fear! After a period of crying, he started to say, "I'm so scared! I'm so scared!" I had no way of knowing what the fear was about. Still, I held him and gave him all the warmth and attention I could. He cried for a very long time. He cried again twice more that day. Each time, I listened and he offloaded.

In the two or three weeks that followed, my son's teachers reported how well he was playing with a few of the boys at his school. They told me he now had a best friend. They were so pleased with his progress. At home, he was initiating play with the neighborhood children we know, and was even going up to boys he didn't know to ask them about the toy in their hand.

He is undeniably the same boy he's always been, yet somehow he's more present and more at ease. There's more that we have to work on. My son is still afraid of a few things, and I'm looking forward to seeing how things will continue to unfold.

———◇———

If these insights about how children recover from their fears are new to you, you're not alone. Most parents, and even many mental health professionals, have not yet been introduced to the healing power of listening to a frightened child. Your child can work his way free from the grip of fear, even if he has struggled with fear-driven behavior for quite awhile. Your warmth and attention is the key.

USING LISTENING TOOLS TO HEAL YOUR CHILD'S FEAR

Most of us were taught to avoid feeling afraid at almost any cost, and when adults tried to help us with our childhood fears, the tools they used were crude. They threw us in the swimming pool when we were afraid to swim, or painted our thumbs with a bad-tasting potion to "cure" us of the thumb-sucking that marked our shy moments. These kinds of experiences give us no feel for the art of truly dissolving fear from our children's minds and hearts! But Hand in Hand's Listening Tools will lead you on a path of discovery as you learn to melt your child's fears, day by day. Here's how!

Step 1. Bring your feelings to a Listening Partnership. To assist your frightened child, you must first tackle your own feelings. Whether you've agonized over your child's fears or hardened your attitude in order to get on with life, living with a frightened child isn't easy. Your feelings might show up as annoyance, or come to you as gloomy imaginings of what he'll be like when he's eighteen. In any case, these feelings will trip you up as you try to be of help. Your child needs your warmth and confidence that he's safe, and a good child through and through.

With a trusted listener, talk about your reactions to your child's behaviors. It's almost always useful to talk about the very start of your relationship with your child. What were your first thoughts when you learned he would be coming into your life? What feelings did you have in the months before he arrived? How was his birth or adoption? What do you remember about his first weeks and months? What was wonderful? What was difficult? Sometimes, certain dynamics between parent and child are set up during these formative times. Now and then, the roots of a child's fears can be found right there at the beginning.

It will also be useful to think back to what was happening for you when you were your child's age. He acquires fears from his own experience, of course, but your responses to him may be influenced by events from your own childhood.

Insights may also come as you talk about what you feel like doing when his fear erupts. What words and actions spring to mind? Who does he remind you of? What do you wish you could tell him, from the bottom of your heart? There are no right and wrong thoughts or feelings. Simply see what's there, and let your own feelings roll. A listener will help you move toward the "I can anchor you" mindset you'll need in order to escort your child to a happier place. There is a road to recovery. You'll be able to find it once his behavior doesn't bug you or worry you so much.

Step 2. Build your child's sense of safety with Special Time. Short but frequent chunks of Special Time can open the door to deeper healing. Your attention and approval will be like warm oil poured on a rusty hinge. As you connect with your child, his limbic system absorbs the message, "All's well here. I'm with you." His behavior will gradually loosen up. You might see a little more laughter. He might tell you more about what he's thinking. And yes, at random times during his days and nights, more tears will begin to fall.

Step 3. Watch for opportunities to help Special Time roll into Play-listening. As your child directs the play, look for the chance to playfully take the less powerful role. For example, in Special Time, be playfully afraid when your son demonstrates his karate chop. Lose at board games, squawking and complaining loudly. Find your child's laughter and promote it! It's a tonic for any child stuck in the muck of fear.

Here's how one mother vanquished her child's fear with the powerful tool of laughter:

———◇———

When my girls were little, I used to bathe with them. We would play with their toys in the tub and have so much fun. When my youngest daughter was about two, though, she became scared of getting water in her face.

We would play with her Barbie dolls in the tub, talking to them, pretending they were our friends, and shampooing their hair. But when it was time for me to wash her hair, she would stand up, crying and screaming, "I don't want water in my face! Stop! I don't like it!"

I started using my Playlistening tool. I would pretend that I was the one scared of getting water in my face. Instead of me washing her hair, she would wash mine. Every time she poured water on my head, I would say, "No, please not in my face! Can't you see that I'm scared? Whatever you do, please don't pour water in my face!" She laughed so hard each time she poured water on my head.

I Playlistened with my daughter like that two or three times. Then one day, while I was pretending to be scared of getting water in my face again, she said, "Mom, it's your turn. Now you pour water on my head." She laughed when I did and said, "Do it again!" And that was the end of her fear of getting water in her face.

———◇———

Step 4. Increase Playlistening, especially in physical play. Safe, high-contact physical play gives children the chance to hone their physical skills and dispel fear through laughter as they play the more powerful role. Games like "I have a hundred kisses for you," where you clumsily chase your child and now and then land a kiss, are great for showing a child he's wanted. With a game like "You can't push me off the bed," you can boast of your strength, but lose the contest every time. As your child laughs, his confidence builds. And when he is accidentally bumped or knocked, you're close by to Staylisten while he offloads fear or panic. Don't try to fix anything unless he actually needs medical attention. You can always bring the ice or a Band Aid when he's done crying. He'll benefit from a chance to work on his physical fears, and over time, you'll see him begin to relax. Little dings will bother him less.

Here's a mother who shows how Playlistening can help a fear come to the surface, so it can be released with Staylistening:

———◇———

My six-year-old son was quite tense when he got home from school. Even his laughter sounded forced. He didn't seem to be himself, and I could see and feel the tears just under the surface. He became very rough with his little brother.

I could feel myself getting a bit agitated, as I dislike it when my boys try to hurt each other. I quickly grabbed a ball and bounced it to my six-year-old. He suggested a game of indoor basketball. We started playing, and I ensured that he had the power and was beating me. He started to laugh, so I chased the laughter, gauging what shots or actions got the bigger laugh. But even after twenty minutes of play, I couldn't detect any shift in the deeper tension he needed to work through.

Five minutes later, I saw it. I had accidentally hit the ball and it bounced off my son's head. It was such a soft ball that I knew that it could not have hurt him, but he started to cry, and fell into my arms while he sobbed. I held him close as he sat in my lap for ten minutes while he offloaded some feelings. Then he got up and was happy to continue playing. His laughter was now free—the tightness had disappeared. He also was happy to pass the ball to his two-year-old brother and include him in our game, encouraging him to get the ball and cheering for him when he caught it.

I also noticed that all of my agitation had gone. I felt so light. It wasn't just the effect of moving my body in play. My own laughter, and seeing my son have those beautiful chuckles, melted my upset.

———◇———

If it seems that your child is scared a lot of the time, set up Playlistening daily and follow the laughter. Over time, you will notice that your child is functioning better. He may reach out more readily for playmates. Or maybe his disruptions in the classroom will become less frequent. I've seen children overcome their fear of strangers, stop biting their nails, stop stuttering, and finally stop wetting the bed as a result of regular Playlistening, along with Staylistening when needed.

Step 5. Bring the limit, early and often. Because laughter, together with your warmth in play, builds emotional safety, a child holding fear is likely to tighten up and become hurtful in the midst of high-spirited play. It's a sign that deeper work on fear will soon be possible. Sometimes bringing a limit will allow the play to continue: you calmly take away the rope your child swings at you and give him a pillow to wield, or if he has picked up a plastic baseball bat, you can say, "Na, na, naaaa!" hold the bat, then tackle him playfully, so he needs both hands for wrestling.

It's also fine to bring the limit without humor. Be gentle but firm, and try to keep your emotional heat at the level you'd use to fold a dishtowel. Hold his pinching fingers; lightly hold his wrist to keep him from hitting; if he wants to bite, put the heel of your hand against his forehead so he can strain toward you, but can't sink his teeth into you. Then listen, so he can cry, laugh, or tremble, and heal. There's no need to blame him for signaling that he's scared. No need to force him to apologize. Simply stop the off-track behavior, and connect with warmth. "I am going to keep things safe," is all he needs to hear. He'll know how to find the troublesome feelings and work them through.

And when you can't think of a calm way to limit your child's fear-driven behavior, it's time to find a good listener for yourself. Children know, subliminally, when their parents' minds are relaxed enough to handle the deep work on fear they need to do. It often happens that shortly after a parent has cried or laughed heartily about *their* feelings, their child will find a small excuse to have a much-needed release of fear. So don't forget your Listening Partnership! When conditions are right, your child will finally dive deep to release his bigger fears. Your opportunity to help him heal will arrive.

Step 6. Staylisten. Most children release heavy fear when an unmet expectation, a tiny accident, or some other minor trigger sets off an extraordinary reaction. Suddenly, your child feels deeply threatened. As soon as you arrive, his limbic system senses the safety you bring, and his body goes out of control. Up comes the impulse to run away or to attack. He'll scream. He may writhe. He will sweat. He may tremble or arch his back. He may battle with you or with unseen forces, screaming all the while. It will look like his mind has left him, and in a way, that's true. Terror infuses his entire being.

This highly charged process can transform your child's life—and yours. But it's challenging. His feelings throw him onto a kind of haunted-house ride through the worst experiences he's ever had. Yet he is fully aware of your presence. In fact, your presence is what enables him to try and shuck this terrible fear. You stand steady against his worst feelings: your willingness to listen heightens his sense of terror. He thrashes, and you pour in your confidence that he is safe and whatever frightened him is over. Your calm presence is all that's needed to shepherd him through this release of held emotion. Your confidence that he's OK will shift how he thinks and feels afterward. Here's why:

Even if, in the original fearful incident, your child didn't suffer harm, the emotion of fear obliterated any sense of security. Now, as he writhes, battles, sweats, and trembles, *that fear finally has an outlet.* It leaps out from his emotional memory and finally runs its course. His emotional bad dream will be over when that fear reaction is finally spent. The impression of your protection will seep into the space that the fear occupied in his memory. Then the data from the frightening incident, emotion-free at last, can be processed.

For example, if your child is working on his experience as a newborn in intensive care, where he lay alone and sick, and was pricked many times a day, the impression he was left with might be, "I am alone in the world, and I never know when someone will try to hurt me. I couldn't get them to stop!" It may have made him cautious and slow to warm, or persistently aggressive. If he flips into a full-out terror response after the doctor gives him a shot at his two-year checkup, he'll get the chance to fight, kick, and howl. This is something his system has been itching to do since his first week of life. If you can anchor him through this intensely physical reaction, his perceptions will change. His behavior will reflect an attitude more like, "Oh, yeah, I was in the incubator, and they pricked me a lot, but I did well. I had help. I got out!" When you support him through the emotional replay of those times, his sense of helplessness and victimization will be replaced by a stronger sense of his own resilience. He will have absorbed the rock-solid support you gave him.

Keeping your perspective through one of these healing episodes is difficult, but it can be done—thousands of parents Staylisten to their children's big fears on a regular basis, and see their children grow in confidence and wisdom as a result.

Here are some basic things to remember while your child is releasing fear.

- **Don't try to talk sense into your child**. His mind has switched into emotion-release mode. Let him blow. He needs your caring, and a tone that says, "I've got your back," to help him banish his fears.

- **Settle in.** Fear does not release quickly. The healing power of your presence will move your child forward, saving you lots of frustration in the days and years to come.

- **Come closer.** How close depends on the situation and your state of mind. If your child is crying and screaming, but he's safe where he is, it's often best not to swoop in. To a child wracked with fear, abrupt external changes feel overwhelming. Try moving closer slowly. Rely on eye contact and the tone of your voice to reassure your child as you approach. You might want to get down on one knee and hold out your arms to welcome him. In response, he may scream and tremble, perhaps jump up and down, or throw himself on the bed or floor. The more calm and reassuring you are, the more intensely he can feel the fear he's working through. You can say something like, "I'm right here. Come into my arms if you want," or, "You're safe. That sound was thunder. It won't hurt you."

- **Slow your movements way down.** Your child needs your full attention during these vulnerable moments. Don't get wrapped up in things like wiping his nose, apologizing to other parents, or whisking him off to another location. Focus on *him*. Let snot fly. If you can, listen to him right where he is for at least five minutes before you move him to a more sheltered spot. This will let him know that he is your sole concern.

- **Tell your child what you plan to do before you do it.** While feelings engulf him, everything will feel like too much. So gently let him know what's going to happen before you make any change. Perhaps you're Staylistening to your child outside as the sun beats down. Tell him that you want to move to the shade, to listen there. If this intensifies his feelings, listen. Then propose moving again, and let another wave of feeling run through him. This "propose, listen, propose again" process allows each suggestion to become a pretext for shedding the same gripping fear.

- **Point your child's attention gently toward the thing he fears.** He won't want to look at or approach the person or situation he fears, so create a gentle counterpoint. "Amy is here, and she's going to take care of you. Want to take a peek at Amy?" Give him time to thrash; then suggest the next small step. "I'm going to put your foot in Amy's lap. There we go." After another ten or fifteen minutes of emotional work, you can go to, "Sweetie, Amy is a good person to be with. I'm going to put both your feet in her lap." It might take a whole hour of fear work before he can allow his feet to rest in Amy's lap, but excellent work is being done safely and slowly. Several Staylistening episodes later, if Amy stays warmly welcoming, he will be able to go off to play with her, and show more confidence in other situations as well.

- **It may help to embrace your child loosely while he's working on fear.** Holding him says, "I'm with you all the way through this." But in embracing him, you run the risk of overwhelming his system with input while he's struggling with his worst fears. You also chance being visited by your own fears. So if you've embraced your child and you feel you need to check how things are going partway through some fear work, let him go, so he can reset the interaction between you. Keep paying attention. Approach slowly, with the message, "I'd love to get a little closer when you're ready." If he's glum and withdrawn, you can hold out your hand, so he can choose whether to stop working on fear and reconnect with you, or start work again by running away or showing some fight.

In this unusual story, a mother tells how her son explained his own fear work when passersby became concerned:

———◇———

Two summers ago, we were at a county fair in Oregon and my then three-year-old fell apart over something. I was sitting on a bench cradling him in my lap and he was screaming something like, "Stop it, Mommy, I need you to stop!" When I next looked up, a crowd of onlookers had gathered to watch us. A security guard approached. The guard ignored me completely and asked my son whether he was OK. It was really uncomfortable for me. The amazing thing was that my son gulped back his tears, sat up, and said something like, "I'm feeling sad but my mommy's helping me and I'm not done crying yet." I hadn't realized that he was so conscious of what was going on.

———◇———

- **Reassure your child that he's safe.** One way to do that is to remind him of your caring and protection with a short sentence every minute or so. Here are some reassurances that highlight your awareness of his terror, as well as the safety of the real situation:

  "I know this is hard."
  "You're a good strong boy (or girl). You get to fight."
  "I'm keeping you safe. I'm watching over you every minute."
  "Whatever scared you is over. It's not going to happen again."
  "You made it. You were strong, and you made it."

- **If he's in a safe place, you can allow your child to run away if his instinct to flee is triggered.** But for him to finish the work he began, he needs to feel your presence. So if you've got the confidence and warmth it takes to support him, follow him calmly. Approach him little by little. Once you're close enough that his crying and trembling start again, stay there, moving closer little by little, and letting him fight you if he must. Outdoors, catch your child quickly if safety is a concern.

- **Keep both of you safe if his instinct to fight is triggered.** He can't track your safety when he's gripped by fear. So don't say, "Now, no kicking!" or "Honey, please don't scratch me, that hurts." He, like other mammals, is built to kick and claw when he feels threatened. It's your job to parry the blows.

  Let me be clear: Any child who tries to hurt himself or someone else is in the throes of fear, and is *asking you* to gently but effectively keep him from doing harm. So you may need to corral him so that he's got room to fight but can't harm his little brother or the friend he's mad at. Let him use his strength, but offer the resistance needed to keep yourself safe. For example, if he's threatening to throw a block or toy, slowly pry it away, saying, "I need to keep us safe." If he's hitting with his fists, brace his arms so he can try to hit, but can't land powerful blows.

- **When your child panics, he is at the point of deepest healing.** Your steady support has brought him to a feeling of immediate crisis. He'll feel like he's *dying* of thirst, or that he *has* to go to bed, or he needs to see his daddy *right this minute*. His eyes will be wide with fear, and his whole body will vibrate with urgency. As far as he can tell, his survival hinges on you *doing* something about his fear. Needless to say, Staylistening through this stage is tricky!

If you hop up and try to ease his fear—say, get him the water he begs for, or let him run to his bed—the healing episode will be over in a flash. He will have gained from the work you helped him do, but to heal completely, he needs your confidence all the way through that feeling of great peril. But don't worry. He'll give you another chance to help him later on!

Here are some ways to respond when healing gets to this powerful stage:

"I'm so hot! I'm burning up—take off my shirt!"
"I see, son. I'll blow on your tummy. Your body can handle the heat."

"I can't breathe!
"I'll make sure you can breathe. I'm watching every breath."

"I'm choking!"
"I won't let you choke. Your body knows just what to do."

"I need to be in my bed! I've got to *sleep*! I want to go there *now*!"
"You're safe here in my arms. You can sleep here if you want to."

When you hang in with a child through this most intense part of offloading fear, you'll often see a pronounced change in his behavior. One two-year-old I met at a play event in a park clung miserably to her mommy for a good twenty minutes while the other children played. She couldn't look at anyone, much less walk anywhere by herself, though she knew most of the families there. Finally, I knelt down, touched her shoulder, and said hello. She began to cry. Her mommy sat down and cradled her, and I said, "Hello, Sandra," every now and then. She worked herself into shedding fear by arching, screaming, and sweating. She was an armful for quite a while.

Then she began making choking sounds as she cried. As her mommy held her, I told her things like, "We're right here. You're safe." And, "This won't go on forever. We'll make sure of that." She was breathing well, but she coughed, writhed, and cried for another good while. Then she calmed, sat up, and contemplated her surroundings. I touched her hand, and she touched mine. We exchanged looks. She looked at her mommy. Finally, she got up and walked over to the swings all by herself, without looking back once for her mommy. As she walked, she gave a little hop. And she hopped several times more. It was as if a huge weight had been lifted from her shoulders. The playground was her oyster for the rest of the afternoon. Her mom later told me that she'd been born with the cord wrapped around her neck twice. When she heard those choking sounds, she felt she knew instantly what fear her child was re-experiencing.

Last, and perhaps most vital, is this proviso:

- **Stop Staylistening the minute you become upset.** Staylistening to a child who is working through heavy fear is challenging! Your own feelings will be triggered. You might flare in anger, become frightened yourself, or suddenly feel a tsunami of resentment. Or another grownup might come along and become upset. In any case, Staylistening is a healing tool only when you can think and care. So when you become upset, get up immediately, tell your child you can't listen any longer, and leave his side. It won't be pretty, but it's necessary. If you've got a Listening Partner, set up a time soon to work on the behavior or feeling that threw you off balance. Your child will present his fears another day, using another pretext, and you'll get a little farther, having shed some of the hurt attached to the button he pushed. This is how we make progress as listeners.

If your child was able to work all the way through the chunk of fear that grabbed him, he'll relax. His body may sink into yours for a good, deep cry. Or he'll calm down, touch your face gently, notice the frost on the window, or ask where the cat went. He won't want to talk about the work he just completed. He'll want to enjoy himself and you again. In the next hours and days, you may detect signs of relief: more affection; more eye contact; better sleep; more adventurousness; easygoing play; more sharing of thoughts and needs; more laughter; or increased tolerance for change.

However, if he seems distant and less trusting after working on fear, you may have missed some of his cues, or communicated some of your own tension as you tried to support him. Back off, and go back to the Listening Tools that build trust and your capacity to listen: Special Time, Playlistening, and Listening Partnerships. It is challenging to help children work through their fear and aggression, but don't give up! Learning to help your child heal from fear is well worth the effort.

CLEARING FEARS AWAY MAY REQUIRE AN EMOTIONAL PROJECT

How long it will take your child to overcome his fear depends upon how scared he is and how safe he feels to show you his fears. If your child has been carrying a load of fear for a while, it may take a couple of months of focus on Special Time and Playlistening before he can begin work on his deeper fears. Then, working through terror may take many rounds of Setting Limits and Staylistening. But each time you use a Listening Tool, you'll learn new things. I call this work over time an "emotional project," and Chapter 8 will help you think about what to plan for.

As you support your child through his work on fear, you'll want to make sure *you're* being supported well, too. You'll need your own outlet for the wide spectrum of feelings you'll experience as he goes through this moving healing process with your help. When you get listening support, too, you will grow right alongside your child. You'll facilitate the change you long for, and you'll relish the results.

THERE'S NO SINGLE FORMULA

There is no one formula for anchoring a child who is working through fear. However, our suggestions have been tested over time. You may benefit from reading about the experiences of other parents in this chapter, on our online Blog, in our online Discussion Group, or on our Facebook page. Whichever strategies you embrace, we encourage you to use Special Time, Playlistening, and your own Listening Partnerships often. Using these connective tools will help to keep a balance between fun, hard work, and focused, caring attention on you.

....

In the following sections, you'll learn how parents have used Hand in Hand tools to help their children overcome some common childhood fears. These parents are regular moms and dads, just like you. They work on their own feelings in Listening Partnerships, do Special Time and Playlistening regularly, set limits when it makes sense, and Staylisten to their children's upsets. I think you'll enjoy their stories and be inspired to try Listening Tools within your own family.

——————— ◆◆◆ ———————

Fear: Nail Biting And Thumb Sucking

THE NAIL-EATING ALLIGATOR

TOOLS: 🐊 PLAYLISTENING   ⏳ SPECIAL TIME   👂 LISTENING PARTNERSHIP

My oldest son has always been a pretty intense guy. I don't mean this in a negative way; he feels everything to the extreme, including joy. From the time he was very young, I noticed that he leans toward what I consider compulsively soothing behaviors. When he was about three-and-a-half I noticed that he had begun biting his nails. A lot. It drove me crazy! I tried everything I could think of to get him to stop. I cut his nails shorter and shorter, but he just bit them more, sometimes to the point of bleeding. I became almost frantic, and, though I tried not to show it to him, he still sensed it. It was as if the more upset I got about this nervous behavior, the more wound up he became, and the more he bit his nails. It was a deeply frustrating cycle.

I eventually realized that I needed to re-evaluate my approach. I soon realized that what made this so upsetting for me was the fact that I had been an avid nail biter in my childhood, and that my own feelings were probably getting triggered. I began to get listening time. With the attention of a warm, caring friend, I was able to look at how frightened and unsafe I felt as a child, how biting my nails became an outward sign of that fear, and how horrible it was to be blamed and shamed for something I couldn't help. I raged about needing help and not getting it. Mostly I needed to cry about how badly I wanted my son's experience to be different than my own, and how I saw his nail biting as a sign that I was failing.

Over many weeks, my reaction to his nail biting lessened. I tried to keep his nails relatively short, but that didn't affect his behavior. I decided to stop trying to prevent the biting for a while. It was too upsetting to me, and I usually ended up making the situation worse. But eventually my mind cleared a bit, I gathered ideas from trusted allies, and I made a plan. To counter his fear, we emphasized more physical play in our house, all day long. I tried to get Special Time in as often as possible, and even during "regular" play I worked to follow his lead more often. I prepared myself for his big upsets, and stayed as warm and present with him as I could when they happened, listening and keeping us safe. And through it all, I kept getting support for myself, mainly through listening time.

The nail biting was one part in a bigger puzzle that I was trying to piece together, and the picture became clear: my son was working on fear. Slowly, over the course of several months, things began to shift. He began playing new and different games with other children and adults, and became more flexible in everyday life. His upsets were less frequent and intense. Then one day, I noticed that some of his nails were growing out.

"Hey," I said enthusiastically, "it's time to cut your fingernails!" He yelled and ran away, saying that he wasn't going to let me. At first I was insistent, but I sensed that this brought up too many bad feelings for him, so a new approach to nail cutting was needed. I came up with an idea to try and make it fun.

I went into our bathroom and got out the nail clippers. "I am so hungry!" I called out in a deep voice, "If only there were something I could eat." My son peeked into the bathroom with a little smile on his face, curious. I held the nail clippers and squeezed them open and shut, making them "talk," turning them toward my own hand and saying, "Ooh, can I eat those? They look delicious!"

"Is that an alligator?" he asked, smiling and knowing full well what our nail clippers looked like.

"Yes," I answered. "It's a rare, nail-eating alligator."

"And I'm hungry!" I made the clippers say.

"Eat Mama's nails," my son said. I continued the game, cutting all of my fingernails while making happy eating sounds, while he laughed. Then I turned the clippers around to face me and had them say, "But I'm still hungry!" I wasn't sure if this little bit of play had been enough to help him feel safe, but I was pleasantly surprised.

Without any hesitation, my son came into the bathroom and said, "Here, you can have my nails," and put his hand in my lap. I made the "nail alligator" noisily munch each of his nails, telling him how delicious they were, until he had tasted each one and was full. I told my son that we would need to feed the alligator once a week, and set a timer on my phone to help me remember.

There has been almost no resistance to nail cutting since then, and when I cut his nails once a week he rarely bites them. More importantly, I can now see his nail biting for what it is: a sign that he is feeling unsafe. When I notice that he has been biting again, I don't say anything about it, but instead give him extra warmth, extra connection, extra play, and extra listening. Without fail, his nails start to grow again. I now feel lucky to have such a visible barometer as to how my son is feeling inside, and I'm proud to have figured out a way to respond.

HOW IT WORKED

Often our children's behaviors trigger upset in us, making it hard for us to help them overcome their struggles. This mom used her Listening Partnerships to let go of the upset she had held since her youth. Then, she could come up with creative ideas for how to help her son with what she came to understand were expressions of fear. She added lots of physical play and Special Time into their daily lives, then concocted the "nail-eating alligator game" and Playlistened her way to happy nail cutting. This was not a quick fix for her son's nail biting, but a change in strategy that allowed mom and son to connect deeply, get rid of old yucky feelings, and shift their behaviors over time.

———◇———

HABITUAL THUMB SUCKING

TOOL: PLAYLISTENING

Just before his fifth birthday, my son started sucking his thumb. I noticed he would sometimes go sit by himself in front of the TV and start sucking his thumb.

I decided that rather than abruptly turning the television off, I would try some Playlistening. I got in close to him and started nuzzling him in his ear. Initially, he pushed me away. Then I told him I had a hundred kisses for him. He took his thumb out of his mouth and said, "No, Mommy, not kisses!" He laughed and laughed as I proceeded to give him little kisses all over. Then he jumped up and, in an effort to divert my affection, invited me and his little sister to come into his room to play. At first, his rejection of my idea felt hard. I have had trouble connecting with him in the past, before I started using Listening Tools. But this time, my desire to connect with my son was stronger than my own feelings, and I continued to offer more kisses as we romped off to his room. And he kept laughing.

That day, I found that my connection with my son is stronger than I thought. Once I showed him I wasn't going away and was ready to play with him, he came back into his playful self. It seems that he switches off with thumb sucking when he feels disconnected from me, but when that connection is offered to him again, he can go back to feeling playful quickly.

That day, my son, daughter, and I went off to play in my son's room. Later that afternoon, I needed to go prepare dinner and my son came to help me rather than going back to watching television and sucking his thumb, which was his usual habit.

HOW IT WORKED

Habitual thumb sucking is just one form of self-soothing, which children use to numb their unpleasant feelings. This mom used a cuddly Playlistening game to help her son laugh away his fear and reconnect with her. Once connected, he was able to think creatively about ideas for play, and even voluntarily participate in making dinner.

———◇———

THUMB SUCKING AND A DAUGHTER'S INSIGHT

TOOL: ● STAYLISTENING

We have raised our six-year-old daughter with Hand in Hand Parenting ideas. One of my daughter's friends sucks his thumb often. Suddenly, she began experimenting with sucking her thumb. She had never sucked her thumb as an infant. For a few days, she went around at home with her thumb in her mouth a lot.

I asked her, finally, why she was sucking her thumb. She told me, "George does it. I do it to keep my feelings in. If I don't do it, my feelings will come right out my mouth."

I went over to her, and touched the hand of the thumb she was sucking. I said, "You can let your feelings out." She burst into tears, and she sobbed long and hard. She didn't tell me what it was about. I listened. Then she stopped. It was over, and she was fine. All she said about it was, "My feelings are coming out of my body. All my feelings are coming out of my mouth."

She moved on. She hasn't sucked her thumb since. But once in awhile, she will tell me, "I'm feeling bad feelings inside." I usually get close and tell her, "You can let them out," and often she will say, "No, I don't want to right now. I want to read," or whatever she wants to do. So she doesn't always have to show her feelings, she just likes me to know that she notices them. She has this vivid perception that her feelings are inside her body, and that they come out of her mouth.

HOW IT WORKED

Sometimes parents new to Hand in Hand have the misconception that we want to make our children cry. In fact, we try not to come to our children with an agenda for how they should feel, or how they should release their feelings. Instead, like this mom did, we want to offer connection and opportunity for our children to let go of feelings that are gunking up their emotional system and preventing them from functioning at full capacity. We offer ourselves and see what happens. Here, Mom used physical connection (touching her daughter's thumb) and offered words that led to her daughter's flood gates opening. She didn't know what the tears were about, and didn't ask, as it didn't matter. What mattered was that her daughter felt better, and the thumb sucking ceased. That connection also led to her opening up to her mother about when she was feeling bad inside. She knew that she would always be met with the opportunity to let those feelings out if she wanted.

Fears Of Differences Between People

FEAR OF A PHYSICAL DIFFERENCE

TOOLS: SETTING LIMITS STAYLISTENING

A visitor came to our preschool one day, and one of the boys was clearly afraid of her. The other children who met her said hello, and went on to play. After he ran away from her, I went to him and asked him why, and he said, "She smells bad. I don't want to talk to her! She smells!"

She had been badly burned in a plane crash. Scars covered part of her face, her hands, and her arms, and a few of her fingers were missing. She certainly didn't smell, but we both surmised that he was frightened by her scars. He was certainly not the first person to react to her appearance with fear, and she understood how to listen to children's feelings. I asked her quickly if we could work together to help him connect with her. She agreed. He hadn't gone outside to play with the others; he was too scared to know what to do.

I put my arm around him, and our guest came over and knelt down about three feet away. I reassured him that he was safe with her. I told him her name, and she spoke gently to him. We both said little more, supporting him as warmly as we could, so he might have a chance to feel the emotions bubbling up. He cried, saying that he wanted his mommy. We listened and told him his mom would come and pick him up at the regular time, and that he could have a good morning here. He cried for about fifteen minutes straight, mostly saying that he wanted to go home.

When his crying slowed down, I gave him a few simple explanations about our guest's scars. I told him that she had been burned in an accident, and that her burns were now healed. I asked her if I could touch her hand where the scars were, and she agreed. She came a little closer, and I touched her hand, fingering her scars. I said that her hands might look different, but that her burns didn't hurt any more. The skin had healed. She told him he could ask her anything he wanted to know. He finished crying, and didn't have any questions.

He seemed unafraid of her at last. She asked him if he would take her outside to see what the other children were doing, and the two of them walked together to the play yard, chatting.

HOW IT WORKED

Helping our children overcome fears about physical differences can be a challenge for parents, as we often carry related fears ourselves. Luckily, not only was there a confident teacher available, but the woman with the burns was able to help as well. This boy's feelings of safety in the arms of a trusted caregiver, along with the presence of the woman whose scars frightened him, allowed him to cry hard. When he had released enough of his fear, he could hear his teacher's explanation, and then head outside, unafraid, with this guest. These were ideal circumstances, but they show how you can foster healing by supporting your child as he faces his feelings of fear, and then offering accurate, age-appropriate information.

———◇———

RESOLVING CONFUSION ABOUT SKIN COLOR

TOOLS: 🚦 SETTING LIMITS   🌀 STAYLISTENING

In the preschool where I worked, there was a little girl, Deanna, who had a hard time making friends with a dark-skinned classmate, Beth. Deanna was two years old. Deanna would say to Beth, "You are dirty, I don't want to be your friend," and other things like that. When I saw that this comment was not just a one-time thing, I decided to try to help Deanna with her feelings. So when she said this again one morning, I came over and got down at her level. I said, as gently as I could, "I see you are having a hard time. What's happening here?"

Deanna said, "I don't want to be her friend, she's too dark." I replied, "You have this idea that she didn't wash her hands?"

"Yes," she replied.

So I said, "Let's ask her if she washed her hands."

I asked Beth, who said, "Yes, I washed my hands."

I then told Beth, "You can go and play with the other children. I'll stay with Deanna right now." And I brought Deanna into my lap, put my arms around her and said, "I see this is hard for you. When you feel someone is dirty, then you don't want to play with them. Tell me more about that." She started crying, and she looked like she felt threatened by my attention. So I said, "I'm not mad at you, Deanna. I just want to understand. I want to see how we can all play together, without having to worry about anyone being dirty." She cried for a while.

When she stopped crying, I opened my arms, but she didn't leave my lap. I put my arms around her again, and I asked her to tell me more about her feeling that the other child was dirty. As she talked, she shifted from saying that Beth was "too dirty," to "too dark." She didn't mind me holding her. She cried some more about another child in the class being "too dark," stopped, then cried again. Then her crying stopped. She cycled through tears on this subject several times. In the end, she melted into me.

She asked, "Are you mad at me?"

"No," I said, "I just want to understand you."

Then she told me, "I want to be really, really white, but I'm not really, really white." She cried hard. I listened.

After awhile, I said, "It's hard sometimes, when you have this idea that dark is dirty. Do you want to check my dark skin for dirt?" We wiped part of my forearm, checking for dirt. She saw that I was dark, but I wasn't dirty. She went and grabbed the dark-skinned dolls, and brought them over to me. We checked them for dirt, and determined that they were not dirty either.

I needed to get back to the group, so I said, "I enjoyed being with you, but I need to go help with lunch. Let's play one game first. Can we invite Beth?"

"I don't know," she replied.

I said, "Let me go first, and you can decide." I went and sat next to Beth, and said, "Can I sit next to you? I'm the mommy waiting for the bus!" Beth and I pretended we were at the bus stop, and Deanna came over to sit with us. Beth made room for her. Deanna hesitated, but she finally sat next to Beth. Deanna and I held hands, then I reached to hold hands with Beth, and together, we got up and ran to another bench, laughing.

After that, lunch was fun, and Deanna was able to pass food around to other children, which she had not done before. She had not wanted to sit next to others and had never eaten much at lunchtime. But after our good time together, she passed the food bowls to others, and ate well. From this day on, Deanna was eager to play with the other children, Beth included.

HOW IT WORKED

This two-year-old had somehow gotten the impression that dark skin was dirty. The teacher realized that the girl was stuck in her feelings and hurting other children, so she brought a limit. Slowly and with a warm heart, she moved in close and asked what was going on. And she assured her that she wasn't angry. After a few minutes, the girl began to cry. At first she cried about other kids in the class being too dark. Then she cried about wanting to have lighter skin herself. When the child had finished crying, the teacher gently offered experience to counter her mistaken impression. Soon they were playing and laughing together.

In the bigger picture, the tears she shed made her more relaxed around the other children in many ways. Racism sits heavy on the hearts of our children of all colors, and assisting them in shedding their fears and reaching for closeness with people of all colors is a vital part of parenting.

———◇———

SHEDDING DEEP FEELINGS ABOUT SKIN COLOR

TOOLS: 🚦 SETTING LIMITS　　◉ STAYLISTENING

My daughter, who is almost four, has had a fear of black people since she was a baby. I first became aware of this when she was about nine months old. My black African hairdresser Nyala walked into the house, and my daughter started screaming. I was surprised, as this wasn't a normal reaction, and I didn't realize it had anything to do with her color at the time. It became obvious later on, when she started to cry every time she saw a black person, including a friend's boyfriend, who we happened to go on vacation with. My daughter was wary of him the whole time. By the time she got to the age of three and was still terrified every time Nyala came to cut our hair, I realized it was time to take some action. We live in a town where few black people live, so there weren't many other opportunities to work on this issue.

I suggested to my daughter that the next time my hairdresser came to cut my hair she could also cut her hair. She said, "OK, maybe," but she also said that she didn't like Nyala, which she has said many times before.

My daughter was fine until the moment the doorbell rang, and then she hid in the corner of the room and cowered in fear. I went to let Nyala in, while my husband stayed close to our daughter. When my daughter heard her enter the house, she started to cry and immediately went upstairs to get away. I asked my husband to keep proposing an expectation, such as "Are you ready to go downstairs and say hello to Nyala now?" and then to listen to her feelings, but not to force her to come down.

While I was having my hair cut downstairs, I could hear my daughter screaming and crying on and off. When my hair had been cut, I went upstairs to see her. She had spent the whole time crying in her daddy's arms with her daddy encouraging her to come downstairs and say hello. He was listening to her cry and reassuring her that she was safe, and that Nyala is a lovely person, and nothing bad was going to happen.

I asked my daughter if she wanted to come down and say goodbye to Nyala because she was about to leave. She said she wanted to, and came downstairs. Nyala was friendly and playful with her. Although my daughter was trembling a little, she interacted with Nyala, and it was very sweet. They were talking about what my daughter was going to be cooking in her play kitchen, and she told Nyala she would make her some food next time she came. They also talked about the new doll she'd gotten for Christmas. This went on for a few minutes before Nyala had to leave. Once she had left, my daughter said that she liked Nyala. Then she said that she loved Nyala, and she began to plan for the next time she came over. She said she would stay downstairs the whole time Nyala was here, and play with her.

I was so happy, because this had been an issue for so long. Staylistening allowed my daughter to move through her fear and feel brave enough to come downstairs and interact with someone she had been very scared of for a long time. My daughter was totally elated after this incident and felt great!

HOW IT WORKED

This mom didn't expect her daughter to "grow out of" this particular fear, which had only gotten stronger over time. Instead, she set out the expectation that her daughter could interact with her hairdresser, but she knew that feelings would have to roll off first. When Nyala arrived, Mom asked her husband to Staylisten without forcing any particular behavior on his daughter. He used, "Propose, and listen; propose, and listen," and accepted the crying and trembling their daughter needed to do. Fortunately, by the end of the haircut, her child had worked through enough fear to interact with Nyala. Mom had previously suggested that her daughter might get a haircut, too, but she didn't push that agenda; she accepted what her daughter could manage. Nyala seemed to understand that this child had fears to overcome, and that she could play a positive role by befriending her.

If her child hadn't been ready to interact with Nyala, this mom could have allowed her daughter to stay upstairs, and simply thanked her for thinking about coming down. She would then have set up another haircut, and another Staylistening opportunity, until the necessary fear work had been done. But one chance had been enough, and her daughter was elated to have overcome her fears. It's so encouraging to know that fears like this child's can be countered with attention, respect, and the understanding that fears can dissolve with listening.

Fear: Performance Anxiety

WHEN YOUR CHILD WANTS TO QUIT AN ACTIVITY HE LOVES

TOOLS: 🚦 SETTING LIMITS   ✺ STAYLISTENING

One of my boys is an avid baseball fan, and, thanks to his grandmother, has been from birth. From as early as I can remember, he's had a baseball in his hand. I can't recall a time when he didn't have a head full of statistics on players and teams, and there is nary a day when I am not asked to play, talk, or otherwise get excited about the sport.

When he was really little, we'd just play ball together in the park. As he got older, there was t-ball, and then Little League. Each year he was a star, by far the most skilled player on the team. Then, when he was about eight or nine, Little League required each child to participate in tryouts. The point of the tryouts was to distribute the children evenly across teams to ensure a fun season, where one team didn't dominate. Every child would be chosen for a team.

When I told my son that baseball season was around the corner, and tryouts were coming soon, I was stunned by his response. "I'm not playing baseball this year. I hate baseball! Why did you sign me up without asking?" At first I was baffled, but then I put two and two together and figured out that he must be nervous about tryouts. I explained to him that the atmosphere would be a relaxed one, and that everyone would be chosen, but his insistence on quitting remained.

I felt confused. On the one hand I knew my son lived, ate, and breathed baseball. There was nothing in life he loved playing more. Yet on the other hand, I wanted to respect his wishes. And ultimately, I wanted to teach him that he could make decisions for himself. I thought about my own life, and the times I had given up on dreams because I was scared of failing or making a fool of myself. I realized that respecting his demand to quit would be doing him a disservice. I would be teaching him to give in to fear rather than teaching him how to move through his fears. So I decided that, come hell or high water, we were going to tryouts. If, after tryouts, he wanted to quit baseball, we could talk about it, but I wasn't going to let him give up on something he loved because he was scared.

On the morning of tryouts, I woke my son at six o'clock. That gave us four hours to get to the dugout.

"Wake up, babe. Baseball tryouts this morning!" I said with excitement. He immediately started to argue.

"No! I hate baseball! I told you I'm not playing this year!"

I Staylistened my way through his upset. When he was done crying, I suggested he get dressed, and he begrudgingly put on his baseball pants and jersey. But when he got to the socks, his fears popped up again.

"These socks bother me," he cried, and again I Staylistened.

After several of these Staylistening sessions with him crying and insisting that he hated baseball and wasn't going to tryouts, and me continuing to listen calmly and assuring him that we were going and that he could do it, we made it to the car.

But when we parked at the field, he refused to get out of the car. Again I held the limit. "Sweetie, you are going to go try out. I know you can do it."

He cried and cried. He held the door shut so that I couldn't open it. He screamed that I was a horrible mother. At a certain point a man walked by with his son and asked if my son was OK. I thanked him, assured him that he was, and told him that he really loved baseball, but was feeling scared about the tryouts. The man stopped, came over to my son, and told him that he remembered feeling exactly the same when he was a boy. My son's eyes lit up.

Eventually, my son agreed to go to tryouts if I would stand at particular points around the field, near each station where he would either bat, pitch, field, or play first base. I agreed to do exactly as he asked.

Together, we headed to the field, and checked in right in time for his turn. I followed the directions he'd given me, and we moved in synch from batting to pitching to outfield to first base. Before we knew it, it was over, and we were walking back to the car together. I asked him how it went, and he said, "Great! I think I'm going to get on the Yankees!" and he looked at me with a big smile.

My son is now thirteen, still passionate about baseball, and getting ready to play high school ball next year. I am so thankful that I had the tools to help him through his fear, so that he didn't have to give up on something he loves!

HOW IT WORKED

One of the most common hesitations I hear from parents about setting limits is that they want to respect their children's desires. But reality is much more nuanced, and we offer our children a gift when, instead of immediately complying with their requests, we take a moment to consider what feelings might be driving them. There is a difference between giving in to our children's feelings and respecting their choices. When we say "yes" to a request that is based in fear, we hold them back in life, keeping them small. And fear can easily masquerade as "I just don't want to." You have to look closely!

This mother paused to consider her son's request to quit baseball, his biggest love. She thought about her son's wishes, and also about her experience as a child. In the end, she decided that if her son really wanted to quit, they could discuss it. But first, she would help him work through his fear of tryouts, so that he could communicate from a place of thinking and feeling connected.

There was a tryout start time, so planning in advance was key to success. Mom woke her son early, anticipating his need for lots of limits and lots of Stay-listening before finally stepping onto the field. And she was right! But her clear limits and loving ear paid off. After shedding lots of tears, her boy was able to step out onto the field and do his best. And as we often see after lots of Staylistening, her son felt pleased with himself, and got on with his day as if those four hours of tryout preperation had never happened. And quit baseball? No way! He wanted to be on the Yankees!

THE SCHOOL PLAY

TOOLS: STAYLISTENING 　 PLAYLISTENING

When he was about nine, my son was given a part in a school play. He had about six weeks to prepare, and it was clear the whole time that he was not eager. He didn't want to be in it, yet he didn't turn back when he had a chance to. Several times, I mentioned preparing for the play, but he would change the subject. I would say to myself, "Well, we'll just deal with it later."

Finally, it was the day before the play and he was really having a fit. He was crying and saying he did not want to be it. To him, it felt like a life and death situation. I listened to him cry, and when he seemed (unhappily) finished, he still wanted me to give him a way out of performing. I said, "Well, let me think about it," and we went to bed.

The next morning his feelings came up again, and I still could not think about how to help him. Then, I got inspired somehow, picked up a toy microphone and began to Playlisten. I pretended that we were on TV and I was a newscaster. I "interviewed" imaginary classmates about the play, pretending that I expected the kids to say how wonderful the play was for everyone to hear. As I interviewed the first imaginary classmate, I was also the voice of the classmate. I had that classmate say, "Oh, it was the most disgusting, awful, horrible, stinky play!" He laughed so hard! Then I went to the next classmate and "they" would say something even more outrageous. In the voice of his classmates, I said all the horrible words I could think of—every classmate had something really bad to say about the play. He laughed and laughed. When I was ready to stop, he asked me to interview some more people about it. I did. Then, he picked up his lunch box, went to school, and did the play. He was still really shy, but he didn't have any problem getting up there!

HOW IT WORKED

Most of us are familiar with walking that tightrope between wanting to step out on stage, and feeling too afraid to do so. After Staylistening with his son, which was part of the solution, this dad came up with a brilliant Playlistening game to restore his son's balance and confidence. By playing with the concept of the whole performance being a flaming failure, he helped his son laugh hard about his fears. Dad created just what his son needed in order to shed enough fear to do the school play.

WHEN YOUR CHILD SUDDENLY CHANGES HER MIND

TOOL:  STAYLISTENING

The evening before my seven-year-old daughter had her audition for a community theater production, she asked me, "Why do I have to go to the audition?" I reminded her that she had enjoyed her theater experience the previous year and had wanted to sign up for this year's show. Her tone became more strident: "I want to quit! I didn't really want to do it!" Ah! I recalled how scary the audition had been for her last year. So perhaps she needed me to listen closely. She spent twenty to thirty minutes growing ever more desperate and angry, shouting that I was forcing her to do something she no longer wanted to do and that I was not listening to her. I reassured her that while I knew it was challenging and scary, I was confident that, with her preparation and prior experience, she would do fine at her audition.

I must admit that when she burst into tears, I felt wobbly and wondered, "Maybe this is truly how she feels, and she's not just letting off anxiety. Maybe I should let her quit now." I decided to keep giving her warmth and closeness as she yelled about how mean I was being. I also decided that it is her life so she should make the decision.

Finally, she petered out and transitioned to something else. I felt the change in her energy, and we went about going to bed. I didn't discuss the outcome with her. I went to sleep wondering whether the next morning would bring more of the same and we'd end up canceling her audition.

From the moment she opened her eyes the next day she was all smiles. When it was time to drive to the audition, she immediately took her dad's hand and went to the car without one word of complaint. For the past month, she has been rehearsing most weekends, and her attitude is always cheerful and upbeat. Perhaps she will need more listening and connection as we approach the first show next month. I will be ready!

I am so grateful to Hand in Hand. Without the insight into how children's emotions work, I would have been much more likely to take her words at face value and let her drop out. It's hard to have your child accuse you of being insensitive! But with my training from Hand in Hand, I wasn't triggered by her outburst and I could give her the warmth and love she needed in order to release her feelings.

HOW IT WORKED

Though she was under fire, this mom thought carefully throughout her daughter's tirade. She listened and managed not to react. She made what might seem like contradictory decisions. She would keep listening, rather than cave in immediately to her daughter's demands; her daughter could ultimately decide what she wanted. Perhaps the wisest thing she did was to let her daughter drop the subject when she was finished crying. Most of us parents push hard to resolve an issue if we've had to devote our time to it. But a good cry can take some time to yield results. Mom let her daughter sleep on it, and in the morning the healing effect of her Staylistening was obvious. Fun and learning followed, yet Mom wisely knows that fear dissolves layer by layer, and another round of Staylistening may be needed as the performance draws near.

Fear Of Doctors And Medicine

SITTING THROUGH A DOCTOR'S APPOINTMENT

TOOL: ⏳ SPECIAL TIME

My two-and-a-half-year-old son had suffered many health problems requiring doctor visits, and at the doctor's office, he could not sit still. He was nervous, fearful, and whiny. It was very hard to get the information I needed from our doctors because my son was such a handful.

One day we had an important appointment with a new doctor. I had many questions, and knew I'd need to give her a thorough medical history of my son. I was nervous about how he would behave for this long visit. So I decided we'd do Special Time for thirty minutes, about an hour before the doctor's visit, to try to help him get through the appointment.

I set the timer and told him we could do anything he wanted. So he grabbed two stuffed animals and said, "Let's play with these, what should we do with them?" I asked if he wanted to pretend that the kangaroo was Dr. Jane and that she was going to examine the teddy bear. He was very receptive, so, I went through a whole exam with the two toys in detail. My son watched with curiosity and attention, then said, "Let's do it again." He grabbed a different stuffed animal and had me do the exam all over again.

After the fourth time, I asked if he wanted to find another animal to examine and he said, "No," and wandered over to his toy pile. He looked at me mischievously and said, "You know what I think we should do now, Mommy?" I said, "What?" And he said tentatively, "I think we should kill Doctor Jane." I enthusiastically replied, "That sounds like a great idea!" I saw an immediate transformation in his whole body. A huge smile enlivened his face. He stood taller. His chest puffed out. His movements were strong. His voice was powerful. He exclaimed, "Yeah! Yeah! That's what we should do; we should kill her! Let's kill her right now!" When I asked how we should kill her, he gleefully answered, "With the potato masher!"

He ran to the kitchen to get it. My husband was there and my son announced, "Daddy, we're killing Doctor Jane! Yup, that's what we're doing right now, with the potato masher!" I was so excited to see my son acting empowered now—a huge contrast to the frightened, panicky stance he took before and during all other doctor visits. I realized we had stumbled into a situation where my son was offloading his fears through getting to play the more powerful role over the doctor. Thankfully, my husband decided not to discourage or interrupt our play.

For the next fifteen minutes, my son enthusiastically mashed the doctor to death many times. After each mashing death, he confidently directed me to help tear her to pieces. He got out a pan to cook up all her pieces, and we pretended to eat her. With a powerful, energetic voice, he kept saying, "We're doing this! We're mashing up Doctor Jane! Yup, now we're cooking her! Now we're totally eating her!" When the timer went off, my son agreed to wrap up the activity, cooked the doctor and ate her one more time, and then was ready for his real lunch. We ate calmly and got ready to go.

I took the kangaroo toy that had been the "doctor" with us. I heard him telling the kangaroo that he had killed her, and that she wasn't the doctor any more. Then he added, "You know Mommy, this isn't really Doctor Jane. It's just a kangaroo toy." I said, "Oh yes, that's true" and smiled.

At the doctor's office, for the first time in his life, my son was thoroughly calm for a full hour—no wiggles, no whining, no interrupting me while I spoke to the doctor. He played quietly with the toys she had there. He was obviously still aware of us, because he asked a few questions politely when he heard us talking about his diet. Because of his calmness throughout that first hour, I easily got all the information I needed from the doctor.

And then, in the exam, he was completely calm and cheerful, too. In fact, he smiled at the doctor and chatted with her.

It was such an extraordinary transformation, and it lasted through the whole visit! I was proud of him, and proud of both of us. Following his enthusiasm and encouraging his power to kill and eat the doctor toy allowed him to work on fears and helplessness that he'd been carrying around doctor visits in general. He knew what he needed to overcome and used that playtime to empower himself so he could relax into this doctor visit.

HOW IT WORKED

Contrary to popular belief, acting out aggression in the company of an attentive, loving adult does not encourage a future criminal. Actually, offering a child the protected space to act out his aggressions playfully helps to eradicate fear that, left to simmer, can drive aggressive behaviors. Using Special Time as a tool, this mom opened the door for her son to create a game that allowed him to shed feelings of helplessness and, for once, take on the powerful role in the doctor-patient relationship. After just a half hour of "kill the doctor," this boy was able to sit through an hour-long doctor's appointment and cooperate fully during his own examination.

---◇---

SHOTS

TOOLS: PLAYLISTENING   STAYLISTENING

I took my four kids to get flu shots at a walk-in clinic. While waiting, my five-year-old asked many questions about the shot and how painful it would be. I demonstrated how it might feel with a light pinch on his arm. He pinched me back playfully, and I reacted with an exaggerated, "Ouch!"

He laughed a lot. This turned into a game where the three older kids tried pinching me and I Playlistened, pretending it was extremely painful. They laughed and released their tension about the shot. We felt connected and happy as we entered the room where they gave the shots.

There were two chairs in the room, and we headed for one. Sitting on the other chair was a child of about six, crying and screaming although the nurse hadn't approached him yet. When she got closer, he screamed louder, trying to escape from his mother's arms. She tried to convince him that it wouldn't be painful at all. His mom held him tight, and he cried loudly as he was given the shot.

I got my shot, and then each of my kids sat on the chair and got their shot. They all sat calmly, showing only a little discomfort after the shot. When it was my little one's turn (she is two-and-a-half), I held her on my lap, told her what was going to happen and that it would be painful but short. She cried in my arms afterward, and I reassured her that it would get better soon. After two minutes she stopped, climbed down, and joined her siblings. A mom with a toddler had arrived and taken the chair next to us. He cried loudly and tried to escape; she tried to hold him with the help of two grandparents.

For us, the whole procedure was pleasant. The huge difference between our experiences and what happened in the other chair was obvious. When we left, my eight-year-old daughter asked me, "Mommy, how come those children are older than our younger ones, and they act like that?" I feel grateful for having the Hand in Hand tools in my parenting. It makes such a difference when children can laugh and release tension before a frightening experience, and are listened to when they feel pain and cry. They feel connected, they develop trust in other people, and they can go through stressful events more easily because they feel supported.

HOW IT WORKED

Shots or check-ups, x-rays or blood tests—our children are bound to need some type of feared medical procedure at some time or another. This mom did everything right. She listened to her children and anticipated their worry about the shots hurting. She followed their laughter in a pre-shot Playlistening game of "pinch." She told them the truth—that it would hurt. And she Staylistened to her child who needed to cry after the shot. Yes, it really can be that simple.

---◆---

BROKEN BONES

TOOL: ⬤ STAYLISTENING

On Easter Sunday, a little boy lifted my three-and-a-half-year-old daughter into a tree and she fell. I heard her cry and ran to her. Her hand was dangling at a ninety-degree angle from her forearm. I knew it was not good. I calmly picked her up and walked to the car. She was crying, "Mama! Mama!" My husband got in the car and we drove to the hospital thirty minutes away. In the car, I held her close to me and immediately started to listen. It was my first reaction to hearing her cry so deeply, thanks to all the Staylistening experience we've had. I calmly said, "I am right here with you. I hear you. We are going to the doctor, and he will fix your hand." I did not give much explanation, and tried to focus on our connection and give her my empathy. She continued crying for a while. Then she slowed to a whine and stopped.

When we got to the hospital we were able to do the X-rays and all the examinations with her on my lap. Three different nurses asked me what pain medication was given to her, because she was so calm and able to cooperate. I replied, "None." She had compound fractures in both of the bones in her forearm. They put her to sleep for sixteen minutes to reset the bones and gave her some pain medication. During the whole experience I kept her really close to me. She woke up sitting on me.

On the ride home she started talking to me about how she fell. The doctor gave us a prescription for her pain. I gave her a half dose the first night to help her sleep, but that was it. The next day she did not want any pain medication or show any signs of pain. She was ready to play! A few days later she was outside, climbing up a smaller tree. I strongly believe she was able to do this because my husband and I were able to calmly and empathically listen to her cry and release her feelings and her fear of the pain. She was able to feel connected and cooperate. She has totally accepted this experience, never asking for her cast to be taken off or complaining about it.

All in all, this potentially traumatic experience has boosted her confidence and deepened our connection and trust. I am so thankful for all that I have learned from Hand in Hand!

HOW IT WORKED

Once you begin to see the healing power of the emotional release process, you wonder why you put so much energy into stopping it! All this mom did was keep her daughter close, listen to her upset, and get her the medical help that was surely needed. The harder part for many of us is remembering what not to do! No need to "shush." No need to convince our child that everything's OK or that it won't hurt for long. This mom let her daughter know that they were on their way to the doctor and then simply listened, welcoming whatever feelings her daughter needed to vent. As often happens when a child is able to cry until she's done, this girl calmed completely, the pain subsided, and she was able to handle the medical procedures easily.

TAKING A COURSE OF ANTIBIOTICS

TOOL: PLAYLISTENING

We were only one day in with nine to go on a course of antibiotics for my two-and-a-half-year-old daughter. We had recently adopted her, and she was fighting us tooth and nail every time a dose was due! Coughing, spluttering, wriggling and thrashing about—we were not welcomed anywhere near her mouth. We had to become overpowering, forceful parents, prying her mouth open and feeling awful about it!

Wondering about Playlistening, I gave my daughter a medicine syringe to play with, thinking she might enjoy using it on her dolls; as we played, the game switched to her giving the medicine to me. "Medicine, Mommy," she said with a smile and a glint in her eye. I caught the look. "No," I exclaimed, and playfully covered my mouth. The giggles began.

"Yes," she insisted, laughing with glee as she inserted the syringe in my mouth and I noisily spat the pretend medicine out. "Ugh! Yuck! Yuck! No more! Please, no more," and on it went. The more I carried on and rejected the "medicine," the more she laughed. Then suddenly, the game would be over, and she would move on to something else, as if a need had been met.

She asked for this game many times a day, both with me and with her dad. We played and we listened, following her laughter. Almost instantly, her rigidity and inflexibility around taking antibiotics began to dissolve. Full cooperation wasn't immediate, but our daughter became more willing.

We learned about empowering instead of overpowering. Playlistening released her fears. Taking medicine is no longer an issue; our daughter cooperates, but she still exclaims, "Yucky!" Who can blame her?

HOW IT WORKED

When children are scared of taking medicine, one dropper of medication can mean an hour of your time and lots of screaming and flailing limbs. Playlistening often provides just the inroad you're seeking. Here, by simply giving her daughter a clean plastic syringe, this mom opened the door to a game her child devised. It was just what she needed! Playlistening over time enabled this toddler to become an expert medicine taker—even if she didn't like the taste.

GETTING THE MEDICINE DOWN

TOOL: STAYLISTENING

Recently, my two-year-old son had a fever in the middle of the night. We cooled him down by putting him in a cool bath; then we tried to give him medicine. Getting medicine into his mouth has always been a struggle, and we've had to hold him down. This fighting feels awful for him and for us.

The day before, I had talked with my husband about Staylistening– about not forcing things, and letting the child show how he is feeling. I wanted to try something different, and convinced my husband to give it a try, even though he was worried about letting our son cry about taking the medicine, and wanted to force him to take it.

So I took a deep breath and said to my son, "I'm sorry that I felt that I had to force you to take this," and just held out the syringe with the medicine where he could see it. I did not try to make him take it. He started to cry hard. When the crying quieted down, I showed him the syringe again, and asked, "Are you ready to take this now?"

After about an hour and a half of crying, we decided that he really needed to take the medicine, and I apologized to him that he had to. When I gave him the medicine, he cried, but not nearly as hard as earlier, and he let us give it to him. We didn't have to force him.

The day after, I had to give him medicine again. He cried some more, protesting that he didn't want to take it, but for much less time than in the middle of the night. Then he let me give it to him. The third time, he cried for only fifteen minutes. The next time, he happily took the medicine, and drank it without any tears at all.

Listening to him through all that crying was not easy. But I kept thinking that he was probably crying about a deeper hurt. As he cried, I felt sorry and guilty. But then, as his crying eased, I could tell that we had done the right thing by Staylistening. I feel a great sense of relief that I no longer have to force him to take medication. That struggle is over.

HOW IT WORKS

Even in situations when we parents need to make something happen, slowing things down, lessening our grip on control, and making room for feelings can move us in the right direction. This mom wanted to stop forcing her son to take medicine, and she used Staylistening to get there. One cry at a time, starting with an apology for past behaviors, Mom helped her son release his backlog of fears. Each time, she told him what had to happen, showed him the medicine, and allowed him time to show her how he felt. After only three or four Staylistening sessions, he was able to take the medicine happily and without protest.

———————— ◆◆◆ ————————

Fear After An Accident

CLIMBING AND FALLING

TOOL: 🌀 STAYLISTENING

I found my four-and-a-half-year-old boy crying hard when I entered his daycare one afternoon. As he nested in my lap, Jen, one of his teachers, explained why he was so upset. "He cut his chin climbing down the ladder above the jumping mat. He wouldn't jump from the top step. He said it was too high for him. Then he hit his chin on the ladder climbing down."

"It's OK," I reassured her, "I'll give him a cuddle."

We were out in the back yard, where no parents or children were near. It looked like a pretty safe environment to Staylisten. "I am here with you. I know it hurts," I said. His cry intensified. Every time his crying waned, I repeated something like, "You cut yourself on the ladder and it hurts," which prompted more tears.

"Don't you think we should try and cheer him up a bit?" Jen asked a few minutes later. "He always feels much better when I allow him to cry for as long as he needs," I replied. Still, her remark made me aware of the fact that she was growing more uncomfortable with his crying. I figured it was almost time to head home, where I could listen to him as long as he needed. But he wasn't ready to stop. After ten more minutes and a few more concerned looks from Jen, I started to feel uncomfortable. My son's cry had softened by then, and I easily convinced him that it was time to go home and enjoy a nice snack.

He'd had at least twenty minutes of crying. When we got home he played, and then decided to inspect his cut in the mirror. This was highly unusual! Up until then, he had always avoided looking at injuries. The rest of the afternoon went smoothly. He was happy and balanced.

The following morning we went back to daycare. As soon as we arrived he pulled me to the back yard to show me the ladder where he got hurt.

He climbed up and, once he reached the top, jumped onto the mattress. "See?" he said, "I can jump from very high!" Then he climbed up to a platform above the ladder, and pretended to walk carelessly and fall off it onto the mat by accident. "See, Mommy? This is what Donald Duck does!"

I realized with much satisfaction that he showed no sign of fear from the previous incident. In fact, he was able to jump from a height that had scared him the previous day. On my way out, his teacher, asked, "Was he OK with the ladder? Does he have any sign of trauma?" I smiled and told her how my child looked more confident than ever, and had jumped from the highest platform onto the mat.

HOW IT WORKED

This boy wanted to jump from high up, but couldn't find the courage, and then got hurt going down the easy way. Mom Staylistened patiently, warding off the well-meaning teacher who wanted to help quiet the boy. The good long cry did wonders! He enjoyed the rest of his day and was able to look at his injury in the mirror, something he'd never been brave enough to do before. But the best outcome was apparent the next day, as he accomplished feats he'd never done before.

BEE STINGS

TOOLS:  STAYLISTENING   PLAYLISTENING

My son was three when he was attacked by yellow jackets in a friend's back yard. I ran over to help. My husband picked him up quickly and the three of us ran inside. The yellow jackets followed him, and when we ripped off his clothes, there was a yellow jacket in his pants, still stinging! My husband and I both got stung, too, but my son was stung eight times. He was in a lot of pain—and really terrified.

We packed ice on his stings, and left for home. He screamed at the top of his lungs for the full half-hour ride. I held him, looked into his eyes, and told him again and again that we were sorry he got stung. I told him we knew it hurt, and that he could scream as much as he needed to. I told him we would stay with him, and that he was doing just the right thing. He screamed a long, long time. I would never wish this experience on any child!

For weeks afterwards, he was so terrified to go outside that he wouldn't leave the house without crying hard. He was terrified of anything that flew, indoors or outdoors. He refused to be outside at all. It was a beautiful summer, and in Buffalo, New York, you want to be outdoors, because the rest of the year you're indoors all the time! So I decided to try both Playlistening and Staylistening to help him with his fear.

I began playing this game with him where I would buzz and "fly" up to him, pretending I was a bee. After a little bit of this playing, he came up with a way to take the powerful role. He would say, "Baba!" which was his version of "Boo!" and I would scream and "fly" away, scared, saying, "What was *that*?! Ohh, I'm scared!" He would laugh hard, and we would begin again. He loved this game. My whole family got into it—my husband played it, my mom played it with him, and sometimes all three of us would play it together. He would scare us and, each time, we would run away "frightened," and he would laugh and ask for more.

I did Staylistening, too. Rather than wait for him to want to go outside—he never wanted to—I decided to take him for a little walk every day. I held him the whole time. He would begin crying the minute we went out the door, and he clung to me for dear life. I told him we would only stay outside for as long as he wanted, but that we needed to go outside, and that he was safe. The first time, he cried for a few minutes, and then wanted to go in, so we did. The second time, he also cried, but it took a little longer before he said he wanted to go in. Every day we did this, and every day he cried hard, but he stayed out longer than the day before. While he cried, I would look at him, hold him, and tell him I was keeping him safe.

We knew he had moved through it when an insect came near him and he said "Baba!" Of course, the insect randomly flew away. He was very proud of himself. He said, "See, Mama! I made it go away!" The final victory came the day he was playing in the yard and he called me, "Mama, come see!" I went over to him, and he showed me a really big bee sitting on his shoe. He said, "Look Mama, there's a bee on my shoe," but he was totally relaxed about it. I said, "Yes, there it is. Do you want to kick it off?" and he said, "Yes," and kicked his foot. The bee flew away, and he kept playing. It was a totally ordinary thing.

I felt like a great Mom! We had figured out how to help him with something that was absolutely terrifying. He has remained unafraid of insects. It's as if that incident had never happened.

HOW IT WORKED

It is very common for children to develop intense and lasting fears after a terrifying experience. Often, because we don't know how to address these phobias, we have to dance around them. If our child is afraid of water, we avoid the swimming pool. If our child is scared of bugs, we hang insect traps all over our yard and decide that camping doesn't really make sense for our family. But doing this only allows fears to settle in more comfortably, affecting our child's daily life and the lives of those around him.

Instead, this mom used Playlistening to help her son laugh away his lighter fears, and Staylistening to allow him to cry away those nestled deeper. When she Playlistened, she played around until her son concocted a way to participate in the game from a place of power. He heard the scary "buzz" sound in the safety of his house, and his mom allowed him to laugh about it, releasing tension. When she Staylistened, she took baby steps, letting him be in charge of saying when to retreat, and allowing him to feel his fear in the safety of her arms each time. Slowly but surely, he recovered his courage, and soon he was able to play happily outside again alongside the bees and other flying insects.

A BIKE CRASH

TOOL:  STAYLISTENING

Our family was on vacation, and my three-and-a-half-year-old son Henry had brought his balancing bike with him. One day, while riding his bike, he rode down a fairly steep hill. The bike went faster and faster, and started to wobble. I couldn't reach him in time, and he took quite a fall on his face (he wore a helmet). I ran over. Henry was crying really hard. I sat down on the ground, pulled him into my lap and started to listen.

His mouth was bleeding freely, and he was swallowing blood. He was quite scared. I knew that the mouth tends to bleed easily, and that it's not common to stitch wounds inside the mouth. People rushed over to offer first aid and ice. I said that we might need it later but that we were fine for now. Some of the people looked at me with disbelief and what I think was disapproval, but I decided to focus on my son. I really wanted to try to listen and be present, as I had heard beautiful stories of how that could benefit the emotional and physical healing process.

When I saw Henry's lip swell and darken, I got a bit scared and nervous. He also swallowed quite a bit of blood. I put those thoughts aside, however, and kept listening to him. People continued to approach us and suggest what needed to be done. I felt that they considered me a really bad mother—in their eyes, I was doing nothing. I kept guarding Henry and our connection, and I focused on us. He was still crying really hard.

The bleeding finally stopped. I could see that all his teeth were intact. Henry started making requests while crying. I listened to him and responded that for now, I just wanted to listen. Once in a while, I said, "You fell off your bike," or "You hurt your lip." The crying went on for about twenty or thirty minutes. Toward the end of his cry, the most amazing thing happened: the swelling in his lip went down, and it turned back to nearly its regular color. I could not believe my eyes. If I had not witnessed this process myself, I would have had a hard time believing it. Finally, Henry was done crying.

I suggested that we continue our walk. Henry said that he wanted me to carry him. I acknowledged what he said and then suggested that he try to walk. He started to walk. Then I said, "If you want to, you can go on your bike." He said, "Yes," and proceeded to get on his bike. It was amazing.

The people who observed us looked very surprised. I wondered what they were thinking now about my parenting style, and I felt pleased with myself. In the afternoon, Henry and I went out again, he rode his bike down the same steep hill, this time with grace. My heart warmed up with gratitude. His lip looked almost normal, and healed entirely within the next few days. I felt I had experienced an almost miraculous way to help my child with a physical injury.

HOW IT WORKED

Sometimes the healing power of crying seems magical. Here, despite the worries of those around her, Mom knew her son's injury didn't require immediate medical attention, and she focused on connecting with him instead. She Staylistened while he shed his fear. When her son started making requests, as kids often do in order to move their attention off of a scary upset, Mom gently brought his attention back to his injury, allowing the crying to continue. When the crying ended, he was ready to hop on his bike and give riding another go. His lip was well on its way to recovery, and that afternoon, he made it down that steep hill just fine.

WHEN YOU'RE BOTH FRIGHTENED

TOOLS: STAYLISTENING   LISTENING PARTNERSHIP

Last Sunday, our morning outing turned into an interesting experience that I'm sure I'll remember for life. My husband, my two-and-a-half-year-old son, and I were having breakfast on a café patio. After my son finished eating, he went to check out the fountain. I went with him and sat down on the edge. We were there for some time when, suddenly, my son slipped and fell head first into the fountain. Immediately, I responded and pulled him out. He was soaking wet and crying hysterically, although I did not see any apparent injuries. I put him on my lap, put my arms around him, provided eye contact, and listened. I did not move him away from the fountain, though the café was full of customers. I remembered that the less you move a child who is hurting, the better the healing process can work. I just made sure he could see me. He let out his upset and fear. I gently touched his head and made some reassuring sounds. I didn't feel it made sense to say much, as his crying was so intense. I focused on being as calm and present as possible, although I, too, had been shocked.

After about five minutes of loud crying, I felt I had to move my son, so I took him to an alley close by. My husband and I knelt on the ground as I kept listening. When his crying slowed, I gently said, "You fell into the water." He continued to cry, and I moved him even farther away. Finally, my husband became worried about our son getting chilled, so we carried him to our car, where I put him on my lap again, and gently took off his clothes. He soon decided to start playing. After about ten minutes, we mentioned the incident again and he said, "I went swimming. Whoosh!" Part of his lip was bruised, and he had a bruise on his cheek, but he said that it didn't hurt. To this day, I'm still amazed how quickly he recovered from an incident that could have easily been traumatic for him.

When we went back to the café later that week, he showed no fear at all. He was mildly interested in the fountain and told us, "I'm not going in today." In his swimming lessons, however, he was more adventurous after this incident than he was before. On my end, I had to devote several Listening Partnerships to this incident, and to some of my memories of his birth and other early challenging experiences he had. He has recovered much more quickly than I have.

HOW IT WORKED

After our child gets hurt, it often takes us parents longer to overcome our fears than it takes our child! Accidents happen, and here, even with an attentive mom by his side, this young one took a big fall into a public fountain. Not seeing any major injuries, Mom chose to Staylisten to her son's upset right where the incident happened. When it felt like a better idea to move his loud cries out of the café, she did that. And she continued to trust her choices and her husband's. She offered simple reminders about what happened to encourage her son to expel any residual fears. One step at a time, they helped their son heal from the accident. In the end, the boy was left with an uncharged, factual memory of the event. "I went swimming. Whoosh! I'm not going in today." And Mom continues to work on her fears and feelings about the event in her Listening Partnerships.

12
Moving Beyond Aggression

WHAT YOU NEED TO KNOW

Almost all of us struggle with our children's aggression. It comes out of the blue, and once it starts, it crops up again and again. What should we do in these difficult, heated moments?

You've probably already found that conventional remedies like reasoning, star charts, Time Outs, spanking, and enforcing "logical consequences" don't stop a child's aggression for long. In fact, the knot of intense feelings that drives your child to lash out can't be dissolved by any of these tactics!

When your child can think, she loves her friends and siblings. Connected, she can let you know when they irritate her by letting out a cry or running to you, upset and asking for help. But when she's in the full grip of big feelings, the things you do and say to correct her actions churn like nonsense in her beleaguered mind.

There is another way!

AGGRESSION IS A SIGN THAT YOUR CHILD FEELS AFRAID

It will be much easier for you to help your child if you realize that she lashes out because she is *afraid*. Children acquire their fears from experiences like a difficult birth, medical treatment, family tension, sudden change, the unhappiness of others, the absence of loved ones, and more. In a situation that overwhelms her, fear sticks in her memory unless someone manages to listen to her cry, thrash, and drain the feelings. An emotional memory doesn't fade with time. So weeks, months, or years later when that memory is triggered by a harmless situation, a full jolt of fear grips her again, although she is perfectly safe. Her reasoning mind shuts down, the survival instinct takes over, and she may lash out.

Aggressive behavior is almost always beyond a child's control, no matter how intentional it may seem. With her fears in charge, her heart goes cold. She will say, "I don't care!" as you point out that she hurt her little brother. She does care, but her trusting nature has been zapped by the feelings of isolation that always accompany fear. In fact, it's useful to think of your child's hurtful acts—biting, grabbing, pushing, hitting, and other senseless, impulsive behaviors—as *signals*. They read, "I'm frightened! Help!"

Your child is good, through and through. She would much rather play and have fun than cause difficulties for others. With Listening Tools, you can reach for her and strengthen her sense that you are on her side. Then, the two of you will be able to partner to release the tension that isolates her. You'll bring limits and compassion; she'll show you the wild emotion she needs to shed. Then she'll relax at last.

HOW TO MOVE YOUR CHILD BEYOND AGGRESSION

Treating an aggressive child aggressively is not a good way to instill the kindness we want her to learn. But in our own heated moments, the behaviors that leap out are often a replay of what was done to us as children. These reactions only make things worse. Our child feels intimidated, and we're not practicing the kindness we preach. The steps we outline here are designed to strengthen the connection between you and your child over time, and to ensure safety all around. You will use each of the Listening Tools to reach for your child, and offload your own upsets often. You deserve at least as much support as your child does! Focusing on connection and keeping things safe will help you find one another and make your way out of the briar patch of prickly feelings that has grown around you.

Step 1. Get listening support. Parenting a child who feels embattled is wearing! To move things forward, you'll need the presence of mind to reach for her, rather than react when she can't think. So with a trusted listener, talk about the first time you ever were spanked or treated harshly. Talk about how you and your siblings were treated, and the "discipline" you witnessed in school or on your sports teams as a child. Talk about how you felt when you were punished, and when you saw other children fall victim to angry adults. Do what you can to release the feelings you come across as you review those memories, and the attitudes that were passed down to you through your family.

During your listening time, imagine that you're in charge at last. You can give any adult who punished you a real talking-to. You can stand up for yourself or even be harsh and demanding with *them*, for a change. Use your imagination to revisit the incidents that paralyzed you, trying out the more powerful role. Shed your tears and let yourself perspire or tremble as you focus on the fact that you are *good*, and always have been. When you went off track as a child, you were simply signaling an adult for help. Working from this perspective will root out both the emotion and the hurtful message it left behind.

Here's a mother who wanted to respond more constructively to her aggressive son. Listening Partnership time, including taking the powerful role, made a big difference for him and for her.

———◇———

My six-year-old son has some separation fears that are rooted in his infancy. The way he releases them best is by "going wild" after I set a limit, or after I hold the limit for him when he tries to hit me. In the beginning, I was always taken aback when it would come to him hitting me. I always tried to protect myself, but sometimes I would yell at him and threaten him to get him to stop. I needed listening time! I wanted to help my son work on his fears, so he wouldn't always have to react in that way.

One listening time, my partner asked me warmly who he reminds me of when he becomes aggressive. I immediately said, "My father." And I began remembering and reliving difficult moments in my past when I felt really hurt, in my heart and physically, too. I cried a whole lot during many listening times about how I was hit by my father. I also took the opportunity to stand up for myself, to use my listening time to yell in protest about what he did to me, and to tell him I never deserved such treatment. This released lots of feelings, too.

After working in this way, I was better at anticipating my son's hitting behavior. For example, when he'd ask for sweets or screen time and I would set a limit, I knew that he'd start trying to hit me. I was calmer, and could protect myself better. And I found I was better able to listen to his feelings. Fewer of my own emotions got in the way. These days, I can ask myself, "Am I fit to handle a big outburst? Or am I too tired to listen to all that fear?" If I am in good shape, I go ahead and set the limit that I think makes sense, and my son gets a wonderful release of his deep fears, followed later by my own listening time where I work on the feelings that came up for me.

By using setting limits and Staylistening, together with lots of Special Time and Playlistening, my son has become more relaxed about saying goodbye. It is now easier to drop him off at school. He spends more time independently, and goes more often to his friends' homes to play. And his aggressive behavior, which we saw daily, now only comes up a few times each month. We are both making good progress!

———◇———

Step 2. Strengthen your child's sense of connection with Special Time. This is your go-to tool for building connection and trust between you. No matter how aggressive your child may be, Special Time is the place to start. Connection is what your child needs, and connection must start on her terms.

Often, you won't have any idea what issue is fueling your child's aggression. But as daily short Special Times continue, she may reveal that hurt by making up a game that portrays it, casting you in the victim role. For example, a child who is bullied at school might use Special Time to play out the name-calling or harassment she experiences. You don't need to grill her about why she wants to call you a stupid-head in Special Time; just keep being a tad muddled—"Are you talking about my head? I thought my head was doing just fine. Hmmm—shall I look in the mirror? Where's the 'stupid' part?" The more befuddled you can be, the more she can laugh. Her laughter releases the lighter layers of fear she's felt. She may never tell you more about the incidents at school, but if she can laugh and cry, the hurt will heal.

Here's a parent whose relationship with her aggressive son shifted greatly after she started doing Special Time exactly as we suggest.

———◇———

I was really struggling. My four-year-old son was trying to hit me often, and needed help. I had been doing what I thought was Special Time, but came to realize it wasn't quite the same activity recommended by Hand In Hand. I'd play with my son and ask him if he wanted Special Time, but I didn't always time it. I would do it intermittently, here and there, but nothing as consistent as every morning. I'd suggest some play or gradually add in my own flair, which would color the play differently. Maybe a big growl from me as I'm chasing him around the house as opposed to just doing the chase he had asked for.

I really saw how the guidelines of timing it, letting the child take the lead, and consistency were all key Special Time components. So I started Special Time first thing the next morning. I announced that it was Special Time and said, "We can do anything you want for ten minutes." I set the timer. He wanted to do a pillow fight. So I was full on, with loving attention to his every move. We had so much fun; there was lots of laughing and running about. When the timer went off, he wanted to play more, but I said that Special Time was over; we could do more after school. He was fine. Our morning went surprisingly smoothly. This was new! I was so happy.

After school, we had more Special Time, and I really noticed the difference. What I used to think was Special Time didn't have the effect I'd experienced in the morning and afternoon. I was onto something transformative here!

I have been doing morning Special Time, and some after school as well, daily for a couple of months and I can't believe the shift in our relationship. It loosened up this knot of fear in my son, and he's been able to move past hitting. We've had lots of Staylistening sessions along the way as well, and these tools together have brought about a newfound healing and deep connection between us. I am ever so grateful to have found a loving way to deal with a difficult behavior that is usually met with even more hurt.

———◇———

Step 3. Show your affection and build closeness with Playlistening. Laughter is a great release valve for the lighter side of your child's fears. And the roughhousing that's often part of Playlistening can be a powerful relaxant. There's nothing like banging up against one another in play to reassure a child that you're strong and that you care. As your child jumps on you, tackles you, chases you, and topples you onto the carpet or the grass, the laughter, affection, and physical contact will do her system a world of good. Vigorous physical play reassures her at a cellular level. Gauge how much strength to use as you play by what lets her laugh. Some children are physically confident, and can handle plenty of challenge. Others must touch and run to maintain their sense of safety. Use your child's laughter as your guide to the amount of strength you use and the amount of contact she can handle as you play.

Here's how one mother uses Playlistening to keep her son's aggression from spiraling downward:

———◇———

When my son, five, is hitting and kicking, I often play this game with him. I say: "My, we have an angry little lion. Hmm, could some kisses tame him?" Then I try to kiss him, which he, of course, resists. At this point, he picks up the role of the lion, groans and roars, scares me, and tries to pull my hair. So I say, "I am sure lions are tamed with kisses. I read it in the encyclopedia! Perhaps this lion needs some *more* kisses!" I pretend to be amazed that he is not yet tamed, and go on trying to kiss him. Or I say, "Maybe a kiss on his *belly* is what he needs. I know lions are tamed by kisses, but I forgot the exact spot where they have to be kissed!" And so on. He loves this game, and laughs and laughs! Three to five minutes of this always helps him to get back on track, so he doesn't act out his discomfort in aggression.

———◇———

Step 4. Set limits right away when off-track behavior crops up. The longer you wait, the more scared and isolated your child becomes, and the more likely she is to be aggressive. You can set the limit playfully, or bring it with a firm, practical tone, but bring it and hold it until your child's off-track energy has been met, heard, and drained.

One good tactic, if your child is pestering but not consumed with anger, is to make yourself the target. Draw the fire away from a child who can't handle it. Roughhousing will do the trick. "Ohh, so *that's* what you say to your sister! Well, I'm gonna have to hang you by your toes for that," said with a grin, is enough to move your aggressive child's attention away from a sibling and on to you. Issue outsized threats, then struggle mightily to follow through. Be friendly and eager throughout. Wet kisses, raspberries, and playful pummeling are all good ways to respond to a child who is sticking out her tongue, calling names, or otherwise badgering another child. As long as your attitude is eager and affectionate, you can probably squeeze laughter from an otherwise edgy situation.

When you roughhouse with children, you create safety. You show them you're not afraid of their bluster. You also make it safe enough to show you their impulse to be aggressive again and again. After she's playfully tested the limits you're setting several times, your child may move to meaner, more hurtful behavior, because there's a deeper upset that's lurking below the surface. Of course, you must bring a limit to keep yourself safe! For example, your child might begin pinching you as you roll around on the floor together. Meet her escalation with an affectionate limit: "Oh, where are those rascally little fingers? I think they must need a kiss— smooch, smooch!" The pinches will recur, but your child's laughter will escalate as you go from kissing your child's fingers to hinting that you might lick them instead. And when she keeps on, the penalty is big, noisy raspberries blown into her tummy. These affectionate paybacks constitute a "fuzzy limit"—you limit the behavior and shower her with affection while she shows you a mild version of her impulse to hurt.

If your child escalates to behavior that you can't or don't want to handle, stop the play, and move close. An opportunity is at hand. She felt safe enough to lose control knowing that you'd be there to bring a firm limit. She's ready to release the feelings that cause her so much trouble.

Bring that limit, perhaps by holding her hands, so she can't hit or hurt you. She will not want to be with you—the emotions that come up will feel unbearable. Tell her, "I can't let you hurt me. Let's stay right here together for a bit." Don't let your child move on to another activity. She will probably feel upset and may want to run away. Big feelings of hurt are rising to the surface. Stay close, even if you must follow her into the farthest corner of the house. She needs to feel your caring. She'll find a way to burst into tears.

Step 5. Use Staylistening to heal the core hurt. I guarantee you that your child's feelings will be intense, and that it will be "your fault!" You will have spoiled the playtime, your breath will be stinky, or you'll be the worst parent in the world because you won't leave her alone. She's itching to unload the big feelings that cause her trouble with others. So listen. Don't defend yourself. Just say, "I know it's hard," "I see you don't feel good," or, "I want to stay with you until things are better." She will cry, sweat, flail, scream, and carry on. This is how fear makes its exit—with noise, hatred, blame, accusations, and then panic. Anchor your child through this, and you'll see some marked improvement, including less aggressive behavior.

Here's how it can work:

———◇———

My five-year-old was goofing around in soccer class and his behavior became disruptive. After a few warnings, the coach grabbed his arm and told him to calm down. My son's response was dramatic. He immediately took a ball from a friend and kicked it away as far as he could. When the coach found a new ball he kicked it, hard. He then ran over to another child and tried to tackle him.

He clearly needed some support so I went over and asked him to take a break with me. He resisted at first but then let me pick him up. As we walked off the field he arched his body backwards and started to fight. I sat with him while he struggled to pull away. There was scratching, kicking, attempts at biting, and he managed to fling my glasses off. I let him know that he was safe and I was right there with him. He was drenched with sweat but not crying.

At one point, he calmed down and asked to rejoin the class. I thought he still had strong feelings about what happened, so I said I'd like to be with him a bit longer. This let him continue to struggle and he started to cry. After crying for a while he said, "It didn't feel friendly when the coach grabbed my arm." I said, "You didn't like that," as he cried some more. When I felt his body relax I asked if he wanted to try returning to the practice. He did, and seemed happy as he participated.

This was a public Staylistening episode—his preschool teacher and a bunch of parents were all nearby. His teacher was surprised by the progression from off-track behavior to crying, and then to being relaxed and happy.

———◇———

These steps will whittle down the hunk of fear that drives your child to lash out. At first, you may find that your child's impulsive behavior increases, because listening to him and keeping things safe has made him hopeful. He wants out of the fix he's in, and he'll signal you often for help. But as you give him opportunities to offload his fears, the relief will show on his face and in his behavior. He might sleep better, eat better, begin to enjoy the brother or sister he felt threatened by, or laugh a little more easily. And eventually, he'll have fewer upsets. Each one will still go deep—that's how he heals, after all—but his resilience will increase. And he'll be better able to signal that he's in trouble by asking for what he needs, or simply bursting into tears. As things improve, you may be tempted to offer less Special Time and Playlistening, but those tools are as important as setting limits and Staylistening in the dissolution of aggression. Each of the Listening Tools meets an inborn need. Each delivers an important facet of your love and reassurance.

FURTHER WAYS TO MOVE YOUR CHILD BEYOND AGGRESSION

Here are some additional strategies that drain the feelings causing aggression, and help your child become more inclusive and flexible in his play with others, including siblings. The process can take time. If you use your Listening Partnership to offload your own fears and upsets, you'll speed things along and tame your own intense feelings as you reach for your frightened child.

1. **Observe.** Under what conditions do your child's fears lead to aggression? Is it after Mommy goes to her evening class? When there have been arguments at home? When other children crowd her? When she's left to play with a sibling in a separate room? When a friend comes over to play, and wants one of her toys?

You may learn to detect subtle signs that your child's fears are rumbling. For example, you might notice that just before she bites, pushes, or hits, the expression on her face goes flat, or perhaps her posture stiffens. The better you are at anticipating her difficulties, the better you'll be at creating strategies that connect the two of you before she erupts.

2. **Abandon false hopes.** We parents sometimes let unrealistic hopes mislead us. Disregard that little voice in your head that says, "Gee, I hope she doesn't go after Joey before breakfast," if your daughter has lit into him before breakfast almost every morning for the past two weeks. The odds are, she'll do it again. Be ready. If your child tends to bite you suddenly during rough and tumble play, be ready. Play so that you keep her head at least an inch from your body at all times. Dart out of the way or provide gentle resistance as she tries to nuzzle in close.

3. Make it *your* job to keep everyone safe. Once you have identified a pattern of aggression, prepare for it by staying close—less than an arm's distance from your child—in case she lashes out.

You're going to try to be alert enough to prevent your child's hand from landing in her friend's hair, or to intercept a shove meant to deck her sister. For example, if your child tends to push the child in front of her on the ladder of the playground slide, put a hand on her tummy as she climbs up. That way, you can keep her a safe distance from the child in front of her. You can say something like, "I need to keep things safe, so I'm going to slow you down just a bit."

If your child becomes upset about the gentle, preventative touch you impose, Staylisten. When your child feels urgent about having things a certain way, it's a sure sign that fear is running the show—there are few things in life that truly must be done only one way, or right this minute! She'll cry because, in her isolation, you feel like an alien, and you've invaded her space. Feeling all alone is what she's used to when she's scared, and the feel of your touch brings those feelings to the fore, without anyone getting hurt.

4. Talk less. Let your presence communicate both caring and limits. Most adults around an aggressive child will issue lots of warnings. "Now today, no hitting when Isabel wants to play with your train set. Remember, hands are not for hurting!" In truth, your warnings aren't needed when your child is feeling connected. And they're useless when she's not. Save your breath! Instead, do a friendly patrol, and bring those invaluable limits when they're needed. Let your limits deliver your love.

5. Elicit laughter when you can. Connecting with a warm adult in play can be a powerful means of keeping a child's sense of connection alive. Don't tickle, but do offer affection, and find ways to take the less powerful role. It's that sense of fun and closeness that will help your child stay on a good track with her friends and siblings, and make it more likely she'll ask you for help when she feels upset.

To help you understand how fear releases, you'll find a fuller explanation in Chapter 11, *Lifting Fear.* There, you'll find some detailed ideas of how to manage Staylistening with a child who is offloading fear in a frantic, trembling, tearful battle.

In the following sections you'll get a peek at the ongoing work of a diverse set of parents who are using Listening Tools to help their children overcome aggressive behaviors.

Aggression: Hitting And Biting

NIPPING AGGRESSION IN THE BUD

TOOLS: ⏳ SPECIAL TIME   ↻ STAYLISTENING

Early one morning, my seven-year-old daughter began to be aggressive with her younger brother. She insisted that he play with her—and on her terms. He did his best to tell her no, but he wasn't getting through. The situation was escalating quickly. I decided to invite my daughter for five minutes of Special Time, as I could see that she was not thinking well.

We went into her room, and she very quickly came at me with scratches, bites, head-butts, pushes, and spitting. Something was really up with her. We started to wrestle, I parried her initiatives with affection, and toward the end of the five minutes my daughter bumped her head on the wall. Then she began to cry.

When the timer bell chimed, she very sadly got up and went to sit in a chair. She reminded me that it was her brother's turn for Special Time. I told her that I would stay with her since she seemed so sad. She half-heartedly told me to go. I stayed, and tried to gently and playfully get close for a hug.

After a little bit, she apologized for being mean to her brother, and told me that it was hard when others didn't want to play with her in the way that she wanted. I nodded and listened. She then opened up and said that sometimes she's felt betrayed by other kids. She was referring to a friendship she was having trouble with at school. I listened some more and stayed close.

When the moment passed, and we went back to our plans for the day, my daughter and son were on good terms again. The five minutes of Special

Time at a tough moment helped my little girl access and connect to something that was really hard for her.

HOW IT WORKED

Of course, we must keep our children safe from one another when tensions arise. This mom saw that her oldest couldn't play cooperatively with her younger brother and needed help. She offered her daughter Special Time, hoping that this would reconnect them and put her daughter back on track. Her daughter's aggression in Special Time confirmed that she needed a safe space to dump her upset, whatever it was about. Mom got right in and played hard physically, a powerful tool in building closeness. A small bump during the connecting play was just what this young girl needed to cry and to heal from the hurts that were driving her aggressive behaviors. When Special Time was over, her daughter was still sad, so Mom continued to stay close. Connected after Special Time and feeling lighter after Staylistening, this girl was able to apologize for her behavior toward her brother, and also open up about the struggle she was facing at school. Had Mom not stepped in early, the sibling conflict probably would have ended quite differently.

LIFTING A PATTERN OF BITING

TOOLS: SETTING LIMITS   LISTENING PARTNERSHIP   STAYLISTENING   SPECIAL TIME

My younger son started biting when he was just over two years old. He would bite really hard when he and his older brother had sharing issues, or when he didn't get his way. He could not assert himself against his brother, who was three years older, more able and verbal, and biting seemed to be his impulsive response.

Resolving the biting issue was a priority over other jobs I had, and I rationed my energy and attention to deal with his new aggression. I reduced the time I spent on my household work, doing the minimum of cleaning, dishwashing, and cooking, to stay close by when my sons were together. I wanted to reach in before things escalated. I would hang out in the same room with them often during the day, or sit between them when they were playing together.

Sometimes, though, when I was in the bathroom or answering the phone, he bit. My older son would be hurt and cry frantically, and my younger son's face would be frozen in guilt. I rushed to them, apologized to them that I wasn't there to keep them safe. Then I would listen to each, one at a time. Often when I Staylistened to one, the other one would try to climb on my lap. So I learned how to hold them both on my lap, keeping them from hurting each other.

My success rate at holding my younger son's forehead away from my older son's body, thus keeping him from biting, increased. I learned to read their very first signals of disconnection, like a slight change in their tone of voice or their mood, so I could prevent an attack. And I patrolled them when they came back together after a long separation.

My vigilant patrols went on for a while. I worked on my embarrassment, guilt, worry, and anger about this challenging situation in my Listening Partnerships, which gave me an insight into the helplessness I felt when I was bullied as a child. My listening partner gave me several chances to stand up and take charge, saying the things I had no power to say as a child, and releasing the anger I'd held for so long. It felt like rewriting my own life history.

I kept offering regular Special Time to both sons, too. In one of the Special Times with my younger son, he bit me hard in the midst of our happy horsy ride. I stopped our play, offered eye contact, though his eyes didn't meet mine, and said, "I can't let you bite." He then started crying. This happened in other Special Times as well—he showed me his impulse, I met it with listening, and he could cry hard.

This work brought gradual change; after six months, he has stopped biting entirely.

HOW IT WORKED

This mom saw that stopping her son's biting would require an emotional project, and she gave herself permission to drop other duties in order to bring her two boys the help they both needed. She took her job as safety manager seriously, and set up as much close supervision as possible. She didn't try to control her son's biting, but instead, she positioned herself to intervene with listening at the moment when his feelings were ready to release. She also lowered her own stress level by using several Listening Partnerships to look at her history as the victim of aggression, and to offload the tension there. Her awareness of the subtle signs that her biting son had stopped thinking grew sharper, which made her more effective at setting limits. All the while, she treated both sons as blameless. One had caught an "aggression infection," and she stayed close so she could bring the healing he so badly needed.

———◆———

AGGRESSION AFTER A TRAUMATIC TIME

TOOLS: SETTING LIMITS   STAYLISTENING

Recently, my entire family caught the stomach flu. It was like being in a really bad movie! The flu took hold while we were on an airplane, and my daughter was desperate to nurse and get water, but every time we gave her liquids, she would upchuck again. To top it off, I began throwing up as well.

My husband held her on the other side of the aisle while she reached for me, begging to be nursed. She must have said "please" about a hundred times. I am certain that watching me throw up was frightening to her as well. Then my oldest threw up, and it was all we could manage to attend to her needs. My baby's needs moved even further out of view.

In the days after the flu passed, my little one was not herself. She was fierce about wanting to nurse. She started hitting, biting, and kicking everyone. I realized that she was dealing with some real issues over her lack of power on the airplane, and with being denied things that felt necessary for survival. At some point she asked me for an ice cube from the freezer and instead of giving it to her, I told her there were not going to be any more ice cubes today. She burst into a violent fit. I was very lucky that my father was visiting at the time and could take care of her sister.

My daughter kicked and then tried to bite herself and me. She howled. She screamed and bucked like a wild animal. It went on and on. Each time it seemed like her rage might subside, she found fresh energy and it just went to a wilder level. I had never encountered anything like it. For an hour and a half, she was sweating profusely, crying, struggling, and fighting. Through it all, I stayed calm and reassuring and told her I was right there, I was listening, and that she was safe now.

Finally, she looked up at me and started playing with my hair. She hid behind it, then said, "Boo!" She giggled. I knew that she was done for the time being. She slid off my lap and went running for her sister and Grandpa. She was full of joy, as if the last ninety minutes had never happened. My father is familiar with Hand in Hand work from previous visits, but even he was amazed at the difference in her, and how light she looked.

HOW IT WORKED

So often, big upsets over little things are actually pent-up feelings desperately seeking a way out. Longing for an ice cube hardly sounds like it's worth ninety minutes of crying and raging, but this girl took the opportunity to free herself from bigger feelings that were preventing her from acting rationally.

Fortunately, there were two adults on hand—one who could listen to her, and another who could care for her sister while Mom helped her do this important emotional work. By simply staying close and assuring this girl that she was safe now, her mother created just the environment that the child needed to release those trapped feelings and move on. As happened here, it is common for a child to cry and sweat and rage for a long time, and then to move on as if nothing out of the usual had happened. This parent was smart not to start a conversation with her child about what happened. Any child who is thinking well knows that not getting an ice cube isn't such a big deal, and that hurting another person is not OK. The ice cube was just a trigger, not the true cause of the upset.

———◇———

WHEN YOUR CHILD TRIES TO HURT YOU

TOOLS: ⏳ SPECIAL TIME   🚦 SETTING LIMITS   🔄 STAYLISTENING

Not long after breakfast, my three-year-old son starts showing off-track behavior: he drops toys, refuses to pick them up, and demands to be served. It is very unusual, as he is a very independent boy.

I decide we'll have a very long Special Time, thirty minutes, and announce it. He turns down the idea.

I feel a bit puzzled—refusing Special Time? It is a first. I take a moment to think, and eventually I say that if he feels like using his Special Time to complain about it, it is OK. I will be right with him, and listen to all he has to say.

His reaction is very strong: he screams, cries, and then tries to bite me. "I won't let you hurt me," I say, holding him back gently but firmly. Obviously, there is a lot of tension and hurt, and he feels safe to release it. He tries to push me onto the floor, then runs to his bedroom. "I don't want you in!" he screams, slamming the door closed. We haven't been using Hand in Hand tools for long. I realize that we have been able to create a safe space for him, and that he is willing to use it, showing us emotions he used to shut down.

I sit outside his door. "I'd like to stay with you. I will wait right here until you are ready to let me in." He cries. "I am right here with you," I say every now and then from behind the door.

After a few minutes of crying, he opens the door. He looks calm and asks me if I can read him some books. We spend the rest of Special Time reading his favorites. When the timer goes off, we are still reading, feeling connected. He is relaxed and balanced. "It is time to get ready," I say. He gets dressed, brushes his teeth without complaining, and goes with Dad to buy groceries.

Special Time, and the Staylistening that followed—in other words, connection and listening—have allowed us go from off-track and aggressive behavior to connection and cooperation in thirty minutes.

HOW IT WORKED

This mom notices her son's extraordinary behavior and rather than punishing him or trying to convince him to behave differently, she swoops in with Special Time. She recognizes his need for connection. As sometimes happens, the boy refuses it. But there is no one right way to use Special Time. As long as you're offering your child complete attention and pouring in your love, he can use his time as he wishes—even to complain about Special Time! A child doing all he can to keep his feelings tamped down is likely to get upset when we keep paying attention. With the feel of his mom's caring, it's nearly impossible for him to keep his emotions buried. So this boy's aggressions spill out in all directions. Mom brings a limit quickly and firmly, but also lovingly, keeping both herself and her son safe. Then, finally, with Mom parked outside his bedroom door, occasionally reminding him that she's there with him, this boy is able to cry away his upsets and regain his relaxed, independent disposition.

HITTING AT SCHOOL

TOOLS: SETTING LIMITS   STAYLISTENING

There was a five-year-old boy in my kindergarten group who had been giving signs of distress for a few days. He threw a few toys, hit a few children, and misbehaved at circle time. He didn't throw hard or hit hard, but I could tell he did not feel good.

One morning when we were in the corridor dressing up to go outside, he started swirling his jacket around, hitting a few children as he did. I took him back into our classroom and told him that we would sit down and wait until there was more room for us to put our coats on. I intentionally used this situation to help him work on his feelings. I was quite sure he wouldn't like the idea of waiting, and he didn't. He tried to run back into the corridor.

I held him back, telling him gently that we would soon go, when there was more room for us there, and he started to cry hard. Tears rolled down his cheeks, and he tried to run away. After five minutes he stopped trying to get away, but kept on crying, now fully absorbed by the tensions he was working on. After another ten minutes, he cried more softly, and gently laid his head on my shoulder.

Within a few more minutes, he was ready to go back into the corridor. As I opened the door, we saw that the children's shoes had left a lot of dirt on the floor. Of his own accord, he took the little broom and cleaned it all up, making everything look nice. He was smiling joyfully, dressing himself calmly, talking to me, and being so very cooperative.

What a change! I was proud of him, and of myself. During this whole time, I was comfortable with listening to him, and I never doubted that we would come to a happy end.

HOW IT WORKED

Even in a school setting, if there is an available adult, Hand in Hand tools can be used to help children overcome aggressive behaviors in a relatively short time. This teacher had noticed a pattern in this boy's behavior, and one day found an opportunity to intervene and help him get free of the feelings driving his aggression. She set a limit so beautifully, avoiding shame and blame altogether by suggesting it would be safer to wait until there was more room to put their coats on. She stayed with him, knowing that if she let him go, his aggression would flare again. The boy started to cry as he tried to get away, but then settled into his loving teacher and cried even more. When he was done, he was a different boy. He was feeling good, connected, and cooperative.

Aggression: When One Sibling Hurts Another

"SHE JUST FELL..."

TOOLS: SETTING LIMITS   STAYLISTENING

This afternoon, I could tell that my four-year-old was going off track. His behavior was erratic, and he couldn't seem to settle. I didn't exactly see what happened, but I heard my seventeen-month-old daughter crying. I walked over and my son said, "She just fell," which he has been saying sometimes when he hurts her. She had his toy in her hand and was upset, but he had caused no visible damage. As I got close to him, I scooped him up I said, "It's really annoying when she takes your toys, but it's not OK to hurt her," and he started to cry really hard.

I held him on my lap and tried to keep some eye contact with him. After a few minutes of crying he said, "She always breaks my toys and that makes me mad!" I told him, "Yeah, she really does break a lot of your toys! That is really annoying." It's true: she does break his toys. I had never heard him make such a blanket statement about how hard it is to have a younger sister around.

He cried hard for a while, intermittently putting his head on my chest. I validated how hard it is that she takes his toys. Eventually, when I said that, he didn't start to cry again, and I imagined that he might be almost done. Soon he poked at my nose. I laughed, and so did he, and he seemed to be done crying.

Amazingly, a few minutes later my daughter was crying about some toy that she couldn't figure out how to work. My son walked over to her and very gently said, "I know how to fix that. Can I help you?" And he gently helped her with the toy. No grabbing, no pulling!

HOW IT WORKED

When our children fight, we'd do well to follow this mother's lead and not worry about what really happened, but move straight into repairing our children's connection with one another. Once reconnected, they will figure out how to make amends. We tend to always run, worried, to the child who got hurt. But if there is no serious injury, it's good for their relationship if we can vary the one we tend to first. Remember, both the aggressor and the victim are hurting. This mom set a limit verbally, letting her son know that while it was fine for him to feel upset, it was not OK to hurt his sister. This limit allowed him to cry hard. When the crying slowed, Mom brought his attention back to the upset so he could cry more. When he felt better, her son signaled her by reaching out gently with humor. Then, he happily helped his sister figure out how to work a toy. They were once again on the same team.

This mom also ignored the fact that her son could not confess to his thoughtless act. The reasons we agree with her are outlined in Hand in Hand's article, "When Children Lie," *available on the Hand in Hand Parenting website.*

FIGHTING FOR ATTENTION

TOOLS:  SETTING LIMITS    PLAYLISTENING   STAYLISTENING

My son, who is five, often gets off to a bad start in the morning, as he and his little sister both compete for my attention. Very quickly, he becomes aggressive with my daughter.

This morning, as he went for her, I put myself between them, playfully kissing him and handling his hits and kicks in a spirited and lighthearted manner. He was really furious at times, shifted into being playful, then into acting helpless and weak. All these emotions came and went quickly. When I provided too much resistance, he started whining and said, "Mom, this isn't how you play the game," so then I let him feel powerful again. This must have gone on for ten minutes, with my daughter nearby. Soon she wanted to join in. She screamed when she got an occasional hit or kick. When I felt I could take it no more, I loudly announced, "Game over—time to get dressed!" I hoped that he would stop targeting his sister when I wasn't around.

He moved on to play with some toys, and I helped my daughter get dressed. He looked back at us and burst out crying. "Why are you getting her dressed first? I wanted to be the first to be dressed!" He sat down on the bed a few feet away from us, crying big tears. I moved closer, and he stopped crying, got angry again, and said, "You should dress *me* first!" I quietly moved back to my daughter and dressed her, often looking at my son, but not saying anything. He needed this cry, and a bit of distance from me to do it. He was crying hard, sitting on his own, but not far away.

When I was done with my daughter, I sat next to him as he cried. I just listened. At one point he asked me to dress him, and so I did, while he kept crying. When this was done, he looked at me and asked me to carry him downstairs like an infant (he weighs fifty pounds). Before doing so, I told him I was not going to be able to listen to him any longer, as I was already late for work. When we got to the kitchen downstairs, he smoothly moved into playing with his sister.

HOW IT WORKED

When our children are struggling with one another, it's crucial to keep them safe. This mom was ready to intercede when her son became aggressive with his sister; she set a limit by moving her body between them and parrying his blows. For Playlistening to work, the child needs to have the powerful role in the play. This mom noticed how her level of resistance affected her son. When she played too hard, his feelings of helplessness arose. She adjusted. With older children, you may find the need to intensify your game so they feel like you're taking them seriously. When Mom was out of steam, she stopped the game, but her son's feel-

ings soon bubbled over. Because they had connected, he could now cry instead of doing battle. She Staylistened from a short distance, because coming closer to her son had stopped the healing process. A bit apart, he could continue to cry. Soon, she moved closer and listened until he was done. By then he could absorb her affection, and play well with his sister.

———◇———

WHEN IT'S HARD TO LOVE YOUR CHILD

TOOLS: 🐾 STAYLISTENING 🐴 PLAYLISTENING

My son is three-and-a-half years old. His behavior had recently become outrageous. He was hitting other children, as well as me, causing disruptions in play with them, and generally making life difficult wherever he went. He never seemed to be reasonable about anything. He was having temper tantrums all the time. Everything seemed to be directed at me. I didn't like him anymore, and I felt guilty about it.

In a Hand in Hand Parenting class, I brought this up, and heard that children's aggressive behavior can often be caused by unmanageable fears. I was asked whether he had experienced any early trauma, such as a difficult birth, medical procedures, or sudden separations in infancy. It was a surprising question, and my answer was that he'd had a very long and difficult birth. He was three weeks late, and I spent three days in the hospital being induced. After I pushed for four hours, he was finally born, but there were signs of fetal distress. It was very hard for both of us. The thought that he might have fears left over from these experiences hadn't occurred to me.

One of the things I learned in the class was that children can release fears through laughter. So it was suggested that my husband and I wrestle with our son, or have a big, silly, pillow fight. We should let him be vigorous and victorious in the play, let him be the winner during most of it, but we should put up a good enough contest that he could laugh a lot during the play. A further idea was to look for any small excuse he might use to have a big cry after this play, to finish relieving himself of the tight feelings that were making him so aggressive.

These suggestions worked wonderfully! The next day, after dinner, my husband and I got down on the floor and had a big pillow fight and wrestling time with our son. He *loved* it! He laughed and laughed and was very excited to play long and hard with us. We did this for two nights in a row, and his behavior began to smooth out somewhat.

The day after the second big play session, he was trying to kick a ball in the air, and became very frustrated. He began talking harshly to himself, "I can't kick this ball right! There, I did it wrong again! Why can't I ever kick the ball right? What's the matter with me!"

I thought, "Here are the tight feelings, coming to the surface. He's being so critical of himself." So I moved toward him and paid close attention, and he went into a major tantrum. I have usually tried to set limits with him around tantrums, or have done Time Outs, or gotten angry. This time, I stayed with him, got close, and he really came undone. He tried to hit me and kick me, crying and thrashing all the while. I hung in through this physical attack, and after awhile, he sat on my lap and sobbed hard for about half an hour.

As he cried, I kept thinking to myself, "This is not about kicking the ball. This is much bigger than that." Sometimes he would push me away, and then cry harder. I stayed with him and kept offering closeness. After a while, I thought maybe he had cried enough, so I got him a drink of water, and he pulled out of it. He was very tired.

Since that big cry, he's been more loving, more physically affectionate, and more verbal. He is a changed child. It's easy to love him again—I feel like I got my son back. He's not finished working on these feelings, but I've made a commitment to spend more time with him playing so he can laugh, and listen to his feelings. The results of listening are so rewarding!

HOW IT WORKED

An aggressive child is almost always scared. When we learn to recognize aggression as a signal for help, it's much easier to feel empathy and to come up with a way to remedy the problem. Once these parents understood that their son was scared, and that there were concrete reasons for his fear, they could experiment with the Hand in Hand tools. Playlistening prompted lots of laughter that led to their son feeling safer and more connected. Then, when he struggled with kicking a ball, he sensed that it was OK for him to finally cry long and hard.

Working through deep fears can take time, but even one half-hour of Staylistening can dramatically transform a child's behavior. This family has learned how to work together to play, connect, and help a good boy untie the knot of fear that was making life miserable for him and those who love him.

"IT'S HER FAULT!"

TOOL: STAYLISTENING

My six-year-old son and four-year-old daughter and I had stopped at a local café for lunch. My son got out of the car and closed the door, not noticing that his younger sister was also on her way out his door. She wasn't injured physically but was hurt by the insult of having the door slammed on her. She began to cry and cry, and at first my son wanted to cast the blame on her and tell her that she shouldn't have come out his door. I stopped him by saying, "She's really upset. Let's just listen to her feelings about what happened."

I put an arm around her, and he came close, and we both just gave her our attention while she cried. I think listening to her cry helped him, because when she finished my son apologized to her instead of offering the lecture he initially wanted to deliver. And she readily accepted his apology, which she won't typically do when she's hurting. They walked arm in arm into the restaurant while my son gently reminded her that she should let him know when she's coming out his door so it won't happen again.

This is a powerful example for me of how listening to someone who is hurt can make way for clearer thinking, compassion, understanding, and love for both children.

HOW IT WORKED

When one child hurts another, he often puts on a veil of indifference or pins the blame on someone else. He's scared. Scared that the person got hurt. Scared that he wasn't able to control himself. Scared of the fallout from the adults around him. But a child wouldn't hurt another if he felt connected to a loving adult. This mom saw her son's goodness, and invited him to be a part of his sister's healing process. He witnessed his mom Staylisten with her, and didn't feel shamed or blamed. His sister recovered from the slight, and he felt close to her again. They were able to make up without prompting, and even have an uncharged conversation about how to help things go differently next time.

Aggression: Meaningful Apologies

WHAT YOU NEED TO KNOW

A forced apology is never meaningful. Think how you'd feel if you'd been wronged by a colleague and your boss stood over her, demanding she apologize to you. When the "sorry" was spoken, would it hold weight? The same is true with our children. Using Listening Tools to focus on helping children rebuild their connection with you and others will help them feel good and think well again. It will also lead to spontaneous gestures of reconciliation that come from the heart.

INTERVENING IN A DISPUTE

TOOLS: 🚦 SETTING LIMITS ↺ STAYLISTENING

I always have the urge to intervene and lecture when my school-aged girls fight. I want to tell them why they should be nice to each other and that they are the only sisters they will have. I want to correct the behavior, but when I do that, I get nowhere. The other day when I heard them saying mean things to each other, I walked into the room slowly and set a limit, telling them that they were not allowed to talk to one another with mean or harsh words. I asked them to explain what happened. Then the magical Staylistening took place. I listened to what had happened, said very little, and let them come to an understanding with one another. They didn't apologize like I may have asked them to do a year ago, but they did listen to each other and admit their wrongdoing. It was lovely. All it took was for me to listen, and then they listened, too. Genius!

HOW IT WORKED

When children are mean to one another, it seems to ignite a fire in parents, leading us to lecture and scold. Here, this mom was able to push those urges aside and move in with a clear limit: "You may not speak to each other harshly." Her loving but firm boundary, and her willingness to listen, allowed her girls to share thoughts and offload feelings in a safe space, ridding themselves of their upset with one another. In the end, they were able to take responsibility for their actions, and feel close to one another again.

———◇———

YOU DON'T HAVE TO LISTEN PERFECTLY

TOOL:  STAYLISTENING

My two girls, ten and six, had a disagreement while playing. The first I heard of it was when my youngest came in from the garden, disappointed because her sister had abandoned their game. She launched into a noisy, angry cry. I listened to her for a while, but began to feel triggered myself, so I asked my husband to step in for a while. He is not on the same page with Listening Tools, so he tried to distract her by suggesting a bike ride. Of course, she didn't respond in a timely fashion, so he got fed up and walked away. The short break had helped me to get back on track, though, so I went back and listened to her. She was incredibly angry and upset. I didn't need to do much. I just listened warmly and occasionally pointed out that she had really wanted to keep on playing with her sister. She cried hard.

After a while, I felt I needed to get dinner started, so I explained that I was sorry, but I couldn't listen to her any more right then. I asked her if she would like to help. I was expecting her to be wobbly because I hadn't waited until she was done. But to my amazement, she happily helped me! Then out of the blue, as we sat down for our meal, she said to her sister, "I am really sorry." Even my husband commented on her transformation.

HOW IT WORKED

In these situations, many of us would run outside and attempt to get to the bottom of what happened. But most of the time it doesn't matter who started

it, or what ignited the argument. The important facts are that the children are
overcome with emotion, disconnected from a caring adult, and unable to access
their thinking. This mom Staylistened to help her daughter heal from her upset.
When Mom felt she was losing her patience, she called on her husband to help.
Then, refueled after a short break, Mom was able to step back in and simply
listen to her daughter cry hard. When she needed to move on to make dinner,
she let her daughter know. To Mom's surprise, her daughter was happy to assist.
And at dinner, without prompting, she could think well enough to apologize to
her sister for whatever happened earlier.

HITTING IN THE CAR

TOOLS: SETTING LIMITS   STAYLISTENING

Both of my kids, now six-and- a-half years old, were off track. We were
on our way to a friend's long-awaited birthday party, and the girls went
from playing to hitting. Fighting in the car is a hard one for me, because
I can't take immediate action to stop it. Shelly was crying hard; apparently
Cassie had hit her.

"Cassie hit me, Cassie hit me," Shelly yelled between sobs. I pulled the
car over, and turned around to examine what had happened. Shelly cried
harder. Pulling the car over was setting a limit. The kids were saying, "I
want to go to the party! Don't stop, Mommy, we don't want to be late!"

Safely stopped, I assessed the situation. Cassie looked stoic, arms folded across her chest, a frown on her face. I could tell that she had indeed hit.
Shelly was wailing. I paused. "Shelly, I'm sorry I couldn't keep you safe,"
I said, looking at her softly and stroking her leg. She grabbed my arm and
cradled it for a few moments.

I turned my attention to Cassie. "Cassie, I'm sorry I wasn't there to
help you stop," I said, looking at her kindly. This was a remarkable mile-
stone for me, as their hitting has triggered me for years. "Your hand just
jumped away from you and hit Shelly. I bet you didn't even know it was
happening." Her eyes welled up with tears and she nodded her head. "You
didn't mean to hit Shelly, did you?"

"No, Mommy, I didn't," she said. "But she was trying to pinch me."

"I'm really sorry I couldn't help you," I said, realizing that she herself had been scared of being hurt. She wasn't feeling connected enough to me to let out all her tears. Nevertheless, I watched her hold in the tears but look at Shelly with renewed softness. They both told me it was over and that I could go. They really wanted to get to the party on time. Although I could have delayed and let them work on their feelings, I didn't have the capacity.

As I started driving again, I heard them talking about being sorry. "But we didn't say were sorry," one girl said. The next thing I heard was both of them saying a spontaneous "I'm sorry" to each other. They meant it.

The party went well, and we all had fun. I'm really glad I stopped and set the limit.

HOW IT WORKED

When we blame one child or the other, it creates tension in their relationship. Instead, this mom set a limit, and then took responsibility for everyone's safety. By apologizing to her children for not being able to prevent this incident, she left the space open for both the aggressor and the victim to heal from their upsets. We forget that children who act aggressively are hurting, too. If this mom had shamed and blamed smug-faced Cassie, another layer of hurt would have set in to separate the sisters. Neither child would have had the opportunity to rebuild their connection.

⚫⚫⚫

Aggression: Bad Words From Good Kids

WHEN YOU CAN'T STAND POTTY TALK

TOOLS: 🐾 PLAYLISTENING   🎭 LISTENING PARTNERSHIP

I began doing Listening Partnerships a year ago, and I feel I am on quite a journey! At first it was strange, watching people step so quickly into laughter or tears or both. Then, as this became familiar and I began to embrace my feelings instead of pushing them away, I experienced the comfort that comes from crying deeply about things that are affecting me.

It has been interesting to observe the sensations within my body when I am talking about things that bring up fear—the need to stretch, the tightness that occurs in my shoulders as soon as I begin, the trembling that I used to put down to being cold, but which I now realize occurs only when I feel threatened. I am starting to allow myself to fully feel.

However, I had not been able to use laughter effectively to release fear until recently. My daughter, who is six, has a tendency to say, "Poo Poo, Wee Wee, Willy" when she is upset. I recognized that this is her way of saying that she doesn't like what's going on, but I was still not able to deal with it calmly and effectively. I had tried all sorts of traditional methods such as sticker charts, rewards, and discussions about how it isn't nice. Since I learned Hand in Hand Parenting, I had tried vigorous snuggles and Playlistening, but I was erratic. Sometimes I could respond effectively, but other times I just got angry.

I brought this up several times in my listening time and this helped in the short run, allowing me to understand the fears I carried. I realized that the words themselves were not bad; however, I was afraid of her saying worse words in the future, or that she wouldn't be able to control her language. And my response was still inconsistent. Then in a parents' listening group I started imitating her, and this immediately made me laugh! I then imagined her as a twenty-year-old who gets upset and shouts these words and that made me laugh even harder. My listeners couldn't help but laugh, too, and this deepened my laughter until I was helpless—laughter, tears, and all. This was a short Listening Time—only four minutes—but it has been amazing to see the after-effects.

Not only did I feel great after, but since then, I have not felt any reaction to her saying those words, except perhaps amusement, because it reminds me of that time! Because of that, I have been able to respond in a playful way, which has been so much more effective than me just telling her to stop, or that it is not OK to talk like that. I can swoop in and playfully offer her a firm hug, or pick her up and throw her on the bed, which she absolutely loves, or chase her around the house to lots of giggles. And as a result, she isn't even saying those things much anymore!

HOW IT WORKED

A parent-child duo with boiling emotions is a recipe for staying stuck in unworkable behaviors. Often, our upsets about our children's unsavory language keep us from thinking well about how to help our children stop using it. Like this mom, we try to explain why we want them to stop, or we get desperate and bribe them with a reward we hope they'll want badly enough to stop. But these strategies don't work for any length of time because they rely upon reason. And when your child is behaving unreasonably, you can assume that she's running on raw emotion. This mom was brilliant to use her Listening Partnership to gain an understanding of her own fears, and then laugh them away. By freeing herself of her own emotional charge, she was able to think well about how to support her child through hers. Playlistening games then helped them strengthen their connection, and her daughter's language improved greatly.

BUTT-TALK TIME

TOOL: PLAYLISTENING

My seven-year-old daughter was using lots of potty language, mostly butt related, in a wide variety of settings, so one night I announced that we were going to institute "Butt Talk Time" (which we called BTT) in our family. Every night, she would have five minutes to say whatever she wanted using whatever words in whatever tone she wanted. The rest of the day she had to use language appropriate to the context. Whenever she'd let something inappropriate slip during the day I'd remind her to save it for BTT.

We've been doing this for a few months and we've had all kinds of entertaining and frankly hysterical BTTs. Sometimes, she'll ask me to sing standard kids' songs while "unintentionally" inserting inappropriate words. She's choreographed dances to one particular word repeated over and over. We've collaborated on raunchy raps. I make sure not to add to her store of "bad" words but I feel free to repeat what she says in whatever way she says it, or I sing it, or say it in various tones of voice, but always in a delighted way. She laughs especially hard when I start to give a very formal and serious talk and then slip with one of the currently hot words "by accident."

My daughter's language has improved dramatically, but what has been great is how much she loves this time. Sometimes in the morning, as she's heading off to school, she'll announce excitedly, "See you for BTT tonight!" She has started to invite people to join her, as if this is the most wonderful treat. I have only allowed other people to participate a couple of times. Her young adult cousin said it was one of the highlights of her recent visit. Her other mom can sometimes handle it, too. The rule when it's just the two of us is that she can say anything she wants, including things about me or directed at me, but when someone else joins she can't say things about other people.

There have been a couple of nights in a row this week that we didn't have time for it and she mentioned that she needed it because things were starting to "leak out" during the day. I told her she could save up the time we've missed. We're planning a really long BTT this weekend. She's so excited to get a whole twenty minutes all at once and I'm actually kind of looking forward to it, too.

HOW IT WORKED

This may sound extreme—letting your child use language that you feel strongly is inappropriate. But offering designated time in a protected space to experiment with taboo words is often just what your young one needs to diminish the charge of all those "bad words." In the privacy of her home, bothering no one else, this mom was freed from feelings of shame, embarrassment, or worry. She could dive into the play fully, staying pleased with her daughter despite the butt talk. And like Special Time, naming this time together gave her daughter a way to ask for what she needed when she noticed herself losing self-control. I've seen parents turn cars, specific rooms, and even bathtubs into safe havens where everyone knows they can let the potty talk flow freely. And it's only built stronger family connections and helped the children's everyday language improve.

WHAT DRIVES NAME-CALLING?

TOOL: 🔄 STAYLISTENING

My three-year-old daughter had been seeking quite a bit of connection from me for the last day or two. She had been employing all of the tactics we've developed over time to get me to snuggle her. Also, she had been whining and exaggerating each time she got a little bump or ran into something. One evening while I was cooking in the kitchen, she pushed my butt, because she knows that if she pushes my butt she gets a "snuggle hug." She pushed me again and again and it was getting hard to make dinner, because I could see that she was seeking connection. Then, at breakfast the next day she called me "pizza head!" A year ago or more, she started experimenting with saying potty words, and I whispered to her that she could say whatever the offending word was, but under no circumstances was she allowed to say "pizza head," an idea I got from Lawrence J. Cohen's wonderful book, *Playful Parenting*.

She was yelling "pizza head" over and over. I saw she needed attention so I scooped her up to take her into the bedroom when her foot knocked the side of the table. Not hard at all, but a *big* cry followed. I carried her into the bedroom and we sat on the bed so I could Staylisten while she cried. We did this for about five minutes and then she said she wanted to be alone. That is a clear signal for me that my daughter is off track and needing me. So I told her that I wanted to follow her. She negotiated that I would stay at her door while she went on the bed. I slowly inched my way onto the bed with her and she was OK with it. She cried a little bit more and then she said, "Those people in Florida were mean."

I asked her which people she was talking about. Three months ago, we'd visited Florida and stayed in a condo for two weeks. The owners of the condo had provided just one garbage bag for our entire stay and when we asked them for more they refused. My husband and I were annoyed that we had to buy an entire box of garbage bags when we needed only three, and she heard us being annoyed. Either the incident was still alive for our daughter or perhaps she was done crying and wanted to change the subject. In any case, that topic came out of nowhere.

Since this Staylistening session, my daughter has been very connected to me. Clearly, she had some bad feelings she wanted to offload. I
spend a lot of time focusing on the tools that we have as parents to stay
connected with our kids. It's nice to know that my daughter also has
tools that work quite well!

HOW IT WORKED

*When we learn to read our children's cues and follow their lead, we quickly
realize how brilliant they are at caring for their emotional selves. This mom recognized her daughter's off-track behavior. She saw calls for help in her daughter's
yelling, her big feelings after a little bump, and in her plea to be left alone. She
Staylistened without probing for explanations or trying to appease her daughter. In
the end, her child offered a peek into an underlying upset that may have been driving some of her troublesome behaviors. Most importantly, this opportunity led to a
stronger parent-child connection, which always paves the way for positive change.*

———◆———

WHEN YOUR CHILD CALLS YOU "STUPID"

TOOLS: LISTENING PARTNERSHIP   PLAYLISTENING

 SETTING LIMITS    STAYLISTENING

After school, my six-year-old was clearly off track and needing to offload some feelings. He had been at his little brother since he got in the
car, and then on the way home, he started calling me "stupid." Normally,
being called "stupid" makes me angry, but I had been working on it with
my Listening Partner and on this day I felt like I could play with it.

So I said to him, "Oh, that's not my secret name! My secret name is
Kombucha Head, but don't tell anyone. It's a *secret*!" So of course, he and
his two-year-old brother started yelling out, "Kombucha Head!" as loud as
they could. I pretended to be horrified, worried that everyone would know
my secret name. This kept going after we got home, but I felt like it was
losing its allure. So I changed tack and said that I had lots of raspberries to

give them. (You give a raspberry by putting your moist lips on someone's skin and blowing hard to make a funny noise.) They both ran and hid under the blankets, giggling together. I pretended I couldn't find them, and ended up leaning on them while they were under the covers. They were laughing and squirming and I sat there blowing raspberries toward them, without being able to actually reach them, pretending to be upset I couldn't land any.

Then, the two of them turned the game around and started trying to raspberry me. So I played it up. "No, no, no! You can't raspberry me! *I'm* the raspberry person around here!" I protested while they landed raspberries all over me. After about five minutes of this, they both got up and went off to play together.

They were fine for the rest of the evening, until just before bed, when my older son kicked me and tried to bite me. So I moved in quickly and held him in my arms, so he couldn't do damage. He started screaming and raging and yelling, "No, no, you are hurting my neck! Don't hurt my neck!" I checked to make sure I wasn't holding or hurting his neck, and my arms were not even near his neck. I repositioned him, just in case I was somehow hurting him, but he continued saying the same things and thrashing. This is a familiar pattern, one that I have been helping him with lately. As far as I can tell, he's working on fears that come from being held down to be stitched after an accident.

After only five minutes, he stopped crying, looked at me and said, "I want to sit next to you, Mom," and we all read a book together. He fell asleep that night quickly, holding my hand. I was amazed at how quickly the Playlistening allowed both of my sons to connect with one another again, after a pretty torrid time in the car. I was also very pleased that the evening ran so smoothly after Playlistening and that the night ended so sweetly after a big rage and release of feelings.

HOW IT WORKED

This mom knew her buttons got pushed when her children called her names. She made sure to work on those feelings in her Listening Partnership, so that her upset wouldn't interfere as she worked to help her children. Here we see how her work paid off. Faced with a child calling her "stupid," she was able to think quickly and offer a silly alternative, which he and his brother both ran with. To keep the laughter rolling, Mom added physical affection to the Playlistening game when they got home.

In the evening, the son whose aggression had surfaced in name-calling felt safe enough to show his fears with more overt aggression. Mom held a limit so that she was safe, yet allowed him to release his feelings in her arms, with crying and struggling. Then, quick as the storm came, it was over. He had swept the fear away, and could connect sweetly again.

PART IV
OUR FUTURE, CONNECTED

13
Connecting When You're At Wits' End

Every parent I've ever known has wondered what to do when their kids push them over the edge. Unfortunately, there is no wellspring of patience to tap in moments like these. But there are things you can do that will help. Even a five-minute exchange of listening time with another parent can mean the difference between hitting or not, yelling or not, blaming or not. When you don't know what to do, it's time to offload your feelings. You've got a good mind, and you know your child well. Feelings are probably in the way of taking a step forward.

Meanwhile, though you don't have any answers yet, use one of the proactive Listening Tools—Special Time or Playlistening—to head things in a constructive direction. Connection is a big part of the solution. When you're too upset to connect with your child, your Listening Partnership will move things along.

THREE IDEAS FOR HANDLING YOUR WORST MOMENTS

In tandem with your regular use of Listening Tools, here are a few practical ideas for handling your fiery parenting moments.

1. Set up emergency listening agreements. Almost every parent struggles with moments of upset, and most of us tend to struggle alone. Chances are good that when you're having an off moment, one of your friends or listening partners is doing just fine. They could listen to you for a few minutes and help you release some tension so you don't have to target your child.

So ask whether they'd be interested in adding a two-way emergency request feature to the partnership you have with them. If you've enlisted a friend who isn't familiar with Listening Partnerships, you'll want to check in with them about how it was for them the first few times either one of you called. Outline the importance of confidentiality, and ask them not to advise you in any way.

I know many parents who have at least two people they can call when they need someone to listen for five or ten minutes. A few parents I know in stressful situations have up to ten! And it turns out to be deeply rewarding to help another hardworking parent navigate a heated moment well.

2. Empower your child with a plan, then conduct an "Anger Drill." Trouble often erupts in a flash. When we try to control ourselves, we become stiff replicas of the parents our children know and love. When our feelings, long fermented, spew forth, the intensity frightens them. They've lost their safe harbor and don't know what to do. You can help your child practice calling for help. We mustn't depend on our children to take care of us, but giving a child permission to reach for help when he's in need hands him a tool and lets him know he deserves assistance.

As with emergency listening, your plan involves making agreements with an understanding friend or two. You enlist one or more people your *child* can call when your anger rises and you have forgotten that there's anyone on your side. Post a list of their names and phone numbers; if your child can't read yet, add a photo of each next to their number.

Then let your child practice calling them. "My Mommy/Daddy needs to talk to you," is the gist of his message. In a tense situation, your child may not remember what to say—simply managing to make the call will be a true victory. So tell your friend to ask to talk with you. This will connect you with someone who knows you're good, and who can listen to you during a hard moment. It moves your child out of the line of fire, and adds an extra resource to the situation even when you can't think to reach out.

Ask your friend to remind you to take the call out of your child's presence, or if that's impossible, to remind you to simply make noise rather than describe your worst feelings out loud. You will still be mad as heck. In fact, with a friend on the line, you'll probably feel more upset than you did before! A willing listener tends to intensify what we feel, and brings our emotion closer to the healing point of release. And a good cry is just what an angry parent needs to transform their day!

Once your child has practiced making calls, you might want to do a full Anger Drill. In a light voice, with comic gestures, play out a silly version of your usual anger routine. Then encourage your child to practice calling your friend. You'll want to see if you can elicit some giggles with your imitation of your fed-up self. You can ask your child how he thinks you should play your angry self—he might have a few interesting tips for you! At any rate, conducting an Anger Drill shows your child that although you lose your composure at times, you're aware of your difficulty, and you're on his side.

3. **Lie down on the spot, and stay there.** A third option for heated moments is to lie down right then and there. If you're not thinking straight, decide to give up trying to be in charge. Don't go anywhere, just lie down, on the kitchen floor if necessary, and let your children continue with the upsetting things they're doing. You're not in shape to help them right now, so as long as they're not running into traffic, you can give up trying.

Lying down can allow you to more fully notice the feelings roiling inside you. When you stop trying so hard to be the parent, you may be able to shed that tension. See what bubbles up. If you can manage to laugh or cry, you'll be on the mend.

Because humans are wired for connection, your children will eventually come closer. They will come to sit on your tummy, ask you what you're doing there, or bring you something they think will help you. They'll act to reset the connection. It's much easier for them to do this when you're on the floor. They feel safer. You seem smaller. And as they come around, you'll all get a fresh start with one another.

Here's how it can work:

———◇———

I am uniquely bad at handling conflict. So when the idea of lying down to keep myself from going off the deep end came up on the Hand in Hand Online Discussion Group, I told my husband I might try it.

Soon after, my kids were arguing about who got to go first at something. I was in the middle of it and became frustrated. I turned and threw myself down on the floor, giving up being in charge à la Patty's suggestion.

My husband was there, too, and knowing that he knew what I was doing added a lot of support. But I didn't find my feelings and cry. I felt such a wave of relief that I laughed harder than I had in a very long time! It was that wonderful uncontrollable belly laughter you just can't stop. I could *not* stop laughing! And the kids *loved* this! It definitely did open up creative channels and defuse the irritation that was starting to build in me.

Afterwards, I had some insights. I think I get into these power struggles with my children because I have this idea that on certain things I have to "be consistent"—and I do think consistency is ideal for things that are important if you can do it in a good way. But I notice that I hold the line even when it *doesn't* matter that much. Now I'm realizing that maybe it's better to be consistently not mean and scary, rather than being a stickler about the rules, if it comes down to one or the other!

I *loved* the lying-down-on-the-floor experience and have to heartily recommend it! It's the most refreshingly unexpected opposite-of-how-you-usually-do-things experience.

———◇———

A mother of five children who are all under nine years old had this experience:

———◇———

It was mid-morning and I was already exhausted. Between the cranky disagreements and random shrill screams from my three-year-old, things seemed off to a bad start with my kids. My seven-year-old insisted I sit on the bed in the guest room to talk with him while he used the bathroom, so I took the opportunity to lie down as I didn't have the energy to do anything else. Within a few minutes, the other four crawled up and lay down around me and on top of me. We all talked playfully and relaxed together. Soon my other son joined us. We lay there for a good fifteen minutes. It completely changed the tone of the morning and my outlook on the day. I wasn't trying to solve anything, but just lying there made the difference. All was well again. They had reconnected with me, and somehow, with each other.

———◇———

When we do get caught up and turn our emotional firepower on our children, it's important to apologize. Children need to hear that we love them, and that we're sorry we got scared or stressed and did things we didn't want to do. They need to hear that we're determined to find a grownup to talk to so we don't get so angry at them. Even our infants deserve our apologies when we've gotten lost in our feelings.

It's not easy to take emergency measures when you're on the edge of anger. But we get lots of chances to try! The strategies outlined here can make your children safer during your heated moments. But it's your Listening Partnerships that will do the most good. Working on your feelings with a listener will reduce the number of heated moments you have, and give you a few added seconds of time to change course before falling into a pit of anger.

14
Building Support for Your Parenting

When you have good support for your parenting, you can sense things moving forward with your children. It's easier to find a moment for your-self. You know where to turn when the day becomes challenging. And often, you have what it takes to offer your children moments of warm attention.

To build the support you need to move mountains such as finding a job you enjoy, handling your children's sibling dramas, or lobbying for needed changes at their daycare center, start with you. How do you *feel*? Many par-ents, when they plunge inward, recognize a few major bugaboos that drain energy and roil their emotions: isolation; trouble reaching out for help; guilt and blame; confusion; and exhaustion. When you make gains on any one of these fronts, your day-to-day burdens will be eased. The energy that was spent on emotion that pooled and festered will flow toward love, play, friendship, and a good night's sleep.

BUILDING YOUR WAY OUT OF ISOLATION

What weighs on you every day? What do you miss from your life before children? Who do you feel close to? Who makes you feel special? Who knows and loves your particular talents? Who sticks by you no matter what? If your support system is stretched thin, how do you get by? What would it take to actually feel supported? Whose support did you have as a child? Who cherished you? If you didn't have much support, how did you find the strength to make it into adulthood?

Here's a mom who noticed how she normally handled her feelings of isolation, and then felt a welcome, positive shift after offloading these feelings:

———◇———

Before I found Hand in Hand, I was very good at turning my head when I felt triggered emotionally. I masked my feelings to the point of isolation and numbness. When I finally learned to allow myself to feel my feelings, I saw that I could then let them go and carry on productively with my mind sharp and my connections with other people strong.

When I finally had a day off with my son, I brought him to the park to play. There, I ran into a friend who had just opened her own hair salon. I have been a hairstylist for thirteen years and have not yet gone out on my own, but I was "happy for her," and stood for twenty minutes as she rattled off all her successes. The rest of the day was shot: I began to feel isolated, became critical of others, and was short-tempered with my son. I tried to cover up the feelings as I had always done: I had a cup of coffee, and called a friend to complain about something unimportant. But I couldn't seem to shake the feeling, and I couldn't be present for my son on our day off together. Finally, I recognized my old pattern of numbing my feelings, so I reached out to a listening partner.

My partner was attentive as I spoke about my day and pinpointed the moment that my mood had changed. I found feelings around accomplishment that were rooted in my childhood. I had been completely unaware that I was carrying a negative impression of myself around for all these years. As I let myself drop into feelings of failure and the incident in my childhood that had sparked them, I began to feel an incredible release. Ten minutes of crying was all it took. My day brightened and I felt as if I had let go of a whole backpack of pain. I turned my attention to my son and played with him the way he deserves.

When I saw my hairdresser friend again, I found I was curious about her business and interested in her successes and challenges. That Listening Partnership made all the difference in my perception of this formerly difficult situation.

———◇———

REACHING FOR FRIENDS, REACHING FOR HELP

Many of us tend to feel personally inadequate when we find ourselves struggling to parent well all by ourselves. But any experienced parent will tell you that we all need time away from our children in order to do our job well. We all need others who care and can help us. We all need the chance to think and talk about the details of life with our children. Being raised in an individualistic society makes asking for help an emotional issue. And if you are a member of a group maligned by racist, sexist, homophobic, or other hurtful attitudes, reaching out is especially hard because you've been the target of unkind and unfair treatment. There is the fear that you may be confirming prejudices by seeking the help every parent deserves.

You'll benefit from using Listening Partnerships as you reach out for fuller connection. Here's a single mom's account of how her Partnerships paved the way for a turning point in her relationship with her mother:

————◇————

I had moved with my daughter to a house close to my own parents. I was about to get a new job, and my parents had agreed to help with child-care. This particular day, my mom was helping me paint the bedroom. As we worked, she said a string of critical things: I hadn't taped the baseboards correctly; I wasn't stroking the paintbrush quite right; I should have opened the window; there wasn't enough food in the fridge for lunch.

I had been working in my Listening Partnership on not giving up on what I thought and what I wanted as a mom. I'd felt like giving up so many times. So when I noticed my spirits sinking, I thought about what to do. I could just let her keep making such remarks, and try to ignore them. Or I could get upset, which wouldn't help our relationship. After all, she was here helping me! Finally, I decided on a third alternative: I would tell her what I wanted. I said, "Mom, I do a whole lot better when I'm feeling good. Can you find a few things you think I'm doing well, and let me know about them when you see them? I think our day will go better that way." She was quiet, but she heard me. The rest of our day went better, and she even said a few positive things to me.

————◇————

COUNTERING GUILT AND BLAME

The job of parenting cannot be done perfectly. We simply don't have the information, the control of our environment, or the help we need to do everything right. But we do have a far more important capability. We can treasure and enjoy our children, and take pride in ourselves as mothers and fathers. Attention on what's good leads us away from dissatisfaction. It helps us make friends and build caring networks around our families.

The regrets we have because we haven't been able to parent perfectly need to be talked and cried about. The past can't be redone, but the feelings from the past can be released. So pay attention to your regrets, but only when you have a listener there to pour in caring while you pour out your feelings of hurt.

Blame is the other side of the guilt coin—it's fault-finding pointed outward. When you find yourself blaming your children for their difficulties, your partner for his or hers, or other parents for upsetting you, big feelings are ready to be shed. Yes, people make mistakes. Yes, our children's behavior often goes beyond what we are able to handle. Yes, if we only had more control over our lives, things would be better. But we *can't* control a child's behavior fully! And we can't fix anything by blaming them, others, or ourselves for the pain we go through.

As you work on feelings of guilt and blame in your listening time, you'll move toward accepting those you care about. You'll have more energy for figuring out how to help them feel safer and more connected. You'll be more proactive as you set limits. You'll be able to listen longer to the feelings they must shed in order to return to their best thinking.

Sometimes, the guilt we feel or the blame we throw stems from specific expectations about what a family is "supposed" to look like. Your partner is "supposed" to come home from work on time. Your older child is "supposed" to be kind to his baby sister. Your neighborhood is "supposed" to be friendlier to young families than it is. Your children are "supposed" to say "please" and "thank you" more often than they do.

When you find that your family isn't the way you think it's supposed to be, try throwing your expectations overboard. When you're working so hard that you can't appreciate yourself or anyone else, give yourself a break! Stop serving hot meals for two weeks, and bring on the carrots, toast, and peanut butter. Let the relatives be grumpy because you decided not to visit this month. Nap during your lunch break, even though people at work will talk. *You* get to decide what's good for you and what's not. When others are triggered into blame mode, hold your head high. You have every right to experiment, and every right to be proud of yourself, your family, and your decisions.

Here are two stories from parents who have tussled with guilt and blame. They show that victory over these energy-zappers is possible:

———◇———

When my older daughter started preschool, I felt anxious and uncertain. I didn't want my feelings to influence her experience of preschool, so I took them to my listening partner to have them heard.

With my listening partner's support, I was able to gain insight into my own fears around separation from my mother when I was a child. I cried and released the feelings that were being triggered as my daughter left me each morning. I also explored the feelings of uncertainty that I had, and found that they rose from feelings of guilt that I often experienced when I was away from my child. Again, I gained insight as I remembered how much I wanted my mother to be with me more. I saw how my present guilt stemmed from not wanting my daughter to have those same feelings. I was once again able to cry about having missed my mother so.

This work gave me relief and insight. I was no longer so triggered by my own story. I'm sure this made it easier for her to separate from me. On the first day, she was happy to go, had a great time, and was eager to go back. Toward the end of the week, I met again with my listening partner to explore and offload feelings. Then, when my daughter did want to cry about some of her feelings around separation, I was able to be there for her and Staylisten without being triggered. All that listening time paid off!

———◇———

Here's the second:

———◇———

I have been using Listening Partnerships to help me with my anger at how difficult it is to find support for my daughter, who has a learning disability. Listening Partnerships have helped, but my anger was still there. I started to direct it at my daughter, and I could not get to the source of it. Why was I now so annoyed with her behavior? So I just kept pushing into that anger in my listening time.

During one session I said, "My mother would have had her on the floor if my daughter acted this way with her!" My partner asked me, "What would your mother have done to her on the floor?" S__t, I thought, do we really have to go there? I choked up and a lot of fear and guilt swelled up. I cried. My mother would have physically gone after her. That is what you do. That is what we do. Kids just don't back talk, not black kids. We had to "do it right." There was a lot at stake. We had to counter stereotypes, we had to demonstrate that we came from a good home, and we had to prove that we are just as good and capable as any of the white kids around us. This is what it felt like for me, coming from a black family in the South. There were threats of a backhand to the mouth, getting hit with Hot Wheels tracks or a switch from a tree. These make funny stories that we now can tell with laughter, but the hard reality of it is that these things hurt our spirits. Now, finally, I get to cry and rage about this.

I love my parents and I could not imagine raising children with no support the way my mother did. There were positives, a lot of them. But I never want to beat the voice right out of my child, shame her, or make her feel like she does not exist. So what do you do when you were raised with, "You don't talk back to adults," and your child begins to talk back in every conversation? You get a little listening and you "go there." You get angry with your mom, you say what you were never allowed to say as a child, and you tell that child within you, "You matter. You are being listened to now." Then you remember that your child's rudeness is really a cry for help amid her own stress and confusion.

Practically, I have started to set a limit. When she speaks rudely I simply come to her and say, "We cannot talk to each other this way." If we need to slide into Staylistening, we do. This is my little quiet space where I get to change the world, one mom and one child at a time. Bring it on, world. I am ready.

———◇———

The bottom line is that even when we've blamed our children or felt bad about ourselves, we've done our best. We certainly need to keep reaching to build good support. But as long as we can keep learning, perfection is not required. We are good parents.

CLEARING AWAY CONFUSION

Confusion often arises over decisions we must make to guide our families. These can be everyday decisions, like what to do when your child wakes up whining every morning. Or it can arise when you're faced with momentous decisions—whether to have another child, whether to take on a job while your children are very young. To help you think more clearly, your Listening Partnership will be invaluable. One excellent strategy is to take several listening times, and devote each one to a single alternative you see before you.

Here are two parents' stories about how Listening Partnerships helped them find the early roots of their dilemma, release the feelings trapped there, and clear up their thinking.

———◇———

I had been feeling anxious about what to do with both kids' school situations. I didn't know where to send my extremely sensitive son, and whether to keep my daughter at her nursery school while it changed ownership. Every time friends asked what we were doing, I would feel overwhelmed and agitated. Should we move away? Should we stay? I couldn't decide. I couldn't think clearly.

I took the issue to my listening partner, just dumping all the confusion and half-thoughts out of my head. She asked me to focus on how I would feel if we stayed. I decided that we wouldn't move away from the area, and she listened while I explored how we could make it work. I got to offload all the concerns I had about the options for schooling, and by the end of the call I felt so much clarity and relief.

Since then, I have been able to take practical steps toward arranging what needs to happen. We so rarely get the opportunity to just dump all our confusion out, and work our way through the muddle, because others interrupt or offer advice. In this case, I got exactly what I needed.

———◇———

And the second story, about a longer emotional project:

———◇———

I had a big decision to make: whether to move my family from the southern part of our state to a northern town. My wife felt strongly that heading north would provide our two- and thirteen-year-olds with good schools and also allow us to spend more time with her parents, who lived nearby. However, I had not moved for almost twenty years and was pretty unsure about all of the newness that relocation would bring.

I took my fears and concerns to my listening partner and focused on my feelings about saying goodbye, which brought up childhood feelings about my parents' divorce. After loads of tears and laughter, the idea of moving began to seem much less ominous. My listening partner suggested that I also spend some time working on my feelings about staying where we were, which brought up my fears about money and my role as a bread-winner in my family. There was plenty to work on!

After several listening times and time to think, I was able to reach the decision to move north. It was one of the best decisions I have ever made.

———◇———

Getting the help of a listener means that you'll feel good about thoroughly exploring your own mind on a subject, and no matter what you decide, you will have absorbed the good will and confidence of your listener. This can give you a head start at feeling good about whichever direction you take! And should you make a mistake, your listening partnership will help you identify it quickly, and change course if you must!

BREAKING THE GRIP OF EXHAUSTION

When you notice that resting doesn't refresh you, you can assume you've become exhausted. A second sign is that you get the most necessary things done, but you don't have the capacity to solve problems creatively. If you've been working hard, you think you have to work harder; if you've been yelling, you decide you're not yelling enough yet; if you spend money you don't have, you think, "If I just get this one more thing, that might turn it around for me." But none of those tactics helps you be pleased with yourself or your children.

An exhausted parent has big feelings, usually of isolation, worry, or hopelessness, mixed in with his tiredness. Taking the time to notice that someone cares about you can lift that emotional load off your shoulders. A good cry may be the result, either during a rest or some time later.

Here's how one parent used a parent support group to address feelings of exhaustion that were interfering with her parenting:

———◇———

There was a period of time when I felt utterly exhausted every time I was with my kids. This made sense as I have twins who at this time were about two. But even the breaks I took did not relieve my fatigue. Finally, I went to a Hand in Hand support group. There, I had a really big cry and some feelings of loss and grief about my own childhood arose. When I left, I felt energized and happy. I rushed home, looking forward to seeing my children and feeling excited to play with them. Afterward, I realized how essential it is to release my own feelings in order to be present and fresh with my kids. I also learned to watch for those feelings of exhaustion and get some listening time for myself pronto!

———◇———

Here's another:

———◇———

It's nine on Friday morning, and I'm sitting in my car in a store parking lot. I'm exhausted and overwhelmed. Thankfully, I have some listening time. My listening partner calls. We have fifteen minutes each, and I go first. I need to.

"I'm here," she says. I just start sobbing. Not just crying. Wailing. No explanation. No rationalization. Just bawling, for the first five minutes. I can't help myself, and while I feel like a freak for just crying on the phone to someone, I'm also grateful that I've set up this support for myself.

I spend the rest of my time spouting about how I just want to cancel everything—all plans with all people for the next month, including Thanksgiving and Christmas. I'm tired and overwhelmed. I just want a break, and I definitely don't want to cook a turkey or bake any pies. My listening partner just listens, occasionally making reassuring murmurs, or saying, "Yup, just cancel it all."

By the end of my time, my brain has come back to rights a bit, and I realize that I'll probably feel better on Monday after a few days rest, and that I don't really want to cancel Thanksgiving.

Then, thankfully, I get to listen to her. It feels good to be able to listen to another mom, and give back some of the loving attention I have so generously received. As for Thanksgiving, Listening Time is at the top of my list of things for which I'm grateful. And, I do cook the turkey, but let a friend bring the pies.

———◇———

It seems to me that a lot of our exhaustion is caused by emotional tension that has no outlet. Once someone has listened and those feelings have been shed, there's just the tiredness. You can relax. You can remember how to rest.

BUILDING ALLIES FOR YOUR FAMILY

Your best allies may be staring at you, bleary-eyed, from across the sandbox, or across the meeting room at work right now! Band together with other parents and help one another. Join a local parent group, play group, or "Park Day" where you and your child can meet other families and begin to build your own parent "village." Having friends join you on your parenting journey can make an enormous difference.

Look for allies within your family, too. It's smart to encourage relationships between your child and grandparents, aunts and uncles, and other family members that allow you a break. Accept help from family members, even the ones you may not agree with on every issue. Even if Grandma is letting them have too much sugar or Aunt Lisa forgets to reapply sunscreen at the park. And don't underestimate the value of paying some good folks to be allies! Teens are often looking for steady part-time work, so if finances permit, find a helper or a weekly sitter so you can take a break.

Here's a Dad who wanted to create links between his family and his daughter's new school, but was told it was impossible. He worked on his feelings with a listening partner, listened well at a school meeting, and then was rewarded when previously closed doors opened up for him.

———◇———

Last spring, months before my daughter started school, the principal and her kindergarten teacher announced that they would allow no parent volunteers in the classroom. I work the night shift, and I can volunteer in the mornings. I really wanted to make my daughter's public school work, and I could tell a lot of other parents did, too. I worked on my feelings in listening time, and decided to speak up.

Several weeks after school began, I went to the local School Council meeting alone and very afraid. I wrote on the open forum agenda, "Parents volunteering in their child's class." Mine was the only topic in open forum and I said a lot. I said things like, "I don't want my daughter's school to be a drop-off place." The council all nodded in agreement and said parent participation sounded good to them, but it would be up to the principal. Well, he got up and really gave it to me for about ten minutes. He said everything from, "We need teachers in the school, not parents," to, "It's time to cut the apron strings," to, "If you feel this way, you could homeschool your child." The whole time I tried to listen, because you could clearly see that he was upset. So I smiled and I nodded, all the time thinking, "What an a__h____!"

During break, the principal came up to me and I listened again. I told him I knew how hard it must be to work all day and stay at night for these meetings. I asked him about himself and his school. I let him know that I had looked into all my options and his school is where I wanted my children to be.

Before I knew it, he was saying, "I've got to get you into the classroom." Then, after the meeting, the teacher and I came up to each other, and I said, "I want to make one thing perfectly clear. I really appreciate you as a teacher." She laughed. I said I knew she could do the job by herself but I just wanted to help her. I would do anything she said. She laughed and laughed. By the end of the conversation, she asked me to come and help next Thursday. So these two people who had insisted for months that I could not be in the classroom said yes!

I actually cried when I got home that night and told my wife the story. Being dressed down like that in public, then treating them well, had taken all my reserves! My time in the class that Thursday went great: I was there from 9 to 11:30! The teacher and I talked, and I felt more comfortable as the morning went on. The children really liked having me there, too.

———◇———

You deserve plenty of help. You deserve good support. Your connection with your children is what makes your family hum. To be relaxed with them, you'll need people who are on *your* side as friends, listeners, and dedicated nurturers. Find them; appreciate them; get to know them; bring them closer. They'll be lucky to have you in their lives. Start small. Meet them in the park, set up a quick game of Sunday basketball, or start up a children's book exchange with them. Go from there. Make them *your* people!

15

The Road Ahead

DO YOUR OWN THINKING ABOUT PARENTING

One of the great hardships in parenting is that, no matter what approach you use, you can't be absolutely certain you're on the right path! Instead, you must experiment, observe, and think for yourself about what's best for your family. Notice how an approach feels to you, whether it reflects your values, and whether it seems to deliver your love. Is it respectful of your child's intelligence and uniqueness? Of yours? Does it advise you to park your love to the side when times get tough, or does it call on you to reach for your child? And does it have anything to say about handling the stresses of parenting?

I think we parents are called to find ideas that bring out the best in us—and in our children. We need ideas that show us how us to reach for one another when times are hard. When you find such ideas, you still have to try them and see how they work for *you* and for *your* children. Then, you must trust your judgment. It's the best a parent can do.

The ideas we have to offer you are simple: listening connects us. And when we feel connected, we feel safe enough to offload emotional hurt so that we can get back to having fun, enjoying one another, setting necessary limits, and doing important work.

At Hand in Hand Parenting, we have learned that by listening we can open one another's minds and hearts, and heal old wounds. Listening can help us find common ground, even when the road is long. Listening can give us the courage to work for justice; it can keep us from giving up on one another. Listening can give us the stamina to solve complex problems; it can help us build better judgment. Listening can build bridges across race, class, religion, age, and circumstance; listening can bring a loved one in from the cold.

LISTENING UNLEASHES OUR CHILDREN'S POTENTIAL

The 130 parent stories you've read show that listening to our children can improve their outlook and their behavior. Several stories even demonstrate that, over time, parents who use Listening Tools can ease a child's whole way of being. It takes work, of course, and a parent's willingness to work on his or her own upsets.

But what comes of the young people raised by these parents who listen? Are they self-involved? Are they emotionally fragile? Do they have good judgment?

We're in touch with some of the young adult children of parents who took our classes or read our booklets in the 1990s. This early group of parents was quite diverse in race, class, and economic status. How are their children doing? The first thing we'll say is obvious—they're not all alike! But here is a brief report of what some of their offspring are doing now, in their third decade of life.

Let's start with a young man who had fulfilled his ardent childhood goal by the age of twenty-two. He played two years of professional soccer in Europe, and has now become a successful personal trainer. One young woman won a full scholarship to college, and a Fulbright scholarship after that. There's a gifted young man who works as a counselor for homeless youth in a large US city. Another young man manages a tattoo parlor, and one young woman manages a department in a major corporation. There's a young woman who set out to work with families, and serves at-risk parents and children as a bilingual child counselor and outreach worker. A young man who has been a civil rights activist since high school is clerking for a judge on the Federal Fifth Circuit Court of Appeals. Another young man has a job he cares deeply about. He was hired to design solar power installations right out of high school. He is paid well, trains new employees, and, at age twenty-one, is the one his bosses put in charge when they go on vacation. One young woman is a dancer and budding neuroscientist who graduated Magna Cum Laude from a highly regarded university. Another young woman found work in India, Italy, and France as she went through university; she is fostering social change through her work in an urban bicycle exchange company.

Many of these young adults come from families that have grappled with outsized struggles. Some come from single-parent families, some of them wrestle with learning disabilities; many have had to contend with racism. They've accomplished a great deal and, with the support of their parents, have overcome major roadblocks to do so.

When several of them were in their early twenties and struggling to establish themselves, one of these young people gathered others she knew who were raised with Hand in Hand. On her own initiative, she started a support group in which they could help one another surmount the effects of poverty and racism, and move their lives forward. They listened to each other weekly for over two years, and anchored one another well. She has since founded a dance and leadership training program for at-risk youth in a major east coast city.

These young adults are not bursting into tears in public places whenever they feel challenged; they're not having temper tantrums when they get parking tickets. They tend to value emotional support and set it up for themselves, formally or informally. And they tend to trust their parents as listeners when major issues arise.

Their parents are pleased and proud of them. These parents supported them during adolescence with love and limits, and persisted in using Listening Tools to stay connected through sometimes trying situations. The young people are engaged with the world, and they feel connected to their parents. They have found ways to do what they love and build healthy lives.

Listening to your child's feelings while getting good support for yourself won't make him walk on water. It won't ward off all difficulties. But from what we see, young people raised in this way are resilient. When they encounter problems, they learn. And they know that feelings of upset can be released; that discouragement is just a feeling; that we become stronger and smarter when we connect deeply with others. These young people are part of a small sample, but the lives of the much larger sample of young people now in their teens look equally encouraging.

And when we look back at our own lives as teens and young adults, it's clear that adult listening fosters intelligence and resilience in children. Any one of us who ever had an adult listen to our feelings during our teen years remembers it! Many of our lives were changed by someone who listened to us. Imagine the loneliness and self-doubt that could be healed, not after years, but after hours or even weeks of listening!

LISTENING UNLEASHES OUR OWN POTENTIAL

When we use Listening Tools to build support for ourselves, our leadership builds. First, we learn to listen, and to lift small and medium-sized difficulties from our children's lives and our own. With the energy we free up, we can move on to tackle bigger issues that affect our self-confidence, our families, neighborhoods, schools, and communities. We bring respect for others and our listening skills with us as we go.

These general findings are illustrated by a parent support group I led for almost three years at a large nearby biotech company. After a series of lunchtime talks, six parents were interested in a Hand in Hand group, and we met for seventy-five minutes weekly at midday. Our group was diverse in race and economic status. It included a maintenance mechanic, his wife, who was a clerk in Human Resources, a secretary, two Ph.D. researchers, and the stay-at-home wife of one of the researchers. All had very young children, a few of whom were enrolled in the company's highly touted childcare center.

In our group, we all listened with respect to each parent in turn. People talked about their parenting bright spots and their upsets. They laughed often, and cried when they felt like it. Deep trust and enjoyment built over time. With Listening Tools, their lives started going better. By the end of the first year, they each had heartwarming successes in parenting, and a few had used the tools well in frightening situations.

By the end of the second year, much bigger changes had come about. The secretary had shed many feelings about a physical difference she'd had since infancy. Newly confident, she set out broader vistas for herself and her career. The stay-at-home mother had dyslexia, and was conquering her fear of reading for the first time in her life. One of the Ph.D.'s had gotten his first promotion in five years, and was surprised to find himself liking his work. The clerk was surer of her own thinking.

The maintenance mechanic had become concerned when his son's two favorite caregivers left the center for other jobs. Listening to other teachers, he learned that many were unhappy with the director, and that the turnover rate was high. He met with the director, who dismissed his concerns. When he learned that additional teachers were planning to leave, he petitioned the company to remove the director. At first he found every door closed. He was almost the only parent who saw that there was a problem. He worked on his frustration weekly in our group. When corporate administrators held a large parent meeting to discuss the center, they disparaged him.

But he persisted. Over time, a majority of parents came to share his concerns. It took almost a year, but they prevailed! New and responsive management was hired. The emotional support this father needed for this exceptional effort came from his wife and our mighty little noontime group.

We consistently see leadership develop in the parents who use Listening Tools regularly. Their confidence in their problem-solving ability grows, and their support networks expand. Connected, they are stronger than when they were laboring alone. And since they are able to connect with their children, the kids grow up more confident, too.

THROUGH PARENTING, WE CAN MAKE CHANGE!

There are indications all around us that an outmoded, destructive human mindset is teetering. Traditional divisions and intense competition between people and groups on the pretext of race, class, religion, economic status, and country of origin have long wasted human energy and intelligence. We need fresh, cooperative, inclusive ways to wage peace, share resources, guide and nurture our children, ensure human rights, care for our planet, build caring communities, and work for justice for all. Parents, and parenting, are a vital part of the solution! After all, we foster the intelligence and good will of our future leaders and innovators.

We can learn from three parent-led shifts in conventional wisdom, law, and common practice over the past sixty years that have benefited us all. The first was the establishment of services, and then inclusion, for children with developmental disabilities. When I was a child, children who didn't have normal IQs were hidden away or institutionalized. My mother led in the grassroots movement to establish and fund services for these children and their parents. Such services are now available in every community. In the process, we have become a more inclusive society, though there is still work to be done.

Mothers Against Drunk Driving (MADD), another grassroots effort, has made it uncool to drink and drive. Legislation, sentencing laws, and social mores have changed to lower public tolerance of impaired driving. Now, appointing a designated driver, unheard of before 1980, is a social norm, and according to MADD, drunk driving deaths in the US have dropped to less than half the number per year at their founding.

Last, parents and childbirth educators have led a gentle but significant shift toward the inclusion of fathers in childbirth over the past generation or two. In the US, a father attending a birth was almost unheard of sixty years ago, but is the norm today, helping fathers bond with their children and take their rightful place as primary parents.

As parents, we are many. As parents, we have influence. When we act in concert with other parents, conventional wisdom and social norms will change. And as parents, it's in our interest to see that building emotional support for our work becomes as ordinary as brushing our teeth!

Listening can connect us. Listening can refresh us. Listening can give us access to one another's best thinking, and help us understand our children in the deep way we always hoped our own parents would understand us. Listening can give us the power to dissolve our children's troubles. Listening builds intelligence.

The time is ripe to replace the focus on command and control in parenting with a focus on connection, sensible limits, and listening. And support for parents is the first step. Support for parents must be the cornerstone of any community that wants to preserve and increase human potential. Hand in Hand Parenting is here to seed this change.

I hope you'll join us. Start with any of the tools I've described. Connect with others. Set reasonable limits with confidence. Listen. Make mistakes, so you can learn. And follow your own best thinking. Your efforts will reap lasting, powerful benefits—for yourself, your family, and our world.

Resources

FREE HAND IN HAND PARENTING SERVICES

All links below are listed at
http://www.handinhandparenting.org/resources

ARTICLES

Over 100 articles on many parenting topics. Select articles are available in Arabic, Chinese, Hebrew, Hungarian, Japanese, Portuguese, Romanian, and Spanish.
www.handinhandparenting.org/article/

BLOG

Parent success stories on how to use Listening Tools to meet many challenges in life with young children. Over 300 entries.
www.handinhandparenting.org/blog/

TO FIND A LISTENING PARTNER

Join a Hand in Hand class to connect with other parents, or go to our Yahoo Discussion Group or the Hand in Hand Parenting Facebook Page and post your particulars.

HAND IN HAND CLASSES, EVENTS, SUPPORT GROUPS, AND TALKS

See our calendar for online and in-person events in the US and other countries. Some are free; some have a fee.
www.handinhandparenting.org/event_category/all/

HAND IN HAND DISCUSSION GROUP

Communicate in a moderated group with over 2200 parents who use the Hand in Hand Parenting approach.
groups.yahoo.com/neo/groups/handinhanddiscuss/info

HAND IN HAND FACEBOOK PAGE

Join our 100,000 fans, and keep up with the latest news and offerings from Hand in Hand.

www.facebook.com/handinhandparenting

HAND IN HAND PARENT SUPPORT FACEBOOK GROUP

Ask questions and connect with other parents.

www.facebook.com/groups/2512990074916600/

LITERATURE REVIEW

Obtain a summary of some of the available research validating the efficacy of each of the Listening Tools.

1djpjq2tu7u32cn9vx36pdku.wpengine.netdna-cdn.com/wp-content/ uploads/2013/08/Full-Lit-Review-2012.pdf

HAND IN HAND MONTHLY NEWSLETTER

New articles monthly, plus all the latest events and news. Sign up at www.handinhandparenting.org/parenting-by-connection-newsletter -and-gift/

TELESEMINARS

Free hour-long talks including Q & A on a variety of parenting topics. Meet our Instructors; ask your questions; join our community. Registrants automatically receive a recording of the call after it takes place.

www.handinhandparenting.org/event_category/free -parenting-by-connection-calls-and-teleseminars/

HAND IN HAND SERVICES AND INFORMATION FOR PURCHASE

HAND IN HAND IN-PERSON STARTER CLASS

Consult our calendar to see if there's one near you. Booklets included.

www.handinhandparenting.org/event_category/all/

HAND IN HAND ONLINE STARTER CLASS

Six-week online class. Videos plus weekly small-group conference call with an experienced Instructor. Class times suit time zones worldwide. Booklets included.

shop.handinhandparenting.org/products/parenting-by-connection -starter-online

HAND IN HAND PARENTING BOOKLETS

Nine booklets outlining our approach. Over 700,000 sold. Available in hard copy or .pdf format. Available in English, Chinese, Hebrew, and Spanish. Other languages coming soon.
shop.handinhandparenting.org/collections/booklets

ONE-ON-ONE CONSULTATIONS

An hour-long call with a Hand in Hand Instructor specially chosen to meet your parenting needs. Booklets included.
shop.handinhandparenting.org/products/one-on-one-consulting

ONLINE PARENT INTENSIVE

Ten weeks of conference-call-based mentoring and instruction based on our Starter Class. Small group mentoring. Booklets included.
shop.handinhandparenting.org/products/parents-intensive-class

ONLINE PROFESSIONALS INTENSIVE

Eight-week class for therapists, social workers, occupational therapists, sleep coaches, and others who work with parents and children. We also offer groups for medical professionals and early childhood education professionals. Groups are led by instructors who are practicing professionals. CEUs and booklets included.
shop.handinhandparenting.org/products/professionals-intensive

SELF-GUIDED CLASSES

Video-based. Six topics. Booklets included.
shop.handinhandparenting.org/collections/self-guided-classes

There's more! Go to **www.handinhandparenting.org** to learn more about joining us on Twitter, YouTube, or Pinterest, attending our Summer Parent Retreats, buying our Podcasts, or applying for our year-long Instructor Certification Program, both online and in person.

BOOKS WE RECOMMEND

The Art of Roughhousing: Good Old-Fashioned Horseplay and Why Every Kid Needs It, Anthony T. DeBenedet, M.D., and Lawrence J. Cohen, Ph.D. Quirk Books, Philadelphia. 2010.

The Aware Baby, Aletha J. Solter, Ph.D., Shining Star Press, Goleta, CA. 2001.

A General Theory of Love, Thomas Lewis, M.D., Fari Amini, M.D., Richard Lannon, M.D. Vintage Books, New York. 2001.

Hold On to Your Kids, Gordon Neufeld, Ph.D. and Gabor Maté, M.D. Ballantine Books, New York. 2006.

I'm Chocolate, You're Vanilla: Raising Healthy Black and Biracial Children in a Race-Conscious World, Marguerite A. Wright, Ed.D. Jossey-Bass, San Francisco. 2000.

Parenting from the Inside Out, Daniel J. Siegel, M.D., and Mary Hartzell, M.Ed. Jeremy P. Tarcher/Penguin, New York. 2003.

Peaceful Parenting, Happy Kids: How to Stop Yelling and Start Connecting, Dr. Laura Markham. Tarcher/Perigree, New York. 2012.

Playful Parenting, Lawrence J. Cohen, Ph.D. Ballantine Books, New York. 2002.

Simplicity Parenting: Using the Extraordinary Power of Less to Raise Calmer, Happier, and More Secure Kids, Kim John Payne. Ballantine Books, New York. 2010.

Waking the Tiger: Healing Trauma, Peter A. Levine. North Atlantic Books, Berkeley, CA. 1997.

Index

CPSIA information can be obtained
at www.ICGtesting.com
Printed in the USA
LVHW021618260121
677550LV00013B/1501